New Directions
in Psychohistory

New Directions in Psychohistory

The Adelphi Papers in Honor of
Erik H. Erikson

Edited by
Mel Albin
Adelphi University

With the assistance of
Robert J. Devlin
Gerald Heeger
Adelphi University

LexingtonBooks
D.C. Heath and Company
Lexington, Massachusetts
Toronto

Library of Congress Cataloging in Publication Data

Main entry under title:
    New directions in psychohistory.
    Papers presented at a conference held at Adelphi University, Oct. 1977.
    1. Psychohistory—Congresses. 2. Erikson, Erik Homburger, 1902-
—Congresses. I. Erikson, Erik Homberger, 1902-   II. Albin, Mel.
III. Devlin, Robert. IV. Heeger, Gerald A. V. Adelphi University, Garden
City, N.Y.
D16.16.N48   901'.9   78-4410
ISBN 0-669-02350-7

Published simultaneously in Canada.

Printed in the United States of America.

International Standard Book Number: 0-669-02350-7

Library of Congress Catalog Card Number: 78-4410

To Professor Erik H. Erikson and the late
Professor Talcott Parsons

Contents

Foreword

I am deeply sorry that I cannot be with you—and see you— for the list of panelists before me promises a most astonishing group of scholars. If my work, in some ways, has been a factor in bringing you together, I do, indeed, feel honored. And if the magic word *psychohistory* played a role in this, so be it—as long as it testifies primarily to the fact that we share in the beauty of a new and convincing kind of data.

But I have questions, which I know you share with me, so let me try to spell them out very briefly. The theme of this meeting is value changes in psyche and in society. I hope that you will discuss, here and there, what value changes, for better and for worse, are implied in the very emergence of a "hyphenated" field such as "psycho-history" and in its wider and sometimes sensational applications.

No doubt, the ever-greater self-awareness of the historical process is of essence in human existence; to add to it is our cause, much as we may differ in some means. But new fields defined by hyphens can all too easily lack some of the rigor of the traditional fields. To a psychohistorian, for example, it might seem unnecessary to define what history was and is. Before long, then, his work may fuse with trends that may just as well be called psychojournalism or psychopolitics—and this is in one of the less savory connotations of these words. A psychobiographer of living beings, in turn, may feel sanctioned to perform premature postmortems. (You know, of course, that I am paraphrasing Mark Twain, who read in the papers that he had died, whereupon he wrote to the editors that that news was a bit premature).

This "psycho" aspect of our work is grounded in psychoanalysis, a field that grew out of clinical work and had to develop some Hippocratic rules of its own. We, too, must be on guard that our eagerness to heal and to change as well as to investigate (and, indeed, to argue) will not involve us in diagnoses and prescriptions that are the province of, say, an ever-renewed political science.

Luckily, our very methods can help save us from going off too many deep ends. First, they will force us, as we go along, to subject our own motivation to a combination of psychological and historical analyses, each tempering the other. And then, we may come to affirm that rather than being in a separate field, we are really part of a great trend that strives for a wholeness of perspective in all fields concerned with human fate and therefore cultivates a complementarity of developing methods.

I regret immensely that, in addition to not seeing you, I will not hear you delineate your ideas within the excellent framework planned by our hosts. As it is, I look forward to reading you. Meanwhile, let me take this special opportunity to say hello to a number of very good old friends—and to wish you all an enlightening experience. Thank you very much.

Erik H. Erikson
Tiburon, California

Preface

Psychohistory's birth pains occurred in the wake of Hitler, the genocidal Nazi death camps, and World War II. These horrors both were too painful for individuals to integrate into traditional moral and emotional modes of defining everyday life and proved too complex for rational explanations by social science. Rationalistic theories emphasizing the significance of class, race, religion, age, sex, or self-interest as predispositional factors for human depravity did not explain adequately the heterogeneous population involved in such barbarous events. Classic liberal tenets about man's cooperative nature, good intentions, or capacity to control his aggression could not make sense of the evil spawned by Hitler and the Nazis.[1]

People could have accepted such events more readily if, on the one hand, they were shown to be unique, a culmination of perverse strains in European social and cultural life or if, on the other hand, they were not unique events endemic to Germanic culture but rather a mass psychosis induced by a group of devious, demented demagogues; man's darker side had once again reared its ugly head. Psychoanalytic theory, it was thought, provided a link between these two realms by uncovering the unconscious sources of social chaos, narcissistic fantasies of omnipotence, and paranoid styles. The writings of Erich Fromm, Wilhelm Reich, William Langer, Alan Bullock, and others employed psychoanalytic psychology both as psychohistorical explanation and as cultural therapy to allay fears of a world gone mad.[2]

These anxieties, however, did not cease after World War II. The continued rise of the Soviet Union under Stalin, the development of the Cold War, and the fear of the spread of communism throughout the world evidenced by the successful Chinese revolution and the Korean War prompted further psychohistories in the service of ideological warfare. Psychohistories compared Stalin, Hitler, and even Mao without drawing distinctions between left- and right-wing revolutions and by reducing all revolutionary behavior to an oedipal/infantile rage that generated a capacity for clandestine organizations and terrorism. Studies of national character also proliferated. These studies were often derived from analyses of the so-called authoritarian family, where similarities in childrearing practices allegedly explained why individuals were prone to demagogic appeals and participation in mass movements.[3]

Under such conditions psychohistory was plagued by a simplistic use of psychoanalytic theory, a disregard for historical, cultural, and social complexity, and the ideological purposes for which it was being employed. Just as Freud had feared that the politicization of psychoanalysis would undermine its scientific credibility, psychohistory's credibility was being undermined by its obvious ideological purposes.

Erik H. Erikson legitimated psychohistory amidst all the chaos. His achievement rested on a judicious use of Freudian theory as well as an emphasis on social, cultural, and historical factors. Erikson developed this conceptual framework in the late forties and early fifties in *Identity and the Life Cycle* and *Childhood and Society*. Erikson's new language for psychoanalysis focused on the concept of identity and adolescent development (as opposed to Freud's child-centered theory and emphasis on sexual conflict) and on the concept of the life-cycle, which he described as the "eight stages of man" (as opposed to the biologically derived three-stage Freudian theory in which personality congeals by adolescence).

The concept of identity had particular salience in the United States, a society engaged in an ongoing struggle with its cultural and social heterogeneity, heightened by the fierce assault of fascism and the ever-present threat of communism. This exaggerated the fear of national "decentering" and served only to increase public and private concern over who we were and what we would become.

In addition, Erikson wrote psychohistories of Luther and Gandhi, whose personal struggles for identity were related to the broader social order and, moreover, were fully compatible with Western liberal morality. Erikson also advanced psychohistory beyond psychobiography by linking leaders with followers through complex patterns of shared and reciprocal needs. *Young Man Luther* and *Gandhi's Truth* were instrumental in the establishment of psychohistory as a respectable academic discipline.

Erikson's emphasis on identity and youth was relevant to another western crisis: the turbulent sixties, the rise of the youth culture and radicalism. Erikson's work during this period and the work of his students, especially Kenneth Kenniston, explored these dramatic developments in some detail. Erikson's centrality to an understanding of the impact of youth in the sixties could, in fact, be traced to *Childhood and Society,* written over a decade before, and his discussions of "momism." Erikson proved to be both historian and prophet, a feat of considerable genius.

Throughout these years, Professor Erikson trained and influenced no less than three generations of psychohistorians. Many of Professor Erikson's students are contributors to this volume. As Professor Erickson's opening remarks in this book suggest, psychohistory needs a house-cleaning, and the group of scholars assembled at the conference at Adelphi University in October 1977 was up to the task. The reader will find that these chapters transcend psychohistory itself and point to many new and creative directions it has taken.

Fred Weinstein's introduction is an analysis of Erikson's contributions both to psychology and psychohistory and to the role of the intellectual in everyday life. Weinstein states that the conceptual language created by intellectuals, in spite of its import, is always flawed as a result of logical errors, moral and wishful contents. Weinstein then describes how Freud's and Erikson's social theories are problematic as a basis for psychohistorical research in spite of their achievements. Erikson's contribution, notes Weinstein, was to rework Freud in novel ways, "creating a language with which people in his own time and place could interpret the events that affected them." Erikson's own energy and talent, furthermore, enabled him to develop "a theoretical reach, clinical capacity and historical imagination unparalleled in his time." Weinstein points out that Erikson's greatest impact is on the wider cultural community. He concludes by arguing that this book and the conference at Adelphi honor Erikson's work "by the promise that those who follow would make an honest attempt to hold on to and amplify what is important, and let go of what is not. The inquiry continues, and everyone who works in the field wishes it to be so, not least of all Erikson himself."

In the seventies, psychohistory came of age and revealed its strengths and weaknesses, as well as the need for further conceptual clarity and empirical verification. This book is intended to be a statement about the state of the art of psychohistory in two areas: the problem of theory and empirical works in the field.

Throughout these chapters theoretical and applied psychoanalytic and nonpsychoanalytic psychology are offered the reader. The emphasis on theoretical models (from Marx to Erikson), explorations of the role of intellectuals, revolutions, political leadership, life history and the artist, the generational transmission of values, and the study of women make this collection unique.

The chapters in part I focus on theory. The two chapters that follow Weinstein's introduction cover three seminal theorists: Marx, Weber, and Freud, and their relevance to the field of psychohistory. Joel Kovel argues in chapter 2 that as a body of thought there is no singular Marx or Freud. Furthermore, each shows up the other—Marx punctures Freud's biological determinism, and Freud deflates the utopian Marxist position that by upending capitalism, alienation is overcome. Kovel argues, however, that this contrariness discloses "a deep affinity." Kovel then develops a sociology of knowledge attempting to grasp the historic meaning of their respective theories as "true scions of the bourgeois age."

The late Professor Talcott Parsons follows, comparing Weber's conception of legitimate order and Freud's metapsychology and explaining how their paradigms of rationality, the social-action system, and the personality are complementary. Throughout, Parsons emphasizes the chaotic nature of personality and the social order and how people contrive a sense of stability. In this regard, Parsons's emphasis on system is less positivistic and more dynamic than is often thought, forcing a reconsideration of the boundaries between personality and human experience.

The next two chapters examine emerging paradigms in psychoanalysis and their relation to the field of psychohistory. Ernest Wolf focuses on Heinz Kohut's conception of a psychoanalytic psychology of the self, pointing to the distinction between reified psychological theories and Kohut's empathic interpretation of behavior, which is of great importance to psychohistorians. "The psychohistorian," Wolf remarks, "would be better served by shunning the application of theories in favor of the kind of deep immersion into his historical material that would evoke in him an emotional involvement and reactions to which he would gain access by introspection." Wolf demonstrates this importance, exploring in detail the psychology of the self and its application to the study of leadership.

Miles Shore's "Emerging Paradigms in Psychoanalysis and Related Fields" contrasts Kohut's selfobject psychology with the contribution of Otto Kernberg, whose focus is on deeper pathological states. Shore surveys various schools of psychoanalysis from Melanie Klein's assertion that psychological development in infancy involves recovery from a normal psychosis to F oy Schafer's action language for psychoanalysis, to an examination of various aspects of the life-cycle and recent work in neurobiology, thereby opening psychohistory to the various ways in which personality is conceived in psychology.

Among Professor Erikson's opening remarks is a reference to the problem of using the psychohistorical approach to understand living political leaders, arguing that this approach may lead to "premature postmortems." In chapter 6 Stanley Renshon comments on the need for a psychology of adulthood to analyze the behavior of political leaders. Until recently, explains Renshon, childhood and youth were made too prominent in the life history of a political leader. In fact, in chapter 5 Miles Shore notes that even the choice of defense mechanisms in adulthood is relatively independent of childhood experiences. Renshon suggests that political scientists and historians draw on Erikson and Levinson in developing a psychology of adulthood.

In chapter 7 Professor Gerald M. Platt addresses the problem of heterogeneity of experience. Platt argues, from data on the English Civil War and German National Socialism, that individuals who participated in these movements came from a cross section of their respective populations and cannot be satisfactorily understood from a prior sociological category (age, sex, class, race, religion, family, and so forth) or psychological category (anality, orality, oedipal conflict, narcissism, and so forth). In an important departure from existing frameworks for analyzing revolutions, Platt draws together elements of interpretive sociology and psychoanalytic sociology, focusing on actor subjectivity as it becomes manifest through language, affect, and ideology. These middle terms, argues Platt, form the bridge between individuals and revolutionary participation.

Part II contains original empirical research in psychohistory. Cushing Strout suggests that the common ground between literary critics, historians, and psychoanalysts is their imaginative participation in other people's experience. Because of this, argues Strout, elements of psychoanalysis, particularly ego psychology and Erikson's concepts of identity and the life-cycle, "may help us to preserve the human concreteness of history, biography, and fiction while freeing us from the prison house of mere language, whether it be structuralist or metapsychological." Strout then applies this theme in a critical evaluation of recent psychobiographies of literary and political figures. Strout addresses the complex movement, back and forth, between the author's life and his text, the essential task of the critic and the biographer.

The next three chapters are about the generational transmission of values. David Musto discusses Freud's and Jung's Lamarkism and the extent to which people are influenced by their environments. Musto situates this dilemma in the family's quest for identity and continuity across generations. He examines four generations of the Adams family begun by John and Abigail Adams in 1764, attempting to understand the family's intergenerational internal stream of identity, which he calls the "family myth," and how it relates to the wider culture.

Howard Feinstein's focus on familial continuity is a blend of Eriksonian developmental psychology, the communications theory of Klaus Riegel, and historical research on the conflicts surrounding work and occupational choice in the family of William James. Feinstein reconstructs the dialogue engaging three generations: young Henry James becoming middle-aged Henry James senior, becoming elderly Henry James senior, in relation to young William James, becoming middle-aged William James becoming elderly William James. At the same time, we should note that young Henry James senior developed his views as artist, scientist, and philosopher in relation to his father's definitions of these terms. Feinstein's point is that value transmission in any family involves at least three generations, and he explains a method for understanding the generational transmission of values.

Lloyd and Susanne Rudolph examine the joint family of the Indian noble Amar Singh through his extensive diaries written between the years 1872 and 1942. The Rudolphs challenge the common beliefs that the nuclear family was a necessary condition or even a cause of modernization and adaptation and that the traditional joint family was oriented toward conservation. Their analysis prompts an assessment of the way affect and authority are organized and distributed, bearing consequences for super ego and ego formation and the forms and fate of noncompliance, evasion, and rebellion in the joint family.

Dominick Cavallo has achieved the synthesis of psychology and history called for by Erikson, making history simply history again, elegantly in-

formed by psychology. Cavallo's study of Jane Addams's childhood and
adolescence focuses on the cultural interfaces where individual life history
meets social history and where biography and collective behavior interact.
Cavallo does this by analyzing how the problems and successes of Addams's
early years were related to culturally prescribed paradigms of moral valua-
tion and social behavior, especially in the ways in which late-nineteenth-century
Americans perceived female and male social roles. Cavallo then shows how
the links between cultural paradigms and Addams's personal experiences,
when placed in the context of late-nineteenth-century urban and industrial
changes, throw light on the relationship between her resolution of private
conflicts and her decision to become a social reformer—and thereby to help
resolve society's public conflicts.

Edward Shorter begins chapter 13 by stating "If women in past times
have been unequal to men, it is partly because they have been so vulnerable
to their own bodies." Shorter then builds a speculative bridge linking his
"provisional" and "interim" findings about women's diseases before 1900
to their mentalities. Shorter concludes by arguing that women "felt uneasy
about sex because of the grim physical consequences which pregnancy,
birth, and abortion could have for their bodies and their lives in general."
Shorter expands this area to include nutritional disorders and various
genital disorders common to women. In short, these problems had an often
profound impact on women's psyches as they engaged in sexuality. Shorter
brings us full cycle, once again reasserting Freud's original point of departure—the biological basis of psychological functioning.

Notes

1. Many of the works done in the fifties reflected this need to understand reality that, from the standpoint of rationality and interest, was
bizarre. The fifties were indeed the Freudian decade. Notable among these
works were: H. Marcuse, *Eros and Civilization* (1955); Ernest Jones's
trilogy in honor of Freud's centenary, *The Life and Work of Sigmund
Freud* (1957); Phillip Reiff, *Freud: The Mind of the Moralist* (1959); Lionel
Trilling, *Freud and the Crisis of Our Culture* (1955); Norman O. Brown,
Life against Death (1959); and Erik H. Erikson, *Childhood and Society*
(1950) and *Young Man Luther* (1958).

2. Although their theories could account for the bizarre, they could
not account for routine everyday life. Biographies of pathological leaders,
not works on collective behavior, have dominated the field for the past
twenty years. What writers failed to produce was a theory rooted in collective behavior, moving beyond the biological theorizing of Freud and his emphasis on individual dynamics to account for the ways in which these events

affect people emotionally, how people maintain control when caught in the struggle between what is predictable and what is chaotic, the range and the intensity of response, and how such feelings are linked to cognition and external reality through a culture. Writers of this period also turned their attention to political and social movements in the United States. See, for example, R. Hofstadter's informal psychological study of the Populist movement in *The Age of Reform*, and *The Paranoid Style in American Politics*.

    3. For a further discussion of these theoretical problems see M. Albin and G. Heeger, "On Turmoil and the Politics of the Third World," *The Yearbook of World Affairs* (London: The Institute of World Affairs, 1979).

Acknowledgments

At the risk of spouting cliches, I must say that Professor Erik H. Erikson is not only a scholar but also a gentleman. In my brief contacts with Professor Erikson he was always cooperative and supportive of both the conference and this book. My gratitude to him extends beyond this endeavor and includes the creativity he brought and continues to bring to the study of history.

The importance of Professor Erikson's contribution to the social sciences and the humanities has a parallel in the long and important career of the late Professor Talcott Parsons, author of works too numerous to mention and founder of Harvard's School of Social Relations. The exuberance Professor Parsons brought to the conference was truly astounding. His vitality is amply demonstrated not only through his creativity (evidenced by chapter 3) and his rigorous analytic abilities, displayed from the floor at various conference sessions, but also through his charm and a subtle, often disarming, sense of humor. Professor Parsons's continued contributions to social theory and its application to psychohistory will be sorely missed.

I must reserve my utmost debt of gratitude to Professor Fred Weinstein, my mentor and friend. Fred is not only central to the directions in which psychohistory moves but he is a teacher of unswerving dedication and a rare human being. For what you have given to me, Fred, I remain indebted.

I want to thank Adelphi University President Dr. Timothy Costello for supporting this conference academically and financially. The conference could not have been held otherwise. Special thanks go also to Harry Davies, dean of the College of Arts and Sciences and Dr. Clifford Stewart, dean of academic affairs, for their generous support.

The early support, cosponsorship, and participation in various conference sessions by members of the Institute for Advanced Psychological Studies at Adelphi University, the Department of Political Studies, and the Department of History provided the impetus for the conference. Special thanks go to my colleagues in the Department of Political Studies for their continuous support of my work and their collegial spirit over the years. I would also like to thank Professors Charles Strozier and William Gilmore of *Psychohistory Review* for their time and effort in making a difficult undertaking manageable and pleasurable. The participants at the conference, too numerous to name here, were superb. Their originality, vitality, and collegiality made it all worthwhile.

My colleagues, Professors Robert Devlin and Gerald Heeger, whose names appear on this book, were continually plugging up the holes in the dike. This book and the conference are much the result of their efforts. Professor Dominick Cavallo offered his usual excellent commentary, guidance, and encouragement on much of this book, as only a friend can do; Professor Frank Miata also deserves special mention for his continuous optimism and friendship over the years as do Professors Hugh Wilson and Regina Axelrod of the Institute for Suburban Studies at Adelphi.

Deborah Heineman, who serves as administrative assistant in the Institute for Suburban Studies, and secretaries Therese Ginty, Marion Manzo, and Michelle Ziza, who typed the manuscript, deserve special thanks because they are highly skilled and underpaid. Finally, I would like to thank the numerous students who helped tremendously in organizing the conference.

Part I
Theory: Psychology and History

1

On the Social Function of Intellectuals: A Consideration of Erik H. Erikson's Contribution to Psychoanalysis and Psychohistory

Fred Weinstein

The social function of intellectuals is to provide the conceptual language people need to bring order to the complex experiences of everyday life. At the least, intellectuals establish for others the importance of conceptual language already available, as teachers, for example; at the most, intellectuals create such language in terms consistent with experience, taking on themselves the task of ordering ceaseless change and novelty, enabling people to integrate the impact of change in imagination, providing the opportunity they need to construct a sense of life as continuous. The ability of some intellectuals to do this stems from a particular talent they have for controlling the effects of change in their own perceptions, acts, images, thoughts, and fantasies, resolving to some useful, although imperfect, degree their own unique conflicts, subordinating fantasy solutions to the cognitive and moral requirements of their time, interpreting those requirements first for themselves and then for the world.

Intellectuals, of course, can come from any social background. And there is no necessary correspondence between personal background and political loyalties, just as there is no one network of interest, morality, and wishful expectation that intellectuals serve, as they may be radical, liberal, or conservative in orientation. But whatever their orientation, they come to represent a constituency, perhaps even competing constituencies, and they serve these constituencies by fulfilling an integrative function, linking past and present in a comprehensive and orderly way, encouraging people thereby to continue to believe in a future consistent with needs and expectations. Political and social activists have often affected to despise intellectuals (the "scribbling set," as the Duke of Wellington referred to them, "shameless scribblers," as Adolph Hitler referred to them, although this is not a prejudice exclusively of the right: V.I. Lenin did not have a high opinion of intellectuals either). Activists despise the apparent passivity of intellectuals, their contemplative style, their lack of physical and technological effect, their willingness to sit and think about the world, and if that, too, is not a form of action and does not have an effect.

Hugely successful intellectuals may dominate centuries with their grand theories about the world, which are felt by them to have primarily cognitive sources and function and are viewed, therefore, as establishing a basis on which people can interpret events objectively and with a fair degree of accuracy. Marx and Freud, two theorists especially useful to consider here, thought that they had discovered and elaborated impersonal, scientific constructions that could serve as fixed standards of objective analysis. But of course they had not done that: their constructions were—inevitably, as with all such intellectual constructions—infiltrated by unobserved moral commitments as well as unobserved residual links to their own wishful expectations.

Indeed, it was the several levels at which these constructions were organized and to which they appealed that make them all at once complex, contradictory, and even confusing.[1] For example, the narcissism that animated, elevated, and confirmed these writers in their uniqueness, and also insulated them against the violent attacks they provoked, freed them for their tasks on the one hand and compelled a certain distortion on the other. Moreover, precisely because people needed their constructed versions of reality, they were confirmed in their high self-regard, but they were also cut off from awareness that their intellectual constructions, like constructions in psychoanalytic therapy, did not need to be objectively true. They needed only to be ordered and, coming from such authoritative sources, emotionally compelling with respect to being able to manage complex events. Their insight was extraordinary, but their symbolic capacity, which quite evidently implicated moral and wishful as well as cognitively disciplined thinking, was even more so, although this capacity was not necessarily under conscious control.

Thus it happened, over long years of struggle, that even intellectuals of the calibre of Marx and Freud sometimes failed, for a variety of personal and social reasons, to sustain the cognitive discipline they valued. Their work, at one point or another, was dominated by moral commitments or wishful expectations that were expressed in the same authoritative style as their disciplined constructions, and for that very reason they also were compelling and also served to help people bring complex events under control. And it happened, too, that many of these people, coming to the work from the standpoint of subjective needs and expectations, often focused attention on the wrong issues.

We may say that the conceptual language created by intellectuals in general is, in these terms, therapeutic and ideological as well as cognitive in import; and because intellectuals in addition may succumb to the force of moral and wishful strivings, their work is certainly not an unmixed blessing for those who follow them.[2] Scanning different bodies of information for connections between different dimensions of reality, they provide justifications for continued personal and social action, but they do so for many, even inconsistent, reasons, and they do so for many, even conflicting, groups. Moreover, as a result of their symbolic capacity and their therapeutic and ideological functions, they can be as charismatic in the intellectual sphere as activists often are in the political, and, against their own best intentions and expectations, they create orthodoxies and guardians of these orthodoxies as well.

Intellectuals codify and abstract experience, they provide the thought content that helps constrain affective responses, they give form to the expression of impulse and interest, they encompass the painful although potentially useful forms of change, they focus attention (necessarily, and perhaps usefully, narrowing it), providing justifications for novel actions or for novel interpretations of familiar actions. But even the very best of them are not as correct as they need to think they are, they routinely overevaluate their own contributions, they can and do err, they are even sometimes confused and they confuse others. Moreover, their real virtues—the extraordinary cognitive, moral and wishful force, the extraordinary capacity for concentration and synthesis, their ability to create novel combinations of ideas leading to novel forms of activity, and their ability to draw people to themselves on these grounds,—often make them oblivious to real defects and indifferent to or even intolerant of real criticisms.

For these reasons, all intellectual constructions, no matter how grand, must be approached with more than a grain of salt. All such constructions are characterized by notable weaknesses as well as strengths, with the added difficulty that the weaknesses are often subtly masked because of the implicated therapeutic and ideological functions. These weaknesses can then become as important, or even more important, than the strengths because of the need people have for these constructions, which leads, among other things, to the unreal expectation that the great intellectuals will have been more cognitively and morally disciplined than anyone really can be. Their own force, and the frailties of their followers, can make them finally as much an obstacle as a spur to further progress in the areas in which they so brilliantly pioneer.

These rather general comments could of course be amplified in a number of directions. But in respect to the conference held in honor of Erik H. Erikson, it is necessary to establish and underscore in the first place the kind of weakness in Freud's work—taking the strengths for granted, for the sake of brevity—that allowed an individual like Erikson not only to broaden the base of a very remarkable achievement but also to rework and expand it in novel and unanticipated ways, serving to create the language with which people in his own time and place could interpret the events that affected them. This must include now by definition some combination of weaknesses and strengths that I have already indicated is characteristic of such endeavor. For if a man of Freud's remarkable capacities did not accurately perceive in many instances the complex interconnections of psychic and social processes, indeed, made very fundamental errors with respect to the analysis of these processes, we could hardly expect Erikson to have done otherwise. And this is said not merely to emphasize the obvious, that everyone fails to some degree, but to emphasize rather that only by identifying the weakenesses and the strengths in any of these writers can we develop some adequate idea of how next to proceed.

One example of the kind of weakness in Freud's work that occurs specifically in his social theory, the area in which Erikson had his greatest impact, will suffice for the purpose of my argument. Freud often mentioned in passing, on the basis of his personal and clinical observations, a variety of social factors that affect psychic processes.[3] But Freud never attempted any systematic integration of social factors in theory because the effects always seemed random and accidental to him, and so they never weighed as heavily in his mind as his conception of phylogenetic inheritance: as far as he was concerned, the origins of morality, religion, and culture lay in the traumatic effects of an actual, historical event, the totem murder.[4]

There were a number of personal and social reasons for Freud's emphasis, but there was also an important theoretical reason for it, and this must be of primary interest here. The problem for theory was that Freud could not explain the recurrent contents of mental life in terms of either instinct or drive. The concept of instinct or drive may refer to somatic or psychic processes, but Freud could not infer and then insist on an exclusive, organized mental content on the basis of these processes. Drives, as Freud noted, are without quality, or as one psychoanalyst has recently pointed out, "A drive energy by itself does not create a mental or cognitive content,"[5] let alone a universally recurring, exclusive (oedipal) content. Freud wanted very much to be able to say that drives can in fact acquire psychical representation as wishes independent of any real, external event, for this was the parsimonious solution; he really could have explained everything about the origin and force of religion, morality, and culture in these terms. And if any wish of Freud's ever threatened to overcome his attachment to scientific discipline, or did overcome it in a way, this was the one. For Freud had actually gone so far as to suggest in *Totem and Taboo* that one aspect of the narcissistic organization of primitive men was the overevaluation of their psychical acts, to an extraordinary degree and, accordingly, "the mere hostile *impulse* against the father, the mere existence of a wishful *fantasy* of killing and devouring him, would have been enough to produce the moral reaction that created totemism and taboo."[6] If that were so, of course, we would not have to think of our cultural legacy as stemming from a hideous crime, the totem murder, we could think of it instead as stemming from drive activity with no damage to the explanatory network linking earliest times to the present day.

Freud's idea that it really may not matter whether the deed actually occurred or was only wished for, along with his idea that the narcissistic organization of primitive men allows them to overevaluate their psychical products, is a particularly rich Freudian joke. Modern men obviously have a similar narcissistic organization, and they may easily do the same thing—and Freud's attempt to derive a specific mental content from a somatic process, or even a psychic process conceived of in drive terms, proves it.[7] Of course, it mattered whether the deed had actually occurred or not: just because the drives are without quality, and because, in his own view, social life (including family life) is too random and accidental in its psychic effects, Freud was compelled to explain the universal, recurrent content he thought he saw on the basis of a presumed historical and social event, the totem murder, the effects of which were transmitted genetically and hence systematically from generation to generation.[8] Freud wrote *Totem and Taboo* to establish this premise.

Freud thus solved his theoretical problem by locating in the remote "racial" past a primal event that structured all human activity thereafter. Freud did not insist on his other, wishful conclusion (drive processes giving rise to specific mental contents), but he developed his sociological position in terms of phylogenetic endowment. This of course was unacceptable, and often enough the wishful conclusion was invoked by others as an alternative explanation to the embarrassing Lamarckism without reflection on its logical and theoretical status. But even so, whatever plausibility the theory had in the first place could only have derived from the relatively undifferentiated nature of psychoanalysis in Freud's time, specifically from the single-minded focus on oedipal dynamics, and once the concepts of ego development, object relations, and narcissism were amplified it became quite clear that much that had been interpreted as oedipal, or as variations on the oedipal theme, was in fact something else.[9] In addition, the basic data of clinical experience with respect to individual manifestations of this presumed universal content cannot be accounted for in any terms presently available. Psychoanalysts have never been able to explain the "choice" of neurosis or defense, or the individual expressions of fantasy, idealization, and selective bias. There is no way to integrate the diverse idiosyncratic results of life's experiences with the overarching concept of unity of motive predicated on a common source of religion, morality, and culture.

Freud's phylogenetic stress, his insistence on the exclusive content of psychic conflict (with whatever idiosyncratic resolutions), and his failure to encompass social factors in systematic theory represent only one aspect of psychoanalysis that could be considered incorrect and/or problematic from the standpoint of an interested observer. There is in fact more that can be so considered and some of this should be noted, however briefly, to put Erikson's contribution in better perspective. Freud, for example, was wrong about the capacity for change after the oedipal period (he thought finally that ego processes could continue to develop but that superego processes could not, except under the special conditions created by the therapy). Moreover, his notion that the patient's transference relationship to the analyst is the pattern for socially legitimated authority relationships in general was based on an unwarranted logical leap, particularly as he would only consider the regressive implications of such relationships; and his integrative theories of internalization and identification are not at all well coordinated to his image of the hostile and frustrating effects of cultural demands on individuals. Finally, his energy concept is of no advantage to a systematic sociology in terms of either integration or frustration, as consistent—application of the concept must lead to a sense of the idiosyncratic and unique resolutions to psychic conflicts.

These comments taken together allow us to see how Freud's thinking was affected, not only by logical errors, but also by moral and wishful contents and how, in addition, such thinking could then come to serve primarily a culturally therapeutic and ideological role, as opposed to, or along with, a scientific one. Freud's position always served the moral and wishful purposes of the "fathers" against the "sons," or of established authority against its subjects more broadly conceived, including especially the authority of men against women. At the same time, however, Freud did provide any number of people with a conceptual language useful for understanding their own behavior and the behavior of others in consistent terms that rendered a bewildering and even bizarre world coherent. This conceptual language is not as objective and correct as Freud had wished and a lot of people assumed. Of course, Freud fundamentally affected the sensibilities of people in this century, the ways in which they use and understand language, the ways in which they view themselves and others as sexual and aggressive beings, and the ways in which they view art, religion, and the wider social world as well. But Freud considered as a cultural force is different from Freud considered as a theorist of human behavior, and whether and to what extent he was objective in his observations and acute in his theoretical constructions is another question. This is not to deny the cognitive utility of Freud's contribution but only to put it in perspective. Freud's conceptual language is still quite appropriate to systematic inquiry into the problems of leadership, ideology, social cohesion and disruption, language, art, and so forth although only when viewed from a standpoint different from the one he preferred.

Further, we can also begin to see the difficulties raised for psychoanalysts, and for other scholars, who want both to maintain a tie to the Freudian tradition and to expand and refine the explanatory power of the Freudian position in systematic cultural and social terms. It cannot be emphasized too strongly that because of the culturally therapeutic and ideological role these difficulties are not exclusively a matter of observation or theory. Saying that Freud was wrong, and even demonstrating within the context of psychoanalysis how Freud was wrong, is no guarantee of objective evaluation, particularly if one wants also to claim that certain moral commitments and wishful expectations interfered with Freud's observational capacities. Things may not work that way with regard to the leading figures in any discipline; they certainly do not work that way in psychoanalysis. For it is quite clear in the psychoanalytic literature that criticism, even from friendly sources, is often perceived and felt to be a matter of cognitively disciplined disagreement.[10]

Thus, where Freud is concerned it is not only a matter of developing a critique of the work, one must also develop a strategy for doing so, or suffer the fate of Adler, Jung, Rank, Horney, and others—expulsion from a valued community. Heinz Hartmann, for example, considered it important to move psychoanalysis closer to systematic sociology, which he thought was indispensable for further progress. Hartmann legitimated this move by giving unwarranted theoretical emphasis to Freud's comments on the ways in which social factors impinge on psychic processes.[11] And, as Paul Roazen has noted, Erikson pursued a similar strategy to get his identity concept across.[12] However, where Hartmann was trying to work out the implications of the psychoanalytic metapsychology in terms of Freud's structural theory and the ego psychology, using language that was already available and acceptable, Erikson meant to change that language, to offer what was in many respects a novel language that people in his own time and place could use to interpret the events that affected them. The rather minor deceptions aside, therefore, it took an individual of considerable force, energy, and talent to manage it.[13]

Erikson broke in important ways from the traditional Freudian position, particularly with respect to the kind of problem in social theory already discussed. And we may view Erikson's contribution as a rescue operation that provided moral and cognitive legitimation for the continued examination of psychoanalytic propositions, as much by example as by insight, and as much cultural in import as theoretical or clinical. In its received form, after all, psychoanalysis could not have continued to command theoretical attention and would have lost its cultural force, except perhaps as a therapy for the few who could afford it, a form of practice with which Freud was not particularly concerned.

Erikson's work, in many respects a critique of Freud as well as a serious, independent contribution, was based on a number of observations including the following: there is not one underlying universal psychic content that people express in their activity; neurotic disturbances are not constant over time, being culturally and historically derived; both family and the wider social structures had changed from Freud's time to his own, leading to a different range of problems to be defined; ego processes are affected systematically by integrative and conflictual social pressures, and it is necessary to have a theoretical (and clinical) orientation to the relationship of personality to social order.[14] Further, it is necessary to establish not only how society makes its priorities effective through the family but also how familial demands are organized at higher levels of generalization so that they may even lose their initially conflicted forms. It is also necessary to establish how it is that people get along in the world (explaining, for example, how neurotics can maintain themselves in life, which Freud observed but did not himself explain), to show how regressive maneuvers may prove to be only temporary and lead to more positive outcomes, and to organize a proper psychoanalytic sociology, because conceiving of phylogenetic inheritance as the source of all morality, religion, and social order is not serious since a purely drive-derived explanation of mental activity is not possible.[15]

This series of abstract propositions was worked out by Erikson in his conception of the psychosocial stages of life, which is not nearly as static and foreshortened as Freud's original developmental scheme (because the later stages of development are not completely or mechanically contained in the earlier ones and because the later stages not only involve phase specific struggles, affected although not determined by what happened earlier, but also harbor a potential for change one could not infer from Freud's original position).[16] It was worked out also with special emphasis on adolescent development in terms of identity and identity crisis, which Erikson noted immediately was as strategic a conception for his day as sexuality was for Freud's.[17] And it was worked out also in the development of what came to be called psychohistory. Psychohistory was developed as a distinctive aspect of a traditional discipline by a number of people, some of whom were not all that familiar with Erikson's work. How all this unfolded has not yet been investigated. But no one can deny Erikson's central role in the process.

Thus, as a critic, theorist, and therapist—but primarily as an intellectual—Erikson had made himself a figure of considerable cultural influence; or as Marshall Berman wrote, as recently as 1975, "Erik Erikson is probably the cloest thing to an intellectual hero in American culture today."[18] However, the relationship of a creative intellectual to his culture is multifaceted and involves a therapeutic and ideological role as well as a cognitively oriented theoretical one, as I have stated. To be sure, Erikson's combined strengths, his theoretical reach, clinical capacity, and historical imagination are unparalleled in his time. But for all that, or perhaps just because of all that, Erikson's greatest impact was not theoretical or clinical, and his work did not have its greatest effect on either the psychoanalytic or the broader academic community. Erikson's work had its greatest effect on the wider cultural community precisely as Berman had stated.

It is interesting to observe in these terms that Erikson never became as much an authority among psychoanalysts as he became among the public at large. Psychoanalysts have routinely complained that they could not operationalize Erikson's observations in their practice, a complaint explicitly confirmed by the response of a number of psychoanalysts to a questionnaire. These psychoanalysts also indicated that although Erikson's formulation of the psychosocial stages is quite important, it is not as important as Hartmann's conception of ego autonomy; and Erikson's formulation of identity (and identity crisis), undoubtedly the most culturally significant aspect of his thought, was not nearly as valued by them as the overall orientation to the life cycle.[18]

It is interesting too that the notion of identity formation, with its special focus on adolescence as a phase of life with certain conflicts peculiar to it, is proving not to have as much significance historically as Erikson might have anticipated.[19] And various critics (Joel Kovel and Edith Jacobson among them) have pointed out that the identity concept has in any case never really been rigorously formulated, as it is used by Erikson in a number of ways to refer to various possibilities. It is not unlikely, then, that Erikson, who worked out the vicissitudes of identity formation in his own life first, overevaluated the significance of the concept in his work.[20] On the other hand, Erikson did provide any number of people in the 1950s and 1960s with a coherent, accessible, and orderly conception of the critical force of adolescent conflicts and their resolutions; his language did establish for people a necessary sense of where youth stood, with all their problems, and hence where their parents stood with respect to them. Erikson's conceptual language was therapeutically and ideologically important whether or not that language turns out to be as correct in the long run as he thought. Identity in particular is one of those concepts that has therapeutic value first and theoretical value afterwards. The concept as we have it may well not stand up to rigorous scrutiny, and it may require reconsideration. But many of Freud's concepts, especially those regarding social process, will not stand up to rigorous scrutiny, being constricted to one degree or another by the cultural requirements of his own day and sometimes even infiltrated and distorted by personal strivings. Still, these concepts were, and for many people still are, a powerful symbolic mode of expression. Judging such concepts only by theoretical standards misses the tension involved in any high-level intellectual construction, which can never be conceived of as being just one thing or another.

However, one cannot gainsay the necessity for evaluating such work in theoretical terms for the purpose of ongoing scholarly endeavor. And from this point of view, Erikson's outstanding elaboration of the life cycle is more important than his singular focus on the problems of identity formation. Erikson's emphasis on socially integrative experience redresses an imbalance in Freud's work, but except at the level of psychobiography, it is not matched adequately by a comparable emphasis on socially disruptive experience, and we cannot yet understand in Erikson's terms how groups are systematically affected when integrative processes are rendered dysfunctional or inapplicable by social change. Erikson's age-graded developmental scheme is far more amplified than Freud's, but it, too, is not yet sufficient for a psychoanalytic sociology. Social movements cut across even the flexible boundaries of the psychosocial stages, and a special set of hypotheses must be provided to explain how people faced by different personal conflicts can be organized, or can organize themselves, in a relatively stable way. Erikson has not provided such hypotheses, nor can we see how they might be derived from his work.[22]

In short, Erikson was no more likely to have been right in his assertions, that is, to have avoided error or to have filtered out one or another kind of distortion even with respect to the most important of them, than Freud was. Erikson has achieved a rare level of intellectual and cultural distinction, but he would not be surprised to learn that a lot of what he said is open to criticism. And developing this criticism, gaining perspective on the weaknesses and strengths of his work, and psychohistorical work generally, is the only effective justification for such a conference as was held at Adelphi University and is now represented by the chapters in this book. Erikson's work was honored, in effect, by the promise that those who follow would make an honest attempt to hold on to and amplify what is important and to let go of what is not. The inquiry continues, and everyone who works in the field wishes it to be so, not least of all Erikson himself.

Notes

1. As I have argued elsewhere, writers like Marx and Freud have such a wide appeal because, paradoxically, they are often contradictory. This allows many different kinds of people to identify with their theories, and the first thing that ideological warriors who struggle in the name of Marx and Freud do is resolve the contradictions, insisting that Marx meant only this or that. In this way, theories that are complex and contradictory, and therefore open-ended in the abstract, become rigid and simplistic in application. Fred Weinstein, "Freud, Marx and the Ordeal of Civility. A Review of John Murray Cuddihy," *Psychohistory Review* 7, no. 1 (1978):38.

2. The concept of ideology is employed here in the sense intended by Marx and Engels: "Ideology is a process accomplished by the so-called

thinker consciously, it is true, but with a false consciousness. The real motive forces impelling him remain unknown to him; otherwise it would simply not be an ideological process'' (Karl Marx and Friedrich Engels, *Selected Correspondence* (Moscow: International Publishers, 1954), p. 541). One interesting thing about this concept is Marx and Engles's unreflected and unexamined awareness that some mental processes go on at some level other than consciousness, and their ability then to turn around and insist that because they had invented the concept of ideology they could not, therefore, have invented other concepts which are themselves ideological. I should note that Freud's conception of childhood sexuality, and of the specific force of oedipal conflicts in childhood, is both a cognitively disciplined as well as a culturally therapeutic and ideological construction. One can more or less usefully observe the behavior of children and adults in the context established by Freud, although the accurate observation of behavior was not the only function of Freud's construction. Freud's idea that sexual and aggressive drives, expressed specifically in oedipal conflicts, are the motive force in history and the true source of morality, religion, and social order, is much less cognitively disciplined than his theory of childhood sexuality, although it has some value in that societies do interfere (in formal and informal ways) with human sexuality by defining and enforcing rules governing arousal as well as expression of it, and it is not clear why—except in some such set of terms as elaborated by Freud. But Freud's idea as it was stated never achieved the status he ascribed to it, and in social terms it is much more therapeutic and ideological than cognitive in importance.

Marx's conception of class may be similarly viewed. Provided the concept is rigorously defined (and Marx did not rigorously define it), one can acquire objectively useful information in terms of it. But Marx overevaluated the importance of the class concept—it is not the highest level of generalization with respect to the interpretation of human activity. Identifying it as the decisive cause of conflict throughout history leads to the anachronistic rereading of events. Marx's conception, however, was morally powerful and culturally therapeutic and ideological in that it helped people to understand what was happening to them in consistent terms and it helped legitimate their organized activity. But that activity never had the anticipated results because the theory was contaminated from the start. Marx's suggestion, moreover, that the bourgeois mode of production would be the last socially antagonistic mode of production represents more a wishful expectation than anything else by Marx's standards (that is, the information he would have needed to make such a prediction was not available to him, and there was no basis in the social order as he knew it for such a prediction, so that it stands as an example of what Marx would call bourgeois idealism). Still, this idea too, dominated though it was by Marx's wishfulness, was important for mobilizing people to organized activity and encouraging them to believe in a future that they could control. Wishful contents sometimes dominated Freud's thinking too, as we shall see.

3. Freud speculated that society would probably one day make psychoanalytic outpatient clinics available for the poor, but psychoanalysts would likely find "that the poor are even less ready to part with their neuroses than the rich, because the hard life that awaits them if they recover offers them no attraction, and illness gives them one more claim to social help." H.P. Hildebrand, "Reflections on the Future of Psychoanalysis," *International Review of Psychoanalysis* 3 (1976):327. Moreover, Freud also pointed out that unfriendly or unhelpful behavior in reality can trigger hitherto latent conflicts, and, of course, there are a wide variety of experiences that can be construed as unfriendly or unhelpful. Sigmund Freud, "Analysis Terminable and Interminable," *The Standard Edition of the Complete Works of Sigmund Freud*, trans. and ed. James Strachey, 24 vols. (London: Hogarth and the Institute of Psycho-Analysis, 1964), 23:222. It is not, in other words, that Freud did not see the effects of social life on people but that he did not see how these could be integrated in systematic theory.

4. See, for example, Sigmund Freud, *Civilization and Its Discontents*, trans. and ed. James Strachey (New York: W.W. Norton, 1962), p. 78; and chapter 9 of this book.

5. I have relied heavily in this section on two papers by Jean G. Schimek, "A Critical Re-examination of Freud's Concept of Unconscious Mental Representation," *International Review of Psychoanalysis* 2 (1975):171-187; and "The Interpretation of the Past: Childhood Trauma, Psychical Reality and Historical Truth," *Journal of the American Psychoanalytic Association* 23 (1975):854-855.

6. Sigmund Freud, *Totem and Taboo*, trans. and ed. James Strachey (New York: W.W. Norton, 1950), pp. 159-160. Italics in the original.

7. This wish was a live one in Freud, although he finally did not give in to it. He wrote to Karl Abraham, 11 November 1917: "Have I really not told you anything about the Lamarck idea? It rose between Ferenczi and me, but neither of us had the time or the spirit to tackle it at present. The idea is to put Lamarck entirely on our ground and to show that the 'necessity' that, according to him, creates and transforms organs, is nothing but the power of unconscious ideas over one's own body, of which we see remnants in hysteria, in short, the 'omnipotence of thoughts.' This would actually supply a psychoanalytic explanation of adaptation; it would put the coping stone on psychoanalysis." See James W. Hamilton, "The Death Instinct," *International Review of Psychoanalysis* 3 (1976):155. As Jean Schimek explains ("Critical Re-examination," p. 179), it may not matter in the actual, current experiences of a child with his parent whether the child

had really done anything or only wished it (as conscious fantasy), with all the interactions and idiosyncratic resolutions that this implies, realizing as well that preoedipal, narcissistic, object-relational and other social factors are also involved. This is quite different from deriving a singular, universal mental content that is systematically experienced by everyone as a result of genetic transformation following the totem murder; and it is altogether different from deriving that content from drive processes independent of any actual, social experience, historical or contemporary. In other words, Freud's basic definitions of drive as somatic need, quantity of energy, or inner sensation of pleasure or unpleasure is first superseded by the definition of drive as unconscious wish or fantasy that is equipped with acquired cognitive contents and their cathexes, biologically predetermined as instinctive knowledge, or phylogenetically acquired schemata. It is then again superseded by the definition of drive as somatic need which just gives rise to mental contents, specifically oedipal contents, independent of any experience. Freud confused a lot of people with his "omnipotence of thoughts."

8. Freud suggested, for example, that as long as the community assumes no other form than the family, conflict is bound to be expressed in the Oedipus complex, so that the conscience and the first sense of guilt might be established, implying that if another form of organization was attempted the cycle could perhaps be broken. But then Freud immediately concluded that even if man organized some other communal form, phylogenetic endowment would retain its supremacy, and the same conflict would be continued in other forms. Freud, *Civilization and Its Discontents*, pp. 79-80.

9. Thus, in object relational terms, "all behavior can be construed as an attempt to prevent losses of objects and to regulate some fundamental susceptibility to depression (loss)." Linda Joan Kaplan, "The Concept of Family Romance," *Psychoanalytic Review* 61, no. 2 (1974):171. Further, with respect to a narcissistic orientation, ". . . one may maintain that conflicts which appear in the foreground at the drive level will actually often prove to be rooted in the deeper level of narcissistic integration." Werner F. Fritz and Bernhard Mitterauer, "Narcissism and Organismic Self-Reference," *International Review of Psychoanalysis* 4 (1977):194. All this challenges the primacy of the Oedipus complex as insisted on by Freud, which psychoanalysts have not failed to notice. See Vann Spruell, "Narcissism: Theories of Treatment," *Journal of the American Psychoanalytic Association* 22 (1974):273. Moreover, the need to integrate these other findings then leads to further complicated efforts to save the original drive theory. Note, for example, the suggestion that perhaps there are ego instincts that parallel id instincts, that is, one object seeking, the other pleasure seeking. These two transcendant classes of instinct would then cor-

respond to the divisions between the ego and the id. And all this does not yet include a systematic orientation to social events that psychoanalysts routinely insist must be developed. But once that is undertaken it is hard to see, even with such rear-guard actions as noted, how there can be very much left of the original emphases, especially because it is hard to see how this can proceed in terms favored by psychoanalysts—ontogenetic development in a familial context. On ego and id instincts, see Arnold H. Modell, "The Ego and the Id," *International Journal of Psychoanalysis* 56, no. 1 (1975):62.

10. Hence the following reports: "In the course of a discussion at a psychoanalytic gathering where I raised some of my ideas, one of the discussants stood up and with an accusing finger pointed the incisive question at me: 'I would like you to tell us frankly whether or not you still believe in the libido.' I was, of course, embarrassed at such an accusation and I stuttered something to justify myself." Pinchas Noy, "Metapsychology as Multi-Model System," *International Review of Psychoanalysis* 4 (1977):10. Or again, "Recently an analyst whom I hold in great esteem wrote to me: 'Now you want to eliminate the concept of drives. . . . Did Rapaport try it?' Staring at these words, I felt strong emotions, anxiety prominent among them, accompanied by images of heretics consumed in fiery pyres. This was natural. I was brought up in the value system of classical psychoanalysis, which has come to recognize the challenge, 'Aha, you are denying drives!,' as indictment, not invitation to inquiry; a basic violation of sacrament is at issue. And in the offing is a gentleman's equivalent of the pyre, perhaps intellectual isolation in the community. So my reflex was a somewhat testy defensiveness, an impulse to cry 'No, no, you misunderstand'—a not untypical plea of the guilty." George Klein, "Freud's Two Theories of Sexuality," in *Clinical-Cognitive Psychology, Models and Integrations* ed. Louis Breger (Englewood Cliffs, N.J.: Prentice-Hall, 1969), pp. 136-137. See also the edited version of this statement in Klein's paper as it was republished by Merton M. Gill and Philip S. Holzman, *"Psychology versus Metapsychology: Psychoanalytic Essay in Memory of George Klein,"* *Psychological Issues* 9, no. 4 (1976):14-15. See also, for example, Heinz Kohut's statement, "Thoughts on Narcissism and Narcissistic Rage," *Psychoanalytic Study of the Child* 27 (1972):366-367.

11. A good example of the strategy of creating a mythical tie to Freud to legitimate a suspect sociocultural position is Gad Horowitz, *Repression: Basic and Surplus Repression in Psychoanalytic Theory; Freud, Reich, Marcuse* (Toronto: University of Toronto Press, 1977), pp. 10-14. Horowitz refers to Hartmann's little deception to justify his own, noting that human growth is "overdetermined," involving five factors: maturation, ontogenetic recapitulation of phylogenesis, universal cultural experience, particular cultural experience, and the inheritance of the culturally

acquired; he noted further that it is very difficult to single out the specific contribution of each factor and assign a value to it. "While Freud is not totally silent on this question," Horowitz writes, "he does restrict himself in the main to the presentation of the sequence of development, without separating out the contributions of the various biological and cultural factors overdetermining that development." Horowitz is joking, of course, as we may infer from the phrase "not totally silent." In fact, Freud could not solve the problem of recurrent human behavior in any terms other than those noted and discussed as well by Musto in chapter 9 of this book. Further, as we can see from the material in note 9, there is more than one strategy that is employed, another favored one being apology and appeasement, showing a reasonable degree of good will, disarming hostile critics beforehand.

12. Paul Roazen, *Erik H. Erikson, The Power and Limits of a Vision* (New York: Free Press, 1976), 11-12, 58-59, 98.

13. Yankelovich and Barrett have written that Erikson's most important contributions remain obscure, one reason being that "he himself has blurred the extent of his divergence from the psychoanalytic movement; it seems he must feel that his debt to Freud is too great to warrant magnifying the differences between them." The authors also note that Erikson presents the curious picture of a prominent psychoanalytic theorist who has ignored most of metapsychology and has used the rest in a very idiosyncratic way. Daniel Yankelovich and William Barrett, *Ego and Instinct. The Psychoanalytic View of Human Nature—Revised* (New York: Random House, 1970), pp. 120, 153.

14. Erikson of course was not alone in his emphasis on ego development—Hartmann and Rapaport made the same point. But although their terms were different, they all recognized that one could not insist on the systematic (inherited) nature of id processes while holding ego processes to be formed principally by "accidental and contemporary events." Hartmann dissolved the antithesis between the ego as the repository of the accidental and experiential, as contrasted with the evolutionary structure of the id, in biological terms (although he was also serious about the social terms); and Erikson did the same in psychosocial terms (although he was also quite serious about the biological foundations of behavior). See the discussion in Modell, "The Ego and the Id," pp. 59, 66.

15. So-called radical critics such as Christopher Lasch often complain about the cultural emphases implied in the "ego psychology" with reference to writers like Erikson or Talcott Parsons. Lasch's statements on Parsons in this connection are certainly incorrect and are equally incorrect with respect to Erikson, who never considered himself an "ego psychologist," and who

always "kept faith with the deepest element in Freud—the biological thrust of his thought." Yankelovich and Barrett, *Ego and Instinct*, pp. 153-154. On Lasch's rather vulgar error in these terms see his *Haven in a Heartless World, the Family Beseiged* (New York: Basic Books, 1977), p. 132; and Gerald M. Platt's critique of Lasch in his "Twenty Lashes for Sociology," *Contemporary Sociology* 8, no. 3 (March 1979):179-180. At the same time, Erikson's work may be distinguished from Freud's in various ways, as noted for example, by Yankelovich and Barrett, *Ego and Instinct*, p. 142.

16. See the discussion in Paul Roazen's *Erik H. Erikson*, pp. 89-90.

17. Yankelovich and Barrett, *Ego and Instinct*, p. 434.

18. Marshall Berman, review of Erikson's *Life History and the Historical Moment*, in *The New York Times Book Review*, sec. 7, 30 March 1975, pp. 1-2, 22. Yankelovich and Barrett refer to Erikson as probably among the very gifted men of the age (*Ego and Instinct*, p. 120).

19. This information is reported by Charles K. Hofling and Robert W. Meyers, "Recent Discoveries in Psychoanalysis," *Archives of General Psychiatry* 26, no. 6 (1972):518-523. The authors report, based on their survey of the opinions of ninety analysts, that "Erikson's work shows a discrepancy between its value as a discovery and its clinical application. Although psychosocial development and identity were rated second and eighth respectively (in a list of fourteen suggested innovations in psychoanalysis since the death of Freud), no technical advances were explicitly associated with his work." (p. 521) On the cultural importance of the identity concept see Yankelovich and Barrett, *Ego and Instinct*, p. 122; Roazen, *Erik H. Erikson*, p. 89; and the Berman review, ibid., p. 1.

20. John R. Gillis, *Use and History: Tradition and Change in European Age Relations 1770-Present* (New York: Academic Press, 1974). H. Ray Hiner, "Adolescence in 18th Century America," *History of Childhood Quarterly* (New York: ATCOM Inc.) 3, no. 2 (Fall 1975):253-280.

21. Identity, providing always that it is rigorously defined, is an important concept. There is something in character that can be understood in these terms, something people feel they might lose or might be willing to sacrifice, or defend, or struggle for. This aspect of character is certainly developed over time and implicates body as well as social processes. However, Erikson's description of identity formation in adolescence, involving a crisis that is age- and phase-specific and is historically observable back, say, to the sixteenth century, is problematic, to say the least.

22. As I have explained elsewhere, the substitution especially of familial socialization for phylogenetic endowment does not go far in the development of a psychoanalytic sociology. For example, contemporary clinical experience suggests that different forms of character disorder are derived from different familial constellations. As there are a considerable number

of such disorders, and as we must also consider normal outcomes, the question of how many family constellations there are becomes very important, a question further complicated when considered in historical terms. Fred Weinstein, "The Transference Model in Psychohistory: A Critique," *Psychohistory Review* 5 (March 1977):16.

2 Marx and Freud

Joel Kovel

There are two points of reference—we might call them theses—from which one should begin examining the problematic posed by Freud and Marx. The first is a recognition that, as a body of thought in distinction to an actual historical figure, there is no singular Freud or Marx. Rather are there Freuds and Marxes, each one determined by the intersection of the actual historical figure—or, more exactly, of a portion of that figure's work—with the activity of an epigone. In this sense there are numberless Freuds and Marxes, every one of whom reflects a particular interest and a particular historical situation. This fact does not make the consideration of Freud and Marx together, any more than the consideratiion of each separately, an arbitrary exercise. But it does force us to realize that an act of interpretation is necessarily involved and, moreover, that our own interests are at stake.

The second point of reference follows from the first. It is the particular construction I choose to put to the matter, namely that although Freud and Marx are taken individually, the two most important thinkers of the modern era, they are also, taken together, locked in a contradiction that is irreconcilable within the terms of either of them. This means that if you regard Freud and Marx equally seriously, then each shows the other up. They do not exactly disprove one another; but each does expose the other in such a way that one can no longer take either thinker as a prophet, that is, as one who has found the singular line to truth and transcendance. A Marxian view, for example, readily punctures Freud's biological determinism as evinced, for example, by his static view of the Oedipus complex. In the same manner, Freud's demonstration of the necessary core of unreason in the psyche puts the lie to any utopian Marxist notion that overcoming the bondage of class might in itself awaken man from the nightmare of history. I happen not to be dismayed by this turn of events, as we have been too long burdened with the notion that our geniuses be gods as well. Whatever their differences, Freud and Marx are united in being demystifiers; and it is perhaps the best homage one can pay to let them bring each other down to earth.

Marx and Freud are indeed contrary to one another. But the contrariness discloses a deep affinity—else one would not be in a position to cast so much light on the other. In this respect they comprise the twinned faces of one Janus-head, with Marx looking outward and Freud inward; Marx observing the societal flux of class warfare and the division of labor while Freud watches the inward play of what Paul Ricoeur called the "semantics of desire"; Marx watching the collectivity, looking toward the movement of the social totality, while Freud gazes at the interiority of the individual psyche at the impression made by "a piece of immortal nature" on the social animal.

Yet they both look from the same place and with the same kind of eye, an unwavering post-Enlightenment gaze, exposing hidden forces that negate the officially established surface. They were both concerned with emancipation and truth; and they each considered that they had arrived at a truth that emancipates. And yet it was a different kind of emancipation they had in mind.

Marx and Freud staked out their discoveries on the line between the human and the nonhuman; and this proved to be the glory and bane of their geniuses. For Marx the nucleus was the transformation embedded in the commodity form, whereby relations between people became relations between things and the human world was swallowed by capital into the exchange principle. For Freud on the other hand, the center lay psychologically at the boundary between the thing-presentation and the word-presentation, the translation point between the inarticulateness of natural urge and the communicable system of speech. These two locations, occupying different positions in the human world, are alike in referring to points of exchange between the realm of ideas; a value, on the one hand, and that of material substance, on the other. From this consideration it may be seen that Marx and Freud have some standing as materialists but also that the term sits uneasily upon them.

Marx and Freud each held themselves to be tough-minded materialist thinkers; and there is ample evidence in their work to support such a label. Consider only Marx's statement from the Preface to *A Contribution to the Critique of Political Economy*: "The mode of production of material life conditions the social, political and intellectual life process in general." As for Freud, we know that he abandoned the *Project for a Scientific Psychology* but never gave up on its goal—that the ultimate explanation for mental processes would be found at the neuronal level.

These examples indicate the presence of materialist thinking in Marx and Freud, but they do not convey a sense of its scope or the kind of influence it had on their doctrines. Here we must distinguish between two aspects that materialist discourse can assume, both of which are reflected in Marx as well as Freud. For purposes of simplicity we may refer to these aspects as the dialectical and the linear modes of materialism. We should be aware here of running aground on other usages of the term "dialectical materialism," some of which may take on a linear aspect according to the terms I am about to define.

Strictly speaking, the materialist is one who holds physical substance to be the ultimate cause of all phenomena. The distinction between the two modes of materialism hinges on the kind of mediation, or transition, between this ultimate cause and the proximate, immediate phenomenon to be understood. If one holds that this mediation is a direct one, so that the same kind of explanation used in understanding the physical world applies, for example, to the human world, then one is being a linear materialist. Marx once wrote, for instance, that "the ideal is nothing but the material world reflected by the human mind." This passage, with its "nothing but" and its notion of simple reflection, is quintessentially a linear type of proposition. It should be added that a good deal of actual Marxist practice down through the years has been informed by just this type of linear materialism. Whenever, in fact, Marx or one of his followers ascribes the same degree of inevitability to a historical process as would belong to law of nature, he is practising linear materialism. Such would be the case whenever purely technological or economic factors are adduced to explain the action of men in society. This kind of materialism is ultimately idealistic, for man is seen as outside nature, acted on by nature and without dynamism of his own—in short, a pale abstraction.

What then is a genuine dialectical materialism—in contrast to the linear materialism that is usually passed off as dialectical? What makes reasoning dialectical is fidelity to a radical concept of mediation. In other words, the mode of explanation shifts in the passage from the physical to the human world. It does so, not to abandon the real physical root of the human phenomenon, but to recognize its unique transformation. A dialectical materialism meets matter halfway. It is poised between subject and object and will not yield to either. And the prime enunciator of this mode of reasoning was Marx himself in his theses on Feuerbach: "The chief defect of all previous materialism (including Feuerbach's) is that the object, actually, sensuousness is conceived only in the form of the object or perception, but not as sensuous human activity, praxis, not subjectivity." The measure of a dialectical materialism lies in its concrete realization of the human phenomenon as sensuous activity. Sensuous activity: a seemingly transparent phrase embodying the profound contradiction at the heart of what is human—that the human essence must be described subjectively as well as objectively; sensuously as well as in terms of action. And sensuousness implies that the core of subjectivity, for Marx as well as Freud, is felt bodily experience. Man is part of nature; and nature becomes to that extent humanized. If this is kept in the forefront, then one can neither slip into linear materialism—for that would be to lose sight of the sensuous, felt aspect of the phenomenon—nor drift off into idealism—for that would be to ignore the question of praxis, of what people actually do, with the necessary implication of changing the material world. Furthermore, praxis—and hence the human essence, as the sixth thesis on Feuerbach holds—is necessarily social, not merely from an objective standpoint, but intersubjectively, as the joined consciousness of sensuous beings.

The contradictions of dialectical materialism are not matters of logic but represent the actual richness of human experience. They are contradictions within a totality, not the abstracted clashing of unmediated forces. And although Marx often lapses into linear materialism, his work remains fundamentally dialectical in this sense. Were it not, he would not have elaborated a synthesis of such world-transforming power.

Freud, too, often appears snarled by linear materialism—and at times seemed to yearn for it, for reasons we shall have to consider shortly. Yet, whatever his natural science preconceptions, Freud became himself by making a break with natural science methodology. His genius lay in making the intersubjective situation of analytic discourse the object of scientific enquiry. In this way he too brought sensuous human activity into view, for the analytic situation is distinctly an objective praxis—characterized principally by speech—yet one turned at every moment toward the eludication of subjectivity. Although Freud's analytic method appears at first glance to bypass activity in the interests of exploring psychic reality, it is in fact deeply true to the principles of a materialistic dialectic. Action is not so much bypassed in psychoanalysis as consciously stilled. In other words, the fusion between sensuousness and activity is shifted to the end of sensuousness, thereby inducing an efflorescence of fantasy out of the thwarting of action. Indeed, the principle involved in the analytic process was anticipated by Marx when, in the course of dissecting the commodity form, he noted that "reflection on the forms of human life, hence also scientific analysis of those forms, takes a course directly opposite to their real development."

This observation leads us to the common notion embraced by Marx as well as Freud, namely, a sense of historical development. Historical materialism is but another term for dialectical materialism; or, to put it another way, the relationship of man to nature, or of subject to object, can only be grasped as historical process, as what emerges in historical—that is, human—time.

Such is the Hegelian root of both Marx and Freud, who each succeeded in grounding Hegel's notion of historical dialectics in the real life of man and woman. Marx and Freud saw the two ends where the arc of human activity touched nature, those two points where we become what we are through the transformation of the material world. Marx recognized the mark of the subject on the object—that is, the active transformation of nature through labor, more exactly, the distortions wrought in this process under capitalism. In Marx the movement is from subject to object, in Freud the reverse direction is discerned, from object to subject. For him the process took the shape of the generation of thinking out of desire, desire for a severed fusion with nature. The urgings of the body that take the shape of infantile fantasy and are given the name of instinctual drive are seen as that which is overcome historically in the emergence of the self—not residues left behind but permanent denizens, moments of perpetual contradiction. "Where id was there ego shall be," wrote Freud. He meant not a linear materialist notion in which two mental agencies wrestle with one another for the same piece of ground but a process of historical differentiation, conveyed best by a literal translation from the German: "where it was, there shall I become"; or, in the language of metapsychology, where thing presentations exist, so may word presentations arise.

These two contact points of the dialectic—from subject to object and from object to subject—are parts of a superordinate historical cycle by which man makes over nature and is in turn made over by it. And Marx and Freud were titans, able to grasp different phases of the cycle; but for whom the relations of the whole remained obscure.

The reasons from this may be discussed from a number of different angles. We may observe, for example, that at each end of the cycle an element of self-alienation is contained in the transformation. Thus at the level of labor—that is, of subject into object—we have the estrangement produced by domination and the division of labor. In the modern age this first takes the form of the alienation of labor and second of the mystification introduced by commodity fetishism, in which the human element drops out altogether. Further, it should be remembered that for Marx alienation cuts a man off from other men no less than from his labor.

In parallel fashion, at the point of object into subject, the dysphasic relationship between infantile and adult mind is expressed in the fact of repression; put another way, the development of a split within the self such that the part that has access to consciousness does not know the experience of the whole.

From a certain angle then, the history of the individual and that of the social group take different courses even though they are elements of the same totality. From this standpoint it would be too much to ask of Marx and Freud that they should have been able to grasp the total flux of relations. Perhaps no human can do so more than abstractly. Indeed it may be necessary to still one end of the cycle to bring the other into consciousness. In other words, Freud had to close his eyes to the historical flux of society to grasp the emergence of the individual psyche, and Marx had to set aside psychological or individual considerations to fix his eye on the track of the dehumanizing commodity form.

This may be true to some extent, but it fails to take into account a historical perspective. The deeper questions are, why Marx and Freud at all, why do they appear at the times they do, and do they express something that is universally true or only the spirit of a particular epoch? We cannot answer these questions adequately here; however, the following may prove suggestive of fuller answers.

All historical categories are themselves historical in a dialectical way. That is, whereas an ahistorical proposition about human affairs is simply false, a historical one is to some extent contingent on its particular time and to some extent universally true. Its relative contingency and universality can only be determined with respect to the total flux of history.

In the case of Marx and Freud, it can be readily seen that there are thinkers who could have only appeared in the West at a certain stage of its development. For the West is the only society in history to become both conscious of itself and estranged from itself. It should scarce be necessary to add in light of the preceding discussion that these two aspects are themselves dialectically related to one another. The root factor expressed by these developments is the relentless objectification that is the most basic feature of capitalism.

Viewed from this historical perspective, Marx represents this society becoming conscious of itself at the moment when productive forces had achieved autonomy and the proletariat its first identity. And his thought embodies this dialectical juncture: now becoming conscious of the track of the productive process, now succumbing to the linear logic of production, at the same time reflecting the creative force of the proletariat along with their stunted self-development, manifest as an immature capacity for reflection.

Freud, fifty years later, represents a new turn in the self-consciousness of bourgeois society, one made possible by the transition from early entrepreneurial capitalism to later monopoly capitalism. This later phrase demands particular attention to the quality of personal experience, to control both productive work and the consumption of commodities. The underlying social movements set going by these developments are the decline of patriarchy, the coordinated surge on the part of women, and a heightened concern for childhood. And the manifestations of these contradictory trends may be summed up as a setting loose of desire in the midst of an ever-increasing need for rationalization.

It is this juncture that Freud explores. In doing so he uses the tools of positivist science bequeathed to him by a bourgeois patriarchy to which he remained loyal even as he demolished its claims to universality. As a result, like Marx, his theory is riddled with that which it also overcomes.

Marx and Freud are true scions of the bourgeois age and ultimately true to its inner schism. Unable to finally free themselves, they took critique as far as it would go, then turned it over to the future.

3 The Articulation of the Personality and the Social-Action System: Sigmund Freud and Max Weber

Talcott Parsons

It has seemed to me logical to assume that the "psycho" in the title of this society referred to considerations about the psychology of the individual and that for my purposes, history could be assumed to concern itself with collective human phenomena at the social and cultural levels. A further circumstance was that, in this particular group, the "psycho" reference has in fact been mainly to psychoanalysis, and this happens to be that branch of psychology in which I am most thoroughly versed.[a]

It always seems helpful, in trying to relate two subjects, to avoid discussion of their relations in general and to look for specific points of articulation which have the promise, if adequately analyzed, of developing more generalized implications. As it happened, when I sat down to consider what I would say in my chapter, I had within weeks given another paper at a conference on the work of Max Weber, which specifically dealt with problems of rationality and rationalization as a historical process in Weber's work (held in Gotslichen, Switzerland in September 1977, under the auspices of the Sociological Seminar, University of Konstanz, Germany).

Although Freud, still by far the most prominent figure in psychoanalytic psychology, has been identified with emphasis on the non- and irrational in human behavior, it occurred to me that the problem of rationality was by no means absent from Freud's thinking. Quite the contrary, the theory of the ego in Freud's sense and of its relation to the reality principle articulates very definitely with modern ideas about rational action or behavior. It therefore seemed to me instructive to take a closer look at both Weber's and Freud's treatment of the problem of rationality and how they articulated with each other either in the sense of positions that were mutually incompatible or stood in some kind of positive relatedness.

Much of Weber's thought in this area and much of the discussion of it have centered on the particular concept which he called *Zweckrationalitat*. Since Weber was a social scientist all his life, and at one stage of his career concentrated on economics, it is not very far wrong to relate closely, if not

---

[a]The "society" Professor Parsons refers to is "The Group for the Use of Psychology in History."

quite identify, the concept of *Zweckrationalitat* with what in the English language has ordinarily been treated as economic rationality. Indeed, in my own translation of Weber's work, I came close to this by using the phrase "instrumental rationality."

A good many of the complicated problems surrounding the concept of economic rationality and related phenomena would lead much too far afield to be considered here. It has, however, traditionally been associated with the analysis of very down-to-earth practical interests and affairs of human beings, in the provision for their everyday needs, including very prominently the instrumentality of market transactions and the use of money. Very gradually, there has built up, at least in certain theoretical circles, something approaching a consensus that economic behavior should be treated as relatively unstable, unless it were controlled within some kind of a normative framework. The most obvious aspect of the normative framework has been the legal order within which economic activities and transactions have taken place. Sociologically, a classic statement of this problem was given by Emile Durkheim in his discussion of the institution of contract; however, it also extends to the vast complex of institutionalized property relationships and much of the field of human occupation and employment. A problem that must be dealt with somehow is how this institutional framework regulating economic—interests and activities can be scientifically conceived. Weber and others made important contributions to these problems.

Before taking up this problem, however, let me give a few bare essentials of Freud's concept of ego functioning in relation to the reality principle. On the face of it, there seems to be no serious reason to doubt that what Freud treated under this rubric was a mode of action and its regulation very similar to what Weber and many others have treated from the social science perspective as economic action. Among the others I may particularly mention Wilfredo Pareto, who made an important contribution in this field, but used the term "logical action"—a broader type in which economic action was included. Freud's ego functioning would come closer to Pareto's logical action and Weber's *Zweckrationalitat* than to "economic action" as such.

This aspect of Freud's thought is particularly highlighted by the contrast he drew between the ego and the id, which was the focus of the "unconscious," in his sense, and was dominated by "impulses" which were quite conspicuously not rationally organized. The contrast, but something of the relationship, was expressed by Freud's famous aphorism, "where id was, there shall ego be," referring particularly to the potentially beneficient results of psychoanalytic therapy.

Again, looking at the problem from Freud's point of view, the question arises, what were the sources of necessary stabilization in ego-dominated action? It would seem quite clear that, from Freud's treatment of the id, this could not be the primary source of such stabilization. Many interpreters of Freud have then described this stabilization as stemming from reality, which Freud himself spoke of as involving the impact of the external world on the ego of the individual. If, however, there is a problem of instability at the level of economic action, which has been theoretically defined, specifically with reference to the concrete external situation, why should there not be a comparable problem of instability of ego-oriented action from Freud's point of view? This is the central problem with which my cogitations concern themselves.

The reality environment that Freud clearly had primarily in mind, especially in his later work, was "social reality." This is to say that social reality in this sense, that is, the individual's interaction with other human beings, is in the nature of the case particularly beset with uncertainty. This is because of the fact that in the mutual stimulation of interacting individuals, the situation in which any one of them acts is contingent on the impingement of his action on the other and vice versa. I myself have devoted a good deal of theoretical attention to the analysis of this double contingency. It very much underlies the famous "problem of order," which has been so prominent in the preoccupations of social theorists, at least since Hobbes.

It is, of course, true that realistically the interaction of any given ego who might be a subject of a Freudian analysis is controlled by stabilizing mechanisms at the social level, independently of that individual's personality constitution. I will come presently to discussing some of the ways in which such social control operates, especially through law.

For the moment, however, I would like to go a little bit further with the structure of the individual personality. This zone of interface between the personality of the individual and the external world is what Freud calls the ego, and it is in his account typically governed by what he calls the "reality principle." In his mature theoretical thinking, Freud attempted to relate the ego in this sense to two other subsystems of the personality.

The one of these just mentioned he called the id, which he spoke of as being governed by the pleasure principle, precisely as distinguished from the reality principle. This clearly cannot be the primary locus of organized stabilization in the structure of the personality. Id impulses, in which what Freud called "wishes" figured very prominently, are very unorganized, if organization is to be measured with reference to the individual's action in a social environment. In fact, the discrepancy, precisely in terms of this sort, between ego and id, has been a major theme of Freudian psychology ever since it was first promulgated.

In Freud's discussions, however, there is a third primary system of the personality, as he often calls it, which he called the "superego." This is an entity of special theoretical interest from the present point of view. Although there are complex problems of interpretation of just what Freud meant by it and how he conceived it to operate, I think certain major points are quite clear. First, whatever may be said about the id and its impulses, it is quite clear that Freud did not conceive the superego to be derived from the biological inheritance of the individual. Parenthetically, however, I should like to say that I think there has been a strong tendency to greatly exaggerate the extent to which Freud attributed biological heredity to the id impulses. The reader will note that I have used the word *impulse* to translate Freud's usual term, *Triebe*, because I think that the common use of the English word *instinct* in this connection tends to bias interpretation in the direction of a biological-hereditary interpretation. Thus, if the attribution of even id impulses to biological heredity is doubtful, it seems to me that no case whatever can be made for a parallel interpretation of the superego.

Indeed, Freud himself is quite explicit as to where the superego comes from. He says it is arrived at through what we now usually call the "internalization" of the parental function. Freud himself used the word *introjection*.

There are two problems of interpretation of the superego. One concerns whether or not Freud confined it to the influence on a child of the father. I think that, although in many of his discussions of the Oedipus complex, he emphasized the father very strongly, in his most careful formulations, in his later writings, he usually used the formula "parental function," explicitly referring to both parents. One aspect of the importance of this point is that in traditional interpretations of Freud, there has been a heavy emphasis on paternal authority. Including the mother, however, it seems to me, significantly mitigates the emphasis on the superego as an authority pattern.

Beyond that, however, arises the further question of whether what was internalized was a personal parental figure or a more general normative pattern. The very fact that in the careful formulations to which I have referred, Freud's reference to parental function suggests an interpretation in the latter direction. He was emphasizing the norms of proper or acceptable behavior, rather than the personal authority of the parents as individuals.

Of the three subsystems of the personality that Freud distinguished from each other—ego, id, and superego—the superego has on the whole received the least attention. My concern at the moment, however, is not primarily with its content, but with its primary function. My suggestion is that this should be conceived to be a regulatory function, not only, as has usually been assumed, in relation to the id, but in relation to the problem from which the present discussion started. This is the problem posed by the fact that the individual person in relation to the external world, that is to reality in Freud's sense, was faced by a problem of uncertainty and instability of proliferating contingencies and the like, which was directly analogous to the kind of problem that social scientists have for some time recognized in the operation of systems of social interaction, perhaps particularly those rather extensive systems where participation by individuals has normally been presumed to be predominantly rational.

If this line of interpretation is basically correct, it would essentially say that mature individuals in their capacity as parents—through some set of mechanisms, the understanding of which presents difficulties for psychological analysis—do typically inculcate in their children a psychological commitment to the observance of normative standards of actions that the parents, presumably, assume to be important. Freud himself often used the word *moral* to characterize these standards. In the interaction between parents and their young children, there of course is no such formal regulatory system as appears in the law at the level of social institutionalization. Nevertheless, it seems to me to be legitimate to establish a quite direct structural and functional connection between the normative system that social scientists have emphasized at the level of social-interaction systems and the superego as a structural component of the personality of the individual.

I might therefore suggest that the relation between Freud's three components of the personality structure is somewhat different from what has ordinarily been supposed. That id impulses, as discussed, are not rationally organized in the sense that makes them appropriate to govern ego functioning in relation to the social environment is a commonplace in the interpretation of psychoanalytic theory. The new consideration I would like to put forward is that there is a certain parallelism between ego and id in this respect. Although the grounds on which they are unstable relative to the functional needs of the personality as a whole differ fundamentally, they share the feature of instability. The instability of ego functioning refers to Freud's category of the input of information from the environment or the external world through the senses. The factor of instability is the contingency of what, to the acting individual, are the significant features of his environmental situation among which the most important is clearly the action of emotionally significant others.

My suggestion about the superego is that its primary function is the mediation of these two sets of instabilities to which the individual personality is exposed and, in psychoanalytic theory, exposed very much from the earliest infancy on. The superego is derived from a special normative source, namely the normative order of the society and culture through the internalization of standards and expectations on the part of either actual parents or other adults who share in the parental function.

Let us now return to the other context, namely that of Weber, in his use of *Zweckrationalitat* and its relation to such categories as economic action. To me, the striking correspondence that prompted the line of thought presented in this chapter was between the broad context of economic rationality in the social science literature and of ego functioning in the psychoanalytic literature. The common feature of the two is some sort of categorization of rationality. The new feature, from my point of view, is the emphasis on the instability of the situations faced by this type of rational action, whether it be viewed from the perspective of the participating personality or that of the system of social organization.

Then, as I have already directly indicated, there seems to be a direct parallel between the personality as an integrating reference, set of mechanisms, or whatever you call them, and the normative system at the social level. In modern societies, by far the most developed and sophisticated part of this normative system is what is ordinarily called law. Max Weber was a major contributor to the understanding of the relations between economic action and law. I think the most significant conceptual point is that Weber clearly treated law as an aspect of what he called "legitimate order." *Zweckrationalitat*, on the other hand, he treated as independent of the category of legitimacy, as governed by interest in the attainment of whatever end or goal the acting individual might be pursuing in the relevant context.

The question now arises of whether or in what sense there is, at the sociocultural level, a second focus of instability of action, so that there would be, in case there is such a focus, a direct structural parallel between personality and social system. I think it can be claimed that, for Weber, there was indeed such a focus. Its place and significance were by no means fully analyzed by Weber, but I think the center of it is his famous concept of charisma.

Weber's fullest discussion of charisma came in the context of his classification of three fundamental types of authority. It should be noted that all three were for him subtypes of legitimate order. The three were traditional, rational-legal, and charismatic authority. I think the concept of traditional authority had, above all, a historical and developmental reference for Weber, but he quite clearly insisted that traditional authority was, in a concept he emphasized a great deal, "routinized." So also was rational-legal authority, and this is the context in which the ordering of social relations through legal machinery found its place. In this connection, it should be remembered that Weber was originally trained in jurisprudence, not in economics or sociology. When he spoke of the rational-legal order, he was speaking from deeply ingrained experience, well beyond that of the ordinary citizen.

By contrast with both traditional and rational-legal authority, however, charismatic authority was primordially uninstitutionalized, as we might say. This has to do with Weber's association of it with individual personalities who pose demands for followership of the precepts they promulgate. Weber always insisted that the charismatic leader treats compliance with his precepts as a duty, not simply as an appeal to economic or other comparable interests. Another very prominent theme in Weber's work concerns what he called the routinization of charisma. This strongly suggests that for him charisma was unorganized, or chaotic, specifically by contrast with the kind of order that a stable system of social relationships demands.

It is in this context that I would like to suggest that the charismatic component, from Weber's point of view, is analogous to the id, from Freud's. Just as id impulses can only be built into normally functioning adult personalities through a process of socialization, as we call it, so I think that charismatic initiatives could for Weber only be built into a structure of a stable social order through routinization. It seems to me that routinization, in Weber's usage, is very close to what a good many social scientists have come to call institutionalization.

It is on this basis that I would contend that in the theory of the social system, or the sociocultural system, using Max Weber's treatment of it as an example, there is therein a three-fold differentiation among structural components of that system, which in functional reference corresponds very directly to Freud's three-fold differentiation of the personality of the individual. From this point of view, the ego and the category of *Zweckrationalitat* in Weber's term, or of instrumentally rational action, correspond to each other. They face each other at the interface between individual personality and the social environment in which the personality operates as an ordinary human actor. In a sense, back of this dual structure, with emphasis on the problematical meaning of back, lies in both cases a system of regulation in terms of normative standards and mechanisms. For the social system, it is the system of normative rules to which action must be oriented, which has, in advanced societies, been institutionalized as a system of law. In personality systems, it is the superego, which is not derivable from the immediate exigencies either of everyday social interaction or of the id impulse system. It is, however, derived in the process of socialization, a point on which Freud is completely unequivocal, from the influence on the growing child of his contact with parental figures, whether they be actual parents or not, in the process that we call socialization.

The new insight that has prompted the present exposition is that there is a third parallel between the two conceptual schemes, namely with respect to the status of the id in psychoanalytic theory on the one hand and of charisma in sociocultural theory on the other. Both are in certain respects more ultimate than the other two in their respective systems, but in addition to being more ultimate, they are less appropriately organized from the point of view of the functioning of the system in question. In certain respects, id impulses are chaotic, seen in the context of the functioning of the normal and healthy adult personality. In a corresponding sense, charismatic initiatives are also chaotic, from the point of view of the functioning of a stable, complex, and differentiated society.

When looked at in this way, an interesting pattern of articulation emerges. Freud's concept of the id arose in connection with his consideration of the boundary and articulating structures between the biological organism and the social and cultural system in which human beings operate. As I have said, the treatment of id impulse, as in a simple sense the operation of biological instincts, is theoretically grossly inadequate. There has to be a complex transformative process in relating what Freud called the "flow of stimulation" from the organism to the psyche, to use his term. This process of transformation clearly involves the attribution as symbols of special meanings to certain surface features of human organisms, the erogenous zones. These are not, however, organs of any one particular individual organism but involve both sexes and two contiguous generations (the principal ones are clearly mouth, breast, vagina, and penis).

The organization of the motivational system of the personality must be articulated with the organization of experience in relation to what Freud called external reality, which is the primary field of ego function, and with respect to which the input that must be structured comes through sensory experience.

To me it is strikingly important that the integrative focus, if this interpretation of Freud is correct, between these two sets of components of the individual personality is derived from the social system in which the individual is, through socialization, in process of being incorporated. It is, in Freud's concept, the superego. The important point for the moment is that the term "ultimate," as used before, refers to the boundary relation between living organism and personality. It connotes motivational ultimacy, which is the inadequate excuse for categorizing it as biologically instinctive.

For Weber, on the other hand, the ultimacy of charismatic impulse, if one may use that term, lies in its relation to what some of us have been calling the "telic" boundary of human action experience. It is the field in which religion is the most prominent cultural and social phenomenon. The charismatic leader in Weber's sense is par excellence the religious leader, especially in his empirical work, *The Prophet.*

There is a hierarchy of levels of organization running throughout the human condition. Although there is the physical world, this may be left out of consideration for the moment, and we may start with the organic. As L.J. Henderson so effectively made clear, there is an order of nature that integrates both the physical and the organic. The organic, however, is the base on which that unique evolutionary product that is called human action has emerged. Only living organisms can act, in this sense; and the resources of the living organism have to be built into their action systems, which in a motivational reference and at the individual level is ordinarily called the personality.

There can, however, be no human personality that is not, in the sense of the current discussion, socialized. We think it has become clear that, in the nature of the case, there can be no normal human being who has not been socialized through internalization as well as environmental experience that is incorporated into a going social system, including its cultural components. It is on this basis that I treat the legal system as the counterpart, for the sociocultural level of the superego, for that of the individual personality. Finally, then, charisma is ultimate in a sense drastically different from that in which the flow of stimulation from the organism is ultimate, but in a theoretically parallel sense in that it concerns the boundaries of the system of action vis-à-vis the telic considerations that have been incorporated in our great religious traditions.

It is significant, therefore, in conclusion, that, although Freud as a medical man was above all concerned with the boundary between organism and personality at the individual level, Weber as a sociologist of religion and an immense innovator in this field was concerned with the boundary between the concrete and empirical modes of life of human beings in this world and the problems of the ultimate meaning of their existence.

4

Psychoanalytic Selfobject Psychology and Psychohistory

Ernest S. Wolf

A few months ago R.W. Southern, president of St. John's College in Oxford, gave the Rede Lecture, a lectureship that was first endowed in 1542 at Cambridge. My attention was caught by the title of Southern's lecture. He named his topic "The Historical Experience," by which he means the historian's experience of history. What Southern calls the historical experience is indeed very close to what psychoanalysts call empathy. I was reminded again how much we psychoanalysts can learn from historians who have struggled with similar problems of method for a long time. However, it is no longer necessary to praise the benefits of interdisciplinary collaboration and empathic science. The true meaning of empathy, namely to really listen to and attempt to understand another person—to bridge the boundaries of race, religion, and nation, of generation, epoch, and time-bound past ages, that is, to transcend individual and group self—has become an ideal not only for many psychoanalysts but for all those who care about their fellow man. Interest in an actual person, not an abstract mankind, is the touchstone for the truly empathic scientist.

In what follows, I will discuss an emerging new paradigm in psychoanalysis, particularly about Heinz Kohut's conceptualization of a psychoanalytic psychology of the self. Let me briefly mention Southern's Rede Lecture again and call to your attention the word "Experience" in Southern's title. I was intrigued to see how much the subjective experience of the historian had become a focus of scholarly interest. For it is also the subjective experience of analyst and analysand that have become increasingly the focus of interest for the psychoanalyst. Of course, the use of empathically obtained insights has always been implicit in psychoanalytic practice from its very inception. Yet, surprisingly, in the 24-hour volume *Standard Edition* of Freud's work the word *empathy* occurs only fifteen times. Freud did not define the concept empathy and never discussed it at length. However, Freud was clearly aware of the importance of empathy in a 1921 footnote, where he stated that it is "the mechanism by means of which we are enabled to express any opinion at all toward another mental life" (Freud 1921).

The reluctance to fully acknowledge the crucial role of empathy in the data collection process of clinical psychoanalysis is also reflected in classical psychoanalytic theory. Traditional psychoanalytic theories of mental processes are constructed in analogy to the models of natural science. For example, the structural theory of id, ego, and superego, that is, of a mental apparatus powered by drives and constrained by defenses, is conceptualized in a natural science model where the analyst-observer studies objects outside himself in his field of observation. It is the essence of psychoanalysis, however, that crucial data are collected introspectively inside the observing analyst, and, in resonating with the analysand, the analyst gains insight into the analysand's inner experience by vicarious introspection, that is, by empathy. Kohut (1959) discussed explicitly the role of empathy as an essential that distinguishes psychoanalysis as a depth psychology from other psychologies based solely on observation of overt behavior or social interaction. It is only with the explicit acknowledgement of the empathic data-base of psychoanalysis that there began that important shift of conceptual focus in psychoanalytic theory formation from emphasis on the facts of what had observedly happened to the experience evoked by what had happened. Equally, the psychoanalyst's heightened sensitivity to his analysand's subjective experience during the analytic session led Kohut to those insights that have found their conceptual statement in the psychology of the self.

The concepts of the psychology of the self thus reflect the newly emphasized position of the psychological observer: no longer is he outside the psychic apparatus, looking at it and describing it in the fashion of the natural scientist who observes objects outside of himself; instead, the psychoanalytic observer of the self is interested in inner experience, whether it is his own experience or whether it is his patient's experience. Within the framework of Kohut's psychoanalytic psychology of the self, therefore, we no longer talk about a psychic apparatus, about id, ego, and superego; instead, we talk about the self and about selfobjects.

The concept of selfobject was introduced by Kohut to bridge the gap between experience and description: aspects of the surround, of the observed social field, which are described by the observer as objects but that are subjectively experienced as part of the self, are termed selfobjects. For example, the elements of essential psychological nourishment that sustain a small child—the caring, soothing, acknowledging, responding, mirroring, admiring, and admirable strength and goodness of the caretaking adult—are not only observed and described but are also experienced by the child as an essential part of its well-being, of its sense of continuity over time and space, in short as its self. When Kohut talks about a child's selfobjects, therefore, he refers to those qualities of the child's environment that are experienced by the child as part of its self and that by virtue of the cohesion they lend to the child's self become functionally and structurally a part of the child's self, at least temporarily. The selfobject concept allows the construction of a model of the self. Based on this model the data of self-selfobject relations can be ordered into theories about normal self-development, pathogenic self-development, self-pathology, self-selfobject transferences, disorders of the self, the psychoanalytic treatment of disorders of the self, and so forth. I shall elaborate on some of these data and theories.

First, however, I want to digress briefly to stress again that the constructs of psychoanalytic self psychology and especially the selfobject concept are derived from the empathic immersion into the clinical data of selfobject transferrences obtained in the psychoanalysis of adult analysands. This stands in contrast to constructs that may be derived by the application of accepted psychological theories, for example, psychoanalytic ego psychology, to observational data. This distinction between empathy-based interpretations, on the one hand, and theory-based interpretations, on the other hand, is of the greatest importance for psychohistorical research also. The application of certain psychoanalytic theories to historical data yields interpretations about the meaning of historical events that are theory-near but experience-distant. Analogous theory-near but experience-distant interpretations sometimes are made in clinical psychoanalysis; they may be correct but often are peripheral to the emotionally invested focus of the examined events. In clinical psychoanalysis these kinds of interpretations do not contribute to moving the analytic process along; in psychohistorical research, I suspect, their effect is equally sterile. They lend themselves to making easy rationalizations that are intellectually satisfying and protect against intense or painful involvement. The psychohistorian, I believe, would be better served by shunning the application of theories in favor of the kind of deep immersion into his historical material that would evoke in him an emotional involvement and reactions to which he would gain access by introspection. These evoked reactions of the historian's self, introspectively perceived and carefully evaluated through the filter of the historian's self-knowledge could become a crucial datum in gaining an empathic entrance to the historical material. Psychohistorical interpretations that lack this empathic content are in danger of being experience-distant and irrelevant. Perhaps, the psychohistorian needs to undergo a training analysis, as does the psychoanalyst, to sharpen his perceptions, to free his creativity, and to improve his judgments by strengthening and by making more flexible the structure of his self.

Let us return to a discussion of self-psychology. Kohut conceptualizes the self as a psychological structure at the core of human personality. The self is made up of three major constituents: (1) a pole of ambition from which emanate the basic strivings for power and success; (2) a pole of values that harbors the basic idealized goals; and (3) an intermediate area of basic talents and skills. These elements of the self and their cohesion into a stable structure are the result of appropriately empathic interactions between the small child and its selfobjects of early childhood.

For example, a small child will thrive with a feeling of well-being and a secure sense of self as long as it experiences a psychologically responsive closeness of selfobject, usually the mother. The psychological absence of this selfobject—for example, an unresponsive or unempathic caretaker—is experienced by the child with distress and results in psychological dysfunctions associated with low self-esteem. A child needs certain psychological functions of the caretaking person to complement and complete the structure of his own psychological functions, to give him a secure sense of self. Empathically attuned selfobjects that are available for appropriately responsive mirroring or for idealization strengthen the self, increase its cohesion, and help protect it against fragmentation. Let me stress an important distinction here. The caretaking person is needed as a selfobject by the child to lend strength and cohesion to the child's self. Of course, the caretaker performs other functions as well. In the physical sphere, he provides the shelter and nutrition needed. In the psychological sphere, he is also the source of the pleasures and pains that go with gratification and frustration of libidinal desires, which have been studied extensively by psychoanalysis. The psychology of the self is evolving from a study of those functions that are reflected in the vicissitudes of self-experience and that have been conceptualized by Kohut as selfobject functions.

Kohut came to the selfobject model of man's psychological structure in two steps. First of these was the discovery during the clinical psychoanalytic treatment of certain patients of a previously unnoticed class of transferencelike phenomena; the second step was the introduction of the selfobject concept. I will briefly review these.

A central phenomenon occurring during psychoanalytic treatment is the repetition by the analysand of the wishes, fears, and attitudes of his early childhood with, however, a significant difference that now the analyst instead of the parent becomes the target for these archaic wishes, fears, and attitudes. This phenomenon is called the transference, and the analysis of the transference, that is, bringing it to the patient's conscious awareness in all its ramifications, becomes an important task in the analytic work. Kohut discovered that, at least in some patients, there developed a set of transferencelike phenomena that are the revival in the analytic situation not of the infantile drives and defenses described by classical psychoanalysis but of archaic needs for narcissistic enhancement. One type, the mirror transferences, are the reactivated needs for acceptance and confirmation of the child's sense of his greatness, perfection, and worth. The other type of transference, the idealizing transferences, are the reactivated needs of the child to share in the calmness and strength of an admired parent by feeling itself merged with the parental image of calm omnipotence and unfailing omniscience. In the analytic situation these reactivated archaic needs become focused on the analyst. Unconsciously, the analysand hopes that the analyst will satisfy the old needs, and, unconsciously, the analysand fears a repetition of the old rejections, frustrations, and humiliations. Characteristically, the patient's sometimes very severe psychological discomfort that brought him to seek analytic treatment, such as low self-esteem, depression, anxiety, hypochondriasis, and so forth, often is greatly ameliorated concomitantly with the emergence of these transference phenomena as long as the analyst makes himself available to try to empathically understand the reactivated needs for confirmation or idealization. This is an activity on the part of the analyst and not a mainly passive posture. The analyst's empathic understanding stance in relation to the analysand quite frequently is sufficiently nourishing to the analysand's self to relieve symptoms. The disruption of these transference relationships—for example, by the physical absence of the analyst or by his functional absence when the analyst, although physically present, is unresponsive to the needs of the patient—results in the return of the symptoms and discomfort.

These observations led Kohut to postulate a structural and functional deficiency of the patient's core psychological structure, his nuclear self. Temporarily, the deficiency was relieved by the emergence of the transference relationship to the analyst; in other words, the functionally responsive presence of the analyst could take the place of the patient's structural deficit, take over the functions of the missing part of the patient's self, and restore completeness and cohesion to the self. Since those aspects of the analyst that restore cohesive wholeness to the patient's self are experienced by the patient as part of his self, the analyst has become for the patient an object that is, at the same time, part of his self. It was this observation that led Kohut to conceptualize the class of objects that are subjectively experienced as part of the self as selfobjects.

In clinical psychoanalysis the discovery of the selfobject transferences, which is Kohut's designation for the class of transferences that consists of the varieties of mirror and idealizing transferences, shifts the analyst's attention to the central vulnerability of these patients, namely to the vicissitudes of cohesion, vigor, and harmony of their nuclear selves. The self is a structure whose state of cohesion, vigor, and internal harmony is reflected subjectively in feelings of well-being, high self-esteem, and joyful function. On the other hand, when the self is in a state of structural fragmentation, depletion, or internal imbalance, then the subjective reflection of this disturbed state of self manifests as experiences of low self-esteem, depression, anxiety, hypochrondriacal fears relating to body or mind, and inefficiently awkward functioning of the person. These symptoms that accompany a pathologically disordered state of the self are extremely distressing and act as powerful motivators to take action to attain or restore a harmonious state of the self. The remedial actions often take the form of a frantic search for substitute selfobjects such as drugs, alcohol, sexual perversions, and other symptomatic behavior. Sometimes the self can be strengthened and relief of symptoms obtained by intense involvement with groups or social movements that symbolically represent selfobjects (this clinical finding may well have some significance for historical research). In clinical psychoanalysis the aim is to strengthen the structure and cohesion of the analysand's self through accretion of new psychic structure via transmuting internalizations. In a well-conducted analysis, usually extending over many months of a working-through process, the selfobject aspects of the transference to the analyst are gradually internalized and become psychic structure, part of the self. The dependence on the analyst as a selfobject is thus gradually replaced by the growth and expansion of the self.

Much data have accumulated after a decade of experience in the psychoanalytic treatment of analysands with disorders of their selves. These data from observed transference phenomena, together with the recovery via memories, dreams, and fantasies of data from the patients' life history and from their self-experiences, have allowed the construction of a psychology of the self. The psychology of the self has grown to include a theory of the normal development of the self, a theory of the bipolar structure of the self, a classification of the disorders of the self, including their etiology, psychopathology, symptomatology, characterology, and treatment. I will summarize some salient points that seem of special importance to historians.

It is difficult to be specific about the beginnings of psychological development without adultomorphizing some very primitive and archaic structures. We assume that a newborn infant has the potentials for the development of a self, but no such structure appears to emerge until about the age of eighteen months to two years. The self that emerges during the second year of life is very fragile, its cohesion is weak, and it tends to revert into its constituent nuclei when the cohesion facilitating ministrations of the selfobject milieu are either absent or faulty. The mirroring selfobject confirms the baby's vigor, greatness, and perfection, for example, when the child feels it is the "apple of mother's eye." The idealized selfobjects are available for the child to look up to and with whom he can merge as images of calm power and incorruptible knowledge. An example would be the soothing calm that would infuse a hurt and upset child as it is picked up gently by a strong, understanding parent. The child's sense of self is strengthened when surrounded by such a selfobject milieu and his self becomes more cohesive by internalizing the functions of the selfobjects. Gradually the self becomes more complete and needs less to rely on the selfobjects to attain wholeness. During the course of normal development the self usually reaches a state of irreversible cohesion around age eight. After that, the self, although still in need of certain selfobject functions and still troubled and suffering without the needed selfobject milieu, no longer runs the risk of regressing into the chaotic precohesive state of the rudimentary self that clinically we recognize as psychotic. If, however, the selfobject milieu failed to provide sufficient responsiveness to the child's need for mirroring and for idealization, then the child's self is left deficient in structure and remains vulnerable to regression leading to a variety of disorders of the self. Major structural defects are associated with propensity for severe regression to the precohesive state of the rudimentary self seen in psychosis and in borderline conditions. Limited structural deficits are associated with dispositions for regression to the fragile self-state seen in narcissistic behavior disorders and in narcissistic personality disorders. Neurosis can be conceptualized as a specific variety of the latter.

However, what I would like to stress is that even after healthy normal development into full-grown maturity, there remains a significant need for an appropriate selfobject milieu, at least for most persons. To be sure, the nature of the selfobject need changes. The infant requires the responsive physical psychological presence of its parents or surrogates. The child learns to accept other adults, such as teachers, as substitutes. Later, there are siblings and friends from the peer group that can be sources of confirmation of self and become available for idealization. Adolescence is characterized by the transition from individual selfobjects to groups as selfobjects. At first it is the peer group that is experienced as part of the self, and peers may become vitally necessary to maintain the cohesion of the self and the sense of well-being. With full adulthood, being part of an in-group is replaced by membershiip in many associations, which are less personal but, in their additive effect on the self, no less needed. Sudden loss of belonging to one's neighborhood or community, or loss of membership in one's professional association, or loss of one's citizenship, can be as devastatingly disruptive to the mature self as the loss of a parent to a youngster. In addition, since these groups are selfobjects, any threat to the group per se is felt as a threat to the self. This provides us with a plausible explanation for the stubborn survival of certain social institutions that have lost all logically rational reason to exist except their selfobject function. It seems to me, for example, that the maintenance of obsolete political boundaries instead of rational regrouping into metropolitan areas is motivated primarily by selfobject needs and fears rather than by economic considerations. On a global scale, the undiminished hold of nationalism is the result of the need of weak selves to draw strength from the identification with the grandeur and ideals of the nation as selfobject.

So far I have mentioned one aspect of the changing selfobject need, namely the diffusion from the individual's person-oriented self-object milieu of infancy to the aggregate of vaguely defined and impersonal relationships to groups in adulthood. Of course, intimate family relationships are also a source of selfobject availability as the adult finds responsiveness in spouse, children, and friendships. However, the family, even the extended family, is hardly sufficient in providing all the aspects of the needed selfobject milieu.

Another aspect of the changing selfobject milieu should be mentioned. In infancy the selfobject's presence is required; for the adult it may be sufficient to have the selfobject represented symbolically. Already the child learns to accept the sound of its mother in another room as a sufficient sign of her presence. In a pathological aberration, the fetishistic child may draw strength the sight and smell of mother's clothing during her absence from the house. The adult's need for selfobjects can often be met by very abstract and symbolic representations, such as a flag or religious ritual and, of course, art in all its forms. It is not hard to imagine the emptiness of life, that is, the emptiness of self, if all these selfobjects were no longer part of one's self. Clearly, selfobject needs do not disappear with normal development. Rather, they change, in general, by becoming more diffuse, more symbolic, and more interchangeable. An important task that remains to be done is to describe the developmental line of selfobjects.

Fragmentation and depletion of the self, as I said earlier, are associated with great distress, such as severe disintegration anxiety, low self-esteem, depression, hypochrondriasis, and so forth. Vulnerable selves, therefore, often are apprehensive and easily traumatized into severe phobic anxiety. They attempt to avoid the suffering by having control of their environment and especially control of their needed selfobjects. Their sensitivity and irritability is such that they react with rage to any threat to their self-image of omnipotent control. This narcissistic rage, as Kohut (1972) has termed it, is an unappeasable and destructive force that needs to wipe out the offending threat to the illusion of omnipotence of the vulnerable self. Narcissistic rage appears to be an important factor not only in the pathological behavior of individuals but also in the quasi-pathological destructive behavior of groups (Kohut 1978). One example is the seemingly unappeasable anger of the Palestinians, whose national group-self has been humiliated by defeat after defeat at the hands of both Arabs and Jews. On the other hand, two thousand years of persecution and the holocaust of recent memory have traumatized the Jewish group self into a hypersensitivity that is expressed in the slogan "Never Again." For groups, as for individuals, narcissistic rage cannot be cured but it will fade away as the availability of responsive selfobjects allows the self to gain strength and confidence.

Briefly, I want to call attention also to the contribution that a psychology of the self can make to the study of leadership. It seems that groups, analogous to individuals, have group ambitions, group ideals, in other words one may postulate a group-self. When catastrophes threaten the group-self in its cohesion and survival, the resulting need for selfobjects to shore up the crumbling group-self may be supplied by a particularly outstanding individual. Kohut talks about messianic leaders who strengthen the group-self by being available for idealization and about charismatic leaders who bolster the group by restoring the threatened sense of grandeur and omnipotence of the group. Churchill after Dunkirk played such a role for Britain. And, perhaps, Martin Luther King did similarly for the American black. In a previous dialogue between historians and psychoanalysts (Wolf 1976) a number of such messianic and charismatic leaders were mentioned (including that giant among messianic leaders, Ghandi, about whom we have learned so much from Erik Erikson). The strength and cohesion of a group-self is continuously reflected in the group's self-esteem. Self-psychology can contribute many illuminating insights into the back-and-forth of the reciprocal psychological needs of the leader for self-confirmation by the group and vice versa.

Tentatively, I would like to offer in the following an interpretation of recent events that was shaped by introspectively perceived reactions that could be ordered into a meaningful view by using the selfobject model. During the decades after World War II, for example, the president of the United States has been the leader of the West, and, like it or not, we have had a ringside seat, or even been intensely involved, in the momentous struggle of the Western world to salvage a new self out of the fragmenting debacle of the war: collapsing empires, wilting ideologies, vanishing religious beliefs in the West. On the horizon was the strange and alien new empire of the East satisfying the need for the idealizable selfobject by offering a quasi-religious commitment to seemingly new ideas and values. In the event, the alien ideal could become a selfobject only for that minority whose individual selves had been injured and who consequently already were alienated from the group-self. The majority incorporated an image of America as a new idealized selfobject, as anybody can witness who has seen the astounding transformation in the appearance and ideals of contemporary Western Europe. (An August 1978 newspaper article talks about Burger King Whoppers in Berlin, a London performance of the American musical "Annie," hot dogs with potato chips and popcorn in Czechoslovakia, not to mention Coca-Cola, Levis, and rock music.) These phenomena have been commented on many times but usually in the context of postulated commercial or political domination. These latter factors may, indeed, be important. However, in my view, the self-psychological dynamics are the decisive ones (see Kohut 1978).

Similarly, one may raise questions about possible self-psychological factors in the precipitation of the turmoil of the sixties in America. How much was America's youth identified with John Kennedy as an idealized self-object? Quite aside from any partisan political issues, the whole country experienced a lift when the beautiful people moved into the White House. Did we not feel a quickening of the pulse, a strengthening of our national resolve, a growing cohesion around our revived idealism? All this was ended in a split second by a tiny piece of metal fired by a mindless nobody. Was the essential weakness and vulnerability of a powerful and idealized self-object ever demonstrated more dramatically, on TV, over and over again? Serious injury was done to the pole of idealization of our group-self. The integrity and strength of this group-self had rested on the incorporation of the idealized president as a selfobject. Am I being too speculative when I wonder whether the turmoil of the sixties had its roots in the disillusionment with a powerful war hero, who turned out to be a rather nice but frequently ill and do-nothing president, and whether this turmoil was then amplified many times as the American group-self was totally shattered by the tragedy in Dallas? As a group we experienced not only depression but fragmentation. Even our language changed by the late sixties. Our news reports began referring to the ragged, drugged, but peaceful flower children protesting the Vietnam war as beautiful people.

I shall not take this line of inquiry any further. As a psychoanalyst I can hardly claim the qualifications needed to answer the kind of question raised. My purpose was to show that one can think of these events in psychological terms and that psychological insights may have a significance beyond the unquestioned importance of political and economic movements. Historians and sociologists with a sensitivity that is attuned to the self-state of individuals and of groups will, in my estimation, make the great contributions here. Therefore, I will summarize my thesis in one sentence: the developing psychoanalytic selfobject psychology can become a powerful tool for illuminating difficult questions in history and the social sciences.

References

Freud, S. 1921. *Group Psychology and the Analysis of the Ego. Standard Edition*, vol. 18. London: Hogarth Press, 1955.

Kohut, H. 1959. "Introspection, Empathy and Psychoanalysis." *Journal of the American Psychoanalytic Association* 7:459-483.

_____ . 1966. "Forms and Transformations of Narcissism." *Journal of the American Psychoanalytic Association* 14:243-272.

_____ . 1971. *The Analysis of the Self.* New York: International Universities Press.

_____ . 1972. "Thoughts on Narcissism and Narcissistic Rage." *The Psychoanalytic Study of the Child* 27:360-400. New York: Quadrangle Press.

_____ . 1977. *The Restoration of the Self*. New York: International Universities Press.

_____ . 1978. *The Search for the Self*. New York: International Universities Press.

Southern, R.W. 1977. "The Historical Experience." *Times Literary Supplement*, June 24.

Wolf, E.S. 1976. "Recent Advances in the Psychology of the Self: An Outline of Basic Concepts." *Comprehensive Psychiatry* 17:37-46.

5 Emerging Paradigms in Psychoanalysis and Related Fields

Miles F. Shore

There are a number of paradigms emerging in psychoanalysis and related fields that, to some, offer new possibilities within a basically psychoanalytic view of human nature. To others, they are developments that assert radically alternative ways of thinking about human psychic functioning, which, as a result, should not be considered as truly psychoanalytic, however useful they may ultimately prove to be.

For purposes of the present discussion I have chosen to consider psychoanalysis broadly. This reflects in part my own position as a psychoanalyst with sizeable administrative responsibilities and an interest in history and social phenomena who has found psychoanalytic concepts to be useful in a great variety of situations outside the consulting room. It also reflects the aim of this chapter—to acquaint historians, social scientists, and other nonclinicans with emerging paradigms that may be helpful to them in their own work.

Some of these new paradigms result from pressures extrinsic to the field. Some are the product of the natural evolution of clinical and theoretical work. A significant number reflect dissatisfaction with current psychoanalytic theory and the results of psychoanalytic treatment, and others, farther ahead in terms of usefulness, are the byproduct of work in entirely separate fields, converging with new data on established psychoanalytic understanding.

The emerging paradigms which I will discuss can be divided into three groups. First, there are those that are related to our efforts to develop new modes of empathic communication with other people. These empathic developments are derived from intensive clinical work, that is, they emerge from the unfolding analytic process that takes place between two people, the therapist and the patient. Second, there are those that are the result of studies of the external validity of psychoanalytic ideas. These are chiefly studies of child development and longitudinal research into the psychological development of the human being over the entire life span. Third, there are developments that, strictly speaking, are not yet psychoanalytic paradigms at all but promise in the future to revolutionize our concepts of human nature. These are chiefly advances in neurobiology, especially neurophysiology and psychopharmacology.

Paradigms Emerging from Clinical Work

The heart of psychoanalysis has always been clinical work. Training in analytic institutes is organized to develop practitioners of psychoanalysis, and, as Astley pointed out in his 1973 presidential address to the American Psychoanalytic Association, an interest in applying psychoanalysis as a general theory of behavior to situations outside the consulting room has generally been regarded as a suspect deviation from dedication to true analysis.[1]

In turn, the essence of clinical psychoanalysis has been the development of an empathic relationship with patients—the progressive tuning and refinement of the capacity to understand the experience of another person especially when under stress or in conflict. It was clinical theory, emphasizing stages of psychological development, that was the center of analytic interest because it could assist practitioners in the empathic understanding of patients.

Originally this empathy was directed primarily toward the oedipal constellation, toward the adult sequelae of developmental issues occurring at ages four through six. But with growing understanding of the defensive functions of the ego the scope of psychoanalysis has broadened. For a considerable period major efforts have been directed to develop empathic understanding of sicker individuals whose more serious pathology reflects a variety of early failures and aberrations in ego development originating in the first and second years of life. The work of Melanie Klein, D.W. Winnicott, Elvin Semrad, Harry Guntrip, and more recently Heinz Kohut and Otto Kernberg has approached a variety of patients from a host of points of view to improve our capacity to tune in to more seriously disturbed individuals.

Ten years ago there was lively debate about the work of Melanie Klein and the English school of analysts. There was great skepticism at Klein's assertion that psychological development in infancy involves recovery from a normal psychosis and that the psyche of the infant consists of highly developed psychological structures—a primitive but elaborate ego and superego bristling with complicated psychological fantasies.[2] Although the structures were suspect and may not actually exist in infants, the mechanisms she described proved useful in understanding patients. Splitting, projective identification, and the depressive and paranoid positions caught on and became the precursors of concepts that, somewhat altered, form our present empathic armamentarium with these sicker patients.

Today, one major area of excitement in the field is provided by the Kohut-Kernberg debate. These two gladiators use similar words to describe different concepts. Like other psychoanalytic investigators they are relatively unconcerned with what epidemiologists call the denominator problem and ascribe universality to observations on what seem to be significantly different populations of patients.

Chapter 4 has given a clear and succinct account of Kohut's work. It would take at least another full chapter to do equal justice to Kernberg's work and a third to compare the two. However, it is possible to sketch briefly some of the differences.

Kohut builds his conceptualization on a sequence of narcissistic development parallel to the development of object libido. Thus his schema includes a range of pathology form sick to normal. Kernberg in contrast is concerned primarily with much sicker people in a more pathological infantile state.[3] This state is characterized by ego splitting (that is, viewing objects as all good or all bad, and feelings are split into love and hate) primitive projection of unacceptable feelings, omnipotence, primitive idealization, and defenses related to envy. For Kernberg, the development of narcissism, that is, self-interest, is intertwined with libidinal development, that is, interest in others, and is not a separate line. A state of normal narcissism is for Kernberg a case of object relationships having escaped the pernicious distortions of primitive aggression and envy. It is certainly not the successful outcome of a normal and separate line of narcissistic development.[4]

Kernberg's psychological landscape resembles an allegorical piece by Hieronymous Bosch. The forces of primitive oral rage and envy clash on a darkling plain strewn with part objects, bad introjects, and grindingly negative transferences. Primitive aggression is a raw id derivative intertwined with early projectively and introjectively internalized object relations, that is, it grossly distorts the persons' view of important people.

Kohut paints a sunnier picture. Aggression arises from the frustration of the child's "absolutarian expectations." This may take place not only in infancy but also in later development. Thus frustration, even at the oedipal period, may derail the course of narcissistic development and damage the sense of self. Kohut's handling of aggression is to undermine it by a "gradual transformation of the narcissistic matrix from which the rage arises."[5] Kernberg in contrast goes directly after the rage and envy, wrestling with them in an attempt to work through and undo the pathological defensive grandiosity to clear the path of normal phallicoedipal development.

Predictably, Kohut and Kernberg differ sharply in their therapeutic suggestions. Kernberg does battle with the primitive forces in his patients. He slices aggressively into the negative transference, exposing the envy and competitiveness beneath apparent idealization. Kohut in contrast is less active and recommends the enhancement of certain narcissistic transference patterns, which become the nidus of what he calls "transmuting internalizations" to restore narcissistic development to its proper track and schedule. Although Kohut in no way abandons the position of analytic abstinence from gratifying the patient's wishes, he does recommend an additional maneuver—the empathic appreciation as well as interpretation of archaic narcissistic needs and demands.

What does one do with these differing approaches? If one's purpose is to construct a consistent theory of human psychological development one concentrates on a careful exegesis and synthesis of the two views. If, however, the purpose is clinical—the understanding of human beings as patients or nonpatients—one applies the concepts when they are useful and help to organize observations that are otherwise baffling. At this level, universality and consistency across theory are not really necessary.

To take a recent, personal psychohistorical example, in my role as a mental hospital director it was my lot to participate as management in a bitter three-day strike of public employees. A Kernbergian analysis, which emphasized splitting and projective mechanisms, was helpful in understanding much that went on. There was a staff of perhaps 150 people who had worked closely together for many years in the care of patients; they knew each other well and had strong feelings of various sorts about one another. The strike split them into two groups; some went out on the picket line, while others defied the strike and stayed to care for patients. The urge on the part of each group to see themselves as simply good and the others as simply bad was alarming, particularly since they would have to work together again after the strike. Both groups felt guilty; the strikers at abandoning patients, the nonstrikers at letting down their fellow workers. Jacques has pointed out how social systems function to absorb persecutory and depressive anxieties.[6] The strike is a deliberate unhinging of the social system to generate distress, and it was clear that both persecutory and depressive anxieties were unleashed and in part projected between the two groups.

In this stressful situation management tried to function as reality-oriented ego to reduce the projection of feelings of both strikers and nonstrikers onto the governor, the taxpayers, and the legislature.

The Kernbergian analysis in terms of primitive mechanisms was very useful. However, one could have done an alternative analysis of the same facts through Kohut's analysis. In that case the aggression would have been seen as the regressive product of disappointment in the fantasies of omnipotence attached to public leaders—the governor, legislature, and so forth. The role of the strikers' humiliation at not being valued enough to be granted better working conditions and the nonstrikers not being assisted by state and hospital officials in caring for patients would also have been important. Thus disappointment in mirror and idealizing transferences of everyday life might have been invoked.

The choice of explanatory schema would be a pragmatic one—which formulation was most useful. Kohut and Kernberg offer both clinicians and historians an array of useful concepts that can substantially increase our ability to feel our way into the experience of other persons and other times.

However, theirs are not the only emerging paradigms. More controversial is the work of Roy Schafer. His approach is regarded by many as so radically different that it falls outside the scope of psychoanalysis.

In a series of papers recently assembled into a book, Schafer has carefully dismantled the traditional scaffolding of matapsychology.[7] His concern is with the terminology of metapsychology, which implies an apparatus with forces that interact impersonally in an instrumental fashion. He feels that the concreteness of the implicit metaphor so distorts the real nature of the phenomena that it is impossible to think accurately about real people who act for reasons at a host of levels and who have lives with varying meanings. His quarrel is with metaphors derived from early body experiences, which, intrinsic to customary language, are pervasively applied to many human experiences including psychological ones. To liquidate such fundamental linguistic habits is no simple task. He is seeking not simply a change in words but a more fundamental change in modes of thought.

He offers as a substitute what he calls "action language," which denotes precisely what people do and which specifies levels of inference. Thus instead of "she has a strong superego," one would say "she reacts guiltily as though she expected punishment as an immoral or dangerous person." Or, instead of "he uses a lot of projection" the action language equivalent would be "he frequently fantasies unconsciously that he is expelling from his body wishes and behavior that he prefers not to acknowledge as his own."

Schafer offers a set of rules to guide this heroic effort and to lubricate what is inevitably a laborious endeavor. One is never to speak of structures or attributes but only of actions. Adjectives are to be replaced by adverbs, "processes" by "fantasies." Psychological events should be understood not as the result of intersecting impersonal forces but rather as the consequences of actions performed for reasons by people who are goal-directed and responsible.

The conceptual distortions introduced by the mechanical metaphor of traditional metapsychology can be corrected and brought closer to real experience by clinicians who are constantly in touch with real patients. Schafer's innovations will be most useful to nonclinicians who, deprived of direct contact with psychological actions, may accept the concreteness of traditional psychoanalytic language all too literally. Thus, I recommend that psychohistorians learn about what he so vigorously and articulately proposes, since it is so firmly in the tradition of listening empathically that I have been discussing.

External Validation of Paradigms

The second set of paradigms emerge from a very different approach to psychological phenomena. In working with clinical data we are more concerned with usefulness than with truth. The experimental validation of psychoanalytic concepts is another matter. I will discuss it briefly.

The tradition of seeking external validation of paradigms derived from clinical experience goes back to Freud's early cases. He often referred to the importance of direct observation of children as a source of corroboration of his findings. Formal child development studies have been highly developed by D.M. Levy, John Bowlby, the Hampstead Nursery Group, and Yale Child Study Center. And, of course, Erikson's work, weaving together direct observation of children and adults with sensitive clinical findings and social data, has broken open the whole field of developmental studies and research into the life cycle and reemphasized the social aspects of Freud's notions of psychosexual development. More recently the work of Margaret Mahler on separation-individuation has provided us with data on early ego development, which is useful in understanding crucial features of later periods of life.[8] And very recently, longitudinal studies of development, which by definition take a long time to mature, are beginning to bear highly significant fruit. George Vaillant's elegant treatment of the early Grant study data and his own extensions of its parameters is an excellent example of this genre.[9] The Grant is a longitudinal study of college men selected for health in the years 1939 to 1941. Vaillant's work is useful both in extending our knowledge of the building blocks of mental health and adaptation and in giving us much stronger evidence of the connections between real life events in childhood and adult behavior, including symptomology. Vaillant finds that the overall quality of childhood is more important for later adjustment than isolated traumatic events, and the presence of ego competences is more important than the absence of problems or symptoms. An even more startling finding is that the choice of defense mechanisms seems to be relatively independent of childhood experience.

Squads of investigators are patrolling the uncharted territory of midlife, filling in its characteristics and providing the now middle-aged survivors of Eriksonian adolescence with new life crises to discuss at social gatherings and to write about in the lay press.

For the clinician and scholar data from longitudinal studies supplement but do not replace traditional formulations that stress the effects of early experience and intrapsychic conflict. It is useful to know that psychological turmoil and crisis related to generativity are common in the fourth decade of life. Full understanding of the onset, form, and resolution of the generativity crisis in a particular individual is impossible without taking into consideration early and later object relationships, patterns of psychological defense, and the characteristic form of intrapsychic conflicts in that person.

Advances in Neurobiology

The last set of paradigms consists really of protoparadigms coalescing slowly in laboratories without couches all over the country. At a memorial service for the late Dr. Grete Bibring, one of the luminaries of American psychoanalysis, she was quoted as saying that if she were beginning her career now she would study neurobiology rather than psychoanalysis. She probably would, for in the early twenties in Vienna, instead of studying the microscopic pathology of neurosyphilis, the conventional thing to do, she and fellow students, Edward Bibring, Otto Fenichel, and Wilhelm Reich made an appointment with Sigmund Freud at *Berggasse* 19 to ask him to clear up their confusion about a work of his they had been reading in a student study group. Modern neurobiology promises the new look at old problems that appeals to lively, curious minds, for it is possible to study nervous system function with new precision, anatomically, physiologically, and biochemically. Technical means are available to track interactions between the environment and the central nervous system to understand in new detail the biological basis of dreaming, consciousness, and perception, and considerable progress is being made in opening up the biology of addiction, the mechanisms of the perception of pleasure, and the metabolic basis of depression. Equally exciting, studies in developmental neurobiology provide a longitudinal aspect to these investigations so that it is possible to study the age at which biological systems develop, mature, and decline, and the correlation between their development and changes in behavior.

Let me give you one brief example, the role of neurotransmitters in depression. Neurotransmitters are chemical substances by means of which nerve cells communicate with one another. Norepinephrine is one of the neurotransmitters thought to be related to depression. In some types of depressions there may be a functional deficiency of norepinephrine at critical receptor sites in the brain. When this functional deficiency is reversed the depression lifts.

How may this occur? The deficiency may be due to too little norepinephrine having been synthesized because of a genetic defect. Or there may have been early developmental influences that caused permanent impairment of the mechanisms of synthesis. Or both may be involved in an interaction over time. Thus a genetic predisposition to depression might be brought to a clinical level by early environmental factors such as repeated failures of adequate mothering. There is suggestive experimental evidence that environmental alternations in behavior can condition the system to produce sustained changes in response pattern. Another possibility is that the synthesizing mechanism of norepinephrine may be intact but environmental stress may cause it to be metabolized more rapidly than usual to cause the functional deficiency that may lead to depression.

There is also a developmental aspect. For instance, the breakdown of enzyme monoamine oxidase increases with advancing age, leading to more rapid breakdown of norepinephrine, which may account for the tendency to depression observable in old age. Finally, population studies may give us information about the distribution of these factors in normal groups and prepare the way for a biologically based taxonomy of reaction types.

This is only a sketch of one biological system that may have great influence on the paradigms within which we order our observations of human beings. Doubtless the pendulum will swing too far toward the biological mode, and a correction back to empathy will be required. But that will be as much a matter for the historian of the psyche as for psychohistorians. In any case as you have seen corroborated by this book, the scope of psychoanalytic inquiry continues to evolve and to gain the interest of students of the human drama from a broad range of intellectual disciplines.

Notes

1. Royden Astley, "Psychoanalysis: The Future," *Journal of the American Psychoanalytic Association* 22 (1974):83-96.

2. Melanie Klein, *Love, Guilt and Separation and Other Works 1921-1945* (New York: Delacorte Press, 1975); Melanie Klein, *Envy and Gratitude and Other Works 1946-1963* (New York: Delacorte Press, 1975).

3. Otto Kernberg, *Borderline Conditions and Pathological Narcissism* (New York: Jason Aronson, 1975).

4. Paul H. Ornstein, "A Discussion of the Paper by Otto F. Kernberg on 'Further Contributions to the Treatment of Narcissistic Personalities.' " *International Journal of Psychoanalysis* 55 (1974):241.

5. Heinz Kohut, "Thoughts on Narcissism and Narcissistic Rage," *The Psychoanalytic Study of the Child* 27 (1972):392.

6. Eliot Jaques, "Social Systems as a Defense against Persecutory and Depressive Anxiety" in *New Directions in Psychoanalysis* ed. Melanie Klein (New York: Basic Books 1955).

7. Roy Schafer, *A New Language for Psychoanalysis* (New Haven, Conn.: Yale University Press, 1976).

8. Margaret S. Mahler, *On Human Symbiosis and the Vicissitudes of Individuation* (New York: International Universities Press, 1967).

9. George E. Vaillant, *Adaptation to Life* (Boston: Little, Brown, 1977).

6

Life History and Character Development: Some Reflections on Political Leadership

Stanley A. Renshon

It is now almost sixty years since Harold Lasswell first reminded us that "Political science with biography is a form of taxidermy" and that intensive life histories were a necessary corrective to the overemphasis placed on institutional, "mechanisms," "structures," and "systems."[1] On the surface it looks as if his advice has been well heeded. After all, the behavioral revolution in political science has as its banner the attempt to "elevate the human being to the center of attention."[2] Yet in spite of the frequently proclaimed importance of the individual, his status in political science remains ambiguous. Clearly, the behavioral movement displaced institutionalism as the dominant paradigm of analytic activity, but it failed to establish the legitimacy of intensive life history analysis. Rather, in place of a detailed and sustained attention to the individual, the behavioral movement focused instead on "aggregated man." To be sure, individuals remain the basis of the thousands of surveys that are conducted, nevertheless the statistical group persists. Given this thrust by one of the most important revitalization movements in the history of political analysis, it is not surprising that the life history focus in political science failed to take hold and develop, in spite of the pioneering efforts by early practitioners (especially Harold D. Lasswell and Erik H. Erikson) to use ideographic means to obtain nomothetic ends.

It is somewhat paradoxical that the failure to develop and maintain a tradition of intensive life-history analysis has impoverished many areas of political research, and few more seriously than the study of political behavior. The importance of case studies as a valuable partner in theory development and validation, rather than a competitor, has been too little appreciated. Instead, the search for generalized propositions has frequently not paused long enough to map the rich diversity of meaning and associations implicit in the relationship between private experience and public life.

Given our intuitive sense of the importance of political leadership, its centrality in political science has been slow to develop. So, for example, although there have been numerous studies of legislatures, voting, and so forth, only 17 of 2,614 articles in the *American Political Science Review* from 1906 to 1963 specifically mentioned political leadership and only 5 had "elites" as a frame of focus.[3]

Lack of attention to leadership originates in part from our cultural ambivalence about its role in American life. On one hand, there is a "debunking" strain in American politics, which is loathe to attribute too much importance or "specialness" to political leaders, a strain that has become increasingly evident in recent years. There is also the impact of Marx and Freud, presenting individuals as subordinated to powerful economic or psychological forces, often beyond their control. So, too, our ideal of democratic leadership in this country requires that a leader be viewed as just one of us who has momentarily been placed in a position to serve our interests.

Our idealization of leaders throughout the life-cycle requires that although they may be in the grip of powerful, impersonal forces, we expect them to persist and ultimately triumph. Leaders may be expected to faithfully execute our preferences, but we also demand that when we are uncertain, anxious, or confused our leaders will be able to do for us what we are not able to do for ourselves.

On its face one would think that if any area of political analysis would profit by taking seriously the intensive life-history perspective, political leadership would have been it. The inherent logic of using this framework is certainly more powerful here than in studies of mass voting preferences (although that perspective is not without relevance). Still, what might have been a mutually productive union has scarcely reached the stage of courtship.

There are a number of reasons to explain why the intensive life-history perspective has failed to gain a hold in the discipline generally and within the area of political leadership more particularly. A number of factors might be mentioned but by far the most important is the equation in many minds of intensive life-history research with depth psychology, and the latter with psychoanalytic theory, not to mention the vast amount of time necessary to accumulate longitudinal data. Political scientists have shared a long, ambivalent, and uneasy relationship with the field of psychology. As Fred Greenstein has pointed out, "for much of the brief history of empirical political science, political analysis has seemed to proceed in quite an acceptable fashion without employing explicit psychological assumptions."[4] Unfortunately, the lack of explicit assumptions is not quite synonymous with the lack of assumptions. James Barber is correct when he says that, "There are probably more political scientists unawaredly writing psychology than prose."[5] The question therefore is not whether to use psychology in political analysis, but what kind of psychology.

Greenstein makes the point that even when political scientists recognize the importance of making explicit their psychological assumptions or turn to psychology for useful models, they find a discipline very much like their own, that is, they soon learn they have simply borrowed unresolved questions.[6]

To those whose time is spent immersed in clinical theory, the broad challenges to the classical model will hardly come as news. For political scientists it soon becomes clear why Greenstein called for the development of psychological models less tied to the assumptive structure of classic psychoanalytic theory. The peristence of classical models within the psychoanalytic community, however, arrested for a time the incorporation of newer models of individual development, and the newer models were further retarded by the difficulty in traversing the rigid boundaries between disciplines. Therefore, I will briefly sketch some of the classical assumptions as they have been related to the study of political leadership, trace some of the newer models of development, and suggest why they are useful in the analysis of political leadership.

Classical Assumptions

The Assumption of Psychopathology

In some ways Lasswell's selection of the title *Psychopathology and Politics* for the first book to systematically introduce the psychoanalytic model to political science was unfortunate. Lasswell, typically far ahead of many who followed him, specifically disclaimed any intention to promote "psychopathography." As he wrote then, "We have not finished when we know that a modern Rousseau suffered from paranoia; that a modern Napoleon has partially atrophied genitalia . . . that a modern Lincoln shows depressive pathology . . . and that a modern Bismark is hysterical."[7] Lasswell was interested in the psychoanalytic model as a framework of analyzing the whole personality, not merely one part of it. Unfortunately, his case materials leave the impression of individuals caught up in conflicts they cannot understand, much less control. Many were understandably reluctant to follow into this "Alice-in-Wonderland" world where what seemed to be was not and what could not be was; but others embraced it all too eagerly and literally. The result in many psychologically oriented political biographies was a turning away from "his reason" explanations to the more difficult and mystifying world of the unconscious. The important question raised by many such studies is how leaders have managed to accomplish anything at all. In some extreme cases, psychological terms have functioned more as epithets than conceptual frames. Thus, one of the less scrupulous excursions in the psychobiography of political leadership asks on the jacket cover whether there is any evidence that "Richard Nixon was anal compulsive," or "whether his continually close relationship with John Mitchell is Symbiosis defined as a mutual reinforcement between two dependent and disturbed individuals."[8] As Alexander George has correctly observed, this is the raw material of "psychoMcCarthyism," not psychoanalysis.

One does not have to travel to this crude extreme to see the unfortunate effects of linking depth analysis with pathological behavior. Another byproduct of this connection has been the more general assumption that psychological theory, and in particular psychoanalytic theory, is useful in analyzing the bizarre and perhaps even the unusual, but not the typical. Even such an astute political psychologist as Greenstein, certainly no Freudian, remarks that "If one is studying 'normal' actors in a familiar culture, it is often convenient simply to look at variations in the setting of politics or merely to deal with the portion of the actor's psychological characteristics that relate to his social position."[9] Convenient perhaps, but ubiquity should not be a signal for neglecting the unconscious. Even assuming for a moment that such uniformities are more real than apparent, basic questions could still be raised about the subjective factors that structure the uniformities of the actors.

The Assumption of Childhood Primacy

Freud found, in the experience of the child, an understanding of the man. The primacy of early experience in classical psychoanalytic theory is well summarized by the aphorism that those who do not understand history are doomed to repeat it. Leaders might be flexible in obtaining power, but eventually unconscious and therefore unresolved conflicts would ultimately prove to be their undoing. From this perspective on developmental processes, adult behavior was less an elaboration than a repetition. Lasswell's analogue of the neurotic being like the car stuck in one gear is apparent here.

Lasswell's own position on this matter, however, is not as straightforward as is frequently thought. On one hand, it is clear that by 1930 he had progressed well beyond the assumption of childhood primacy. He specifically states for example the purpose of his book, "is not to make a hit and miss collection of isolated anecdotes about the relation between early experiences and specific traits and interests," but rather, "to discover what developmental experiences are significant for the political traits and interests of the mature."[10] The appendix of the 1977 edition of *Psychopathology and Politics* and the question list of political practices, however, is curiously devoid of references to childhood experiences. The questionnaire is almost completely given over to a detailed examination of the private experience of public activities. Yet, strangely little of this material found its way into Lasswell's case studies. The result is a series of brief profiles in which the "here and now" of political life and experience is little in evidence.

For many less rigorous scholars who subscribed to the twin assumptions of depth psychology, the best explanations of leadership behavior were those that emphasized the unconscious and earliest childhood experiences. The task of leadership studies was to discover (one might say uncover) the voice of the child in the behavior of the adult. This trend persists to the present. So, for example, a recent psychological analysis of President Carter predicted that he would soon lead us into war because of an unresolved "birth trauma." Here is psychological analysis as Greek tragedy par excellence. Deeper and earlier you can hardly get!

The problem with such assumptions is not only that they are difficult or impossible to verify, but also that they ignore the wide range of adult experiences independent of childhood.

Until recently, a psychology deeply rooted in the past has not been very helpful in providing models for the present, let alone the future. With no alternative model[s] to serve as a guide it is hardly surprising that studies of political leadership and of political socialization, even where psychologically oriented, have remained tied to the primacy of early experience. Where they are not so tied, they have specifically avoided attention to psychological processes.

Nonbiographical studies of political leadership present something of a paradox. On one hand, there seems to be recognition of the importance of diverse developmental experiences; on the other hand, the psychological implications of such experiences have been largely ignored. We have, therefore, numerous studies that chart the developmental trajectories of political leaders mostly in terms of broad sociological categories such as class, education, and formal political attachments. Unfortunately, these sociological indicators have functioned as implicit stand-ins for psychological processes. Thus, we have large amounts of background information on elites and leaders, without much understanding of the meaning of these experiences to the individuals involved and the ways that they fit into their private development as well as public careers. This is surely a mistake since studies by Edinger and Searing[11] and later Searing,[12] have demonstrated that many of the background variables used in leadership analysis are unreliable guides to leadership attitudes even within the same political system.

The problem, to state the point again, is the assumption that the meaning and effect of these experiences remain stable. This implies that changes resulting from differences in perspective cannot and do not occur. Herein lies the crux of the difficulty over time in exploring the adult sources of adult behavior. The classical psychoanalytic model downplayed the evolution of perspective in adulthood, because the unconscious made us all perpetual children. Such a view is supported neither by our own experiences as we move through the life-cycle nor by recently reported research.

Part of the problem lies in equating adult and childhood experience. For Freud, the two most important and prototypical experiences were toilet training (raising the problems of autonomy and control) and the oedipal conflict (raising questions of the appropriateness of affective investment). In both cases, however, it is worth pointing out that the conclusion is never in doubt. It is a rare adult that has not learned to control his bowels, and few, if any, children succeed in displacing the father (although given the prevalence of one-parent families, this may have to be reevaluated). So, from the start, the theory informs us, the child is doomed to failure, whatever his resources, strengths, or strategies.

Childhood and adult experiences are simply not analogous. Childhood experiences with authority, involve a high degree of affective organization; adult experiences with authority are organized to a greater degree cognitively. This means that one does not treat all authority figures as one's father. To be sure, there are still plenty of "powerful others" in adulthood, but the development of personal strengths and capacities, the skillful use of accumulated experiences, and sometimes just plain luck make outcomes that were impossible during childhood at least plausible for adults. This is not to say that many of the same issues are not involved in the important "marker" experiences of adult life. In some sense, every personal challenge involves questions of mastery (can I do it?) and esteem (what does being able or unable to do it mean about me?). It seems unlikely that these two core axes of human character will be missing from any age-significant task, however such tasks may differ in other ways. The question of the similarities and differences between childhood and adult marker experiences awaits some more basic agreement about the nature of adulthood itself.

In some ways it seems curious that Freud did not devote more attention to adult life. His closest formulation of a concept of mental health was to remark that it consisted of the ability to work and love, which at least implies in the case of the former a concern strongly rooted in the adult world.[13]

If Freud can be credited with at least pointing us in the right direction, it is to Erikson that we owe understanding of the first broad contours of adult development. His eight-stage theory of the life-cycle is by now familiar, and there is no need to explicate it here. It should be noted, however, that although the theory does deal with the human life cycle, only three of the eight stages deal with adulthood. Erikson's model focuses on the development of the ego through time and is principally internal in emphasis. Each stage is characterized by the development of dilemmas that are anchored by personal and social coordinates and reflect major conflicts that must be resolved. For the stage of young adulthood the struggle is between intimacy and isolation, for the stage of adulthood it is between generativeity and stagnation, and for old age the critical issues are between integrity and despair. There are, for Erikson, inner laws of development summarized in the epigenetic principle whose unfolding will reflect the "goodness of fit," between personal character and social institutions. Where the two are not in synch, a crisis period develops.

Out of these discrepancies between self and one's place in the world, according to Erikson, social transformations are forged. The "fit in the choir" suffered by a young Martin Luther who was struggling with his religious beliefs and his identity helped to usher in the Reformation.[14] A middle-aged Gandhi suffering through a mid-life crisis created a new political form, the nonviolent revolution.[15] One of the lessons of Erikson's work for the study of political leadership is that the internal development of individuals can produce profound alternations in their relationships with conventional institutions. The change from individual to leader (great man) takes place when these inner dialogues reflect and anticipate as yet unarticulated public concerns.

But not all political leaders are great men, and Erikson's accounts of Luther and Gandhi lead one to wonder whether theories of adult development have much to say about more typical political leaders. Here it is helpful to turn to the recently published work of Daniel Levinson. Like Erikson, Levinson uses the intensive life history approach, but with a major difference. In Levinson's words:

> We regard adult development as the evolution of life structure; our developmental periods are successive phases in the process of building, modifying and rebuilding that structure. Erikson's mode of analysis too, is concerned with the interconnectedness of self and world. He regards development however as a series of stages in ego development. . . . Erikson's ego stages refer to the self as it is engaged in the world, but their primary focus is *within the person*. Our approach makes use of Erikson's but shifts the focus somewhat. The concept of the life structure is centered more directly on the *boundary between the self and the world*.[16]

Levinson's theory grew out of research conducted over a ten-year period with forty men from varying socioeconomic positions. The adult life cycle is characterized by an alternating series of stable and transitional stages whose major function is to develop, reexamine, and where necessary reconstruct the life structure. The concept of the life structure is crucial to Levinson's theory and refers to the "underlying pattern or design of a person's life at any given time."[17] The life structure has numerous components including occupation, love relationships, marriage and family life, relation to self, and roles in a great variety of social contexts. Work and family, however, are usually the most important and changes in either of these areas can trigger profound changes in the other elements of the life structure. The primary task of each stable period is to build a life structure that is valued by the self and for which there is space and support in the social world. While Erikson's tasks seem global and heroic, the tasks of Levinson's model are concrete, even mundane. The elements of the life structure are nothing more than the incidents of everyday life.

The adult stages that Levinson has articulated can be briefly noted. The early adult transition begins at age seventeen and ends about twenty-two. The task is to separate from home and move out into the adult world. The next period, getting into the adult world, covers the years from twenty-two to twenty-eight, in which the task is to "fashion and test out a provisional structure that provides a workable link between the valued self and the adult society." These initial choices are tested and reexamined in the next period, the age thirty transition (twenty-eight to thirty-two). To the extent that the first structure was flawed, it must be redesigned and changed implying a conscious architecture. Settling down, ages thirty-three to forty marks another period of stability, where the major tasks are finding a "niche" in society and making it. The next stage, the mid-life crisis, provoked a strong crisis in about 80 percent of Levinson's sample. Here, under the increasing pressure of time, the choices already made and discarded must be seen for what they have made us miss as well as what they have provided for us. Levinson's study ends with getting into middle adulthood, but he believes that there may be another late adult transition occurring between sixty and sixty-five.

But how is Levinson's work useful for the study of political leadership? First of all, unless we are willing to believe that our governments are run by children in adult guise, a theory that points to the adult sources of adult behavior will prove useful in dealing with adult phenomena.

The key point of the adult development theorists like Erikson, Levinson, Gould,[18] and others, is that adult development means a change in personal perspective, with an accompanying shift in values, concerns, and the allocation of energy and time. Political leaders at different stages of development might and probably do have different public and private concerns. Roger Gould reported an empirical study in the *American Journal of Psychiatry* that documented changes in values and preferences as a function of life stage.[19] Since it would be foolish to suppose that political leaders are somehow exempt from the laws of psychological development, these changes might lead to policy changes, changes in importance of issue areas, or changes in the latitude of acceptance and rejection in policy disputes.

One implication of the preceding point is that changes in perspective can best be understood as a function of situated activity. One of the very important aspects of Levinson's theory is that it points us directly toward the world of work, as both an important source of adult experience and the arena in which many dreams and deeds are played out. It is surprising how little is actually known of a systematic and comparative nature about political work, how leaders spend their days, and what it means for them to do so. It would also be interesting to know not only their daily routine but what they are thinking as they go through their days and careers. This should not be taken for granted, and it is not as difficult to learn as might be thought. Researchers at the University of Chicago analyzing daydreaming have given their subjects beepers, and asked them to write down their thoughts (or lack of them) when "beeped." This is a modern adaptation of Harold Lasswell's old, unheeded idea to get political leaders to keep track of how they spend their days, who they see, what they talk about, and so forth.

Related to Levinson's concern with the world of work is his emphasis on the "dream" and on mentoring, two concepts with important implications for the study of political leadership. The dream evolves during adulthood and is less than a fantasy but more than a wish. It is a vision of the self in society that imparts drive and direction to the task of building a life structure. Not everyone has a dream, nor are all dreams articulated in a way that allows completion.

The lack of a dream deprives the individual of an important source of energy and satisfaction, as well as a way in which to measure his progress toward his concrete self-selected goals. For political leaders, the dream will likely include visions of the kind of society in which he or others can create a viable place. As Levinson notes, there are only limited ways available in which one can build a life structure compatible with the self and acceptable to society. Creative leadership may spring from the sense that the self can never be satisfied in the present social structure, hence the push for social change. Those leaders with impoverished dreams may transform societies to reflect their own distorted visions, and those with no strong dream are likely to be found far from the center of power.

Levinson also calls to our attention the role of mentoring. The mentor relationship is one of the most complex and developmentally important that a man can have in early adulthood.[20] The mentor is at once a guide, advisor, friend, and sponsor, but it is really more. It is best viewed as a "love relationship," and Levinson states quite strongly that "poor mentoring in early adulthood is the equivalent of poor parenting in childhood."[21] We are just beginning to explore the importance of the mentoring role in political life. Kellerman's recent article documents the important role of mentoring in the career of Willy Brandt, and one can easily think of other relationships, as for example, Hubert Humphrey and Walter Mondale, or Sam Rayburn and Lyndon Johnson.[22] No full account of adult socialization and political leadership can be written without attention to the mentoring relationship.

Another valuable aspect of Levinson's theory is that it focuses attention on the concrete, conscious, or at least preconscious, dimensions of the adult world. The self involved in constructing a life framework and carrying out its implicit design is in most cases influenced, not dominated, by the unconscious. Levinson's subjects revealed a considerable degree of awareness of their plans and scripts and the problems experienced during transitional phases. It is well to recall here that the technique was the intensive interview, not the survey question.

The importance of this is that it orients our studies of political leaders—not only to the world of political work they inhabit, but also to the ways in which they carry out what they have to do. The chief task for most leaders is decision making about complex issues in an arena of high stakes and great uncertainty about both facts and outcomes. An integrated theory of adult development focuses attention on the conscious and preconscious strategies or standard operating procedures used in doing the essential work of political life.

Let me summarize the intervention implications of this research for the study of political leadership. To the extent that political life is dominated by the unconscious, the methods for introducing change are limited (in fact, to some form of therapeutic procedure) and the chances of success small. To the extent that theories of adult behavior push us to focus on the nature of the work world, its design, and the standard operating procedure used to work within it, there may be more room for change and more chance of success. Decision makers may be more amenable to procedural redesign in the name of more effective decision making than they will be in entering therapy to deal with "deep-seated" distortions of their thinking process, although hopefully redesign could be combined with some sort of insight analysis.

The last aspect of adult development and political leadership that I want to touch on concerns the nature of crucial experience. I mentioned that childhood and adult experiences are not synonymous, and one of the very important insights of adult development theorists is that important developmental crises occur, with regularity for some, after childhood. Not all politically relevant experiences, however, need be a monumental crisis. Barber's emphasis on first independent political success fits in well with developmental theory. Such experience provides a first lesson in facing a problem and (primarily) solving it successfully on the basis of one's own work and strategy. It can be a heady experience and one not soon forgotten. (Childhood theorists might do well to borrow a page from adult theory and look for the precursors of "independent success.") It is clear that these adult experiences have great importance for political leaders. One need only think of the Hiss case for Richard Nixon or his brief sojourn in the government bureaucracy. The major point here is that each person learns "his own lessons about life," many of which come directly from his own adult experiences. Moreover, adult development theory suggests that the meaning of these experiences may well change throughout the life cycle so that different lessons are drawn at different stages of life.

Conclusion

In this chapter my focus has been on where we should be going rather than where we have been. In doing so, I do not wish to leave the impression that the experiences of childhood must now be cast aside in the rush to chart the course of adult political development. It seems far too likely that echoes of childhood will prove to be an important part of adult development and psychology since it at least implies an attenuation of strength over time.

Political leaders, like the rest of us, live in a world of great uncertainty, high personal and public stakes, and shifting sets of private and public priorities. They meet these challenges with finite, but potentially expandable, personal resources. Just how they negotiate these public and private currents during their political careers is likely to be an important and profitable focus for building a theory of adult political development and behavior.

Notes

1. Harold D. Lasswell, *Psychopathology and Politics* (Chicago: University of Chicago Press, 1930), p. 1.

2. David Easton, *The Political System* (New York: Knopf, 1953), p. 203.

3. Glenn Paige, *The Scientific Study of Political Leadership* (New York: The Free Press, 1977), p. 12.

4. Fred Greenstein, *Personality and Politics* (Chicago: Markham, 1969) (reissued 1975), p. 12.

5. James Barber, "Strategies for Understanding Politicians," *American Journal of Political Science*, Spring 1974, pp. 38-61.

6. Greenstein, *Personality and Politics* p. 12. Greenstein notes " rather than finding *a* psychological science upon which to draw for insight, he (the political scientist) finds congeries of more or less competing models and frames of reference, with imperfect agreement about the nature of man's inner dispositions, on the appropriate terms for characterizing them, and on the appropriate methodologies for observing them."

7. Lasswell, *Psychopathology and Politics*, p. 7.

8. Arthur Woodstone, *Nixon's Head* (New York: St. Martin's Press, 1972).

9. Greenstein, *Personality and Politics*, p. 12, [emphasis added].

10. Lasswell, *Psychopathology and Politics*, p. 8.

11. Lewis Edinger and Donald Searing, "Social Background in Elite Analysis: A Methodological Inquiry," *American Political Science Review*, Fall 1967, pp. 428-445.

12. Donald Searing, "The Comparative Study of Elite Socialization," *Comparative Political Studies*, January 1969, pp. 471-500.

13. Paul Roazen, *Erik H. Erikson: The Power and Limits of a Vision* (New York: Free Press, 1976), p. 136. Roazen has remarked that this phrase gets deeper the more you think about it, and he is right, but even so, it hardly serves as a detailed guide.

14. Erik H. Erikson, *Young Man Luther* (New York: Norton, 1958).

15. Erik H. Erikson, *Gandhi's Truth* (New York: Norton, 1969).

16. Daniel Levinson with Charlotte Darrow, Edward Klien, Maria Levinson, and Braxton McKee, *The Seasons of a Man's Life* (New York: Knopf, 1978), p. 323.

17. Ibid., p. 42.

18. Roger Gould, *Transformations* (New York: Simon and Shuster, 1978).

19. Roger Gould, "The Phases of Adult Life; A Study in Developmental Psychology", *American Journal of Psychiatry*, 129, 1972, pp. 521-531.

20. Levinson, *The Seasons*, p. 97.

21. Ibid., p. 338.

22. Barbara Kellerman, "Mentoring in Political Life: The Case of Willy Brandt," *American Political Science Review*, 72 (1978): 422-435.

7

Thoughts on a Theory of Collective Action: Language, Affect, and Ideology in Revolution

Gerald M. Platt

Introduction

Regrettably, much that passes for sociological, psychological, and psychohistorical studies of revolution have been professional glosses. These empirical glosses are the result of inadequate theory, not poor research. The goal of this chapter is to develop an alternative theory to overcome professional glossing. However, to achieve this end a theory of revolution must take as its point of departure the subjectivities of revolutionary participants. Extant theoretical approaches to revolution cannot systematically examine subjective perspectives of revolutionary participants.[1]

The shortcomings of extant theory reside in their epistemologies based in traditional analytic categories such as class, age, religion, psychological types, and so forth as the sources for motivating revolutionary participation. Such analytic categories do not describe subjective orientations to action but rather are analysts' objective categories superimposed on perspectives of the real actors in the world. Such analyses produce only statistical relationships between the analytic categories and the composition of revolutionary participation. This assertion regarding analysts' objective categories replacing the real subjectivities of actors obtains for sociological and psychological theories, although those who employ psychological categories erroneously assume they are dealing with subjectivities of persons in the real world. I will establish that these assertions are correct in my discussion of the epistemology of categorical analysis.

I will illustrate the shortcomings of contemporary sociological and psychological approaches by their failures to adequately explain the Nazi movement. I will illustrate a typical sociological failure through a discussion of Lipset's work on Nazism and a typical failure of psychological approaches with the work of Peter Lowenberg on the "Nazi Youth Cohort." Subsequent to these illustrations I will draw on Weinstein's recent psychological analysis of the Nazi movement to demonstrate, in a positive fashion, the existence of psychological diversity or heterogeneity rather than psychological unity among Nazi participants. A positive example of the sociological diversity of heterogeneity of revolutionary participants will be illustrated through a discussion of the social class composition of the English Civil War.

Although these many examples have a certain persuasiveness, illustrations can never be ultimately convincing. Therefore, I will turn to a formal discussion of the epistemological failure of categorical approaches to revolutionary participation. This formal analysis addresses itself to the universal shortcomings of sociological or psychological theories of revolution based in categorical analyses.

Finally, I will offer an alternative theory of revolution. This theory builds on existing approaches and on my previous work in this area. Thus, the alternative theory will subsume categorical approaches, advancing my own work by suggesting reasons for the heterogeneous psychological and sociological perspectives of revolutionary participants.

Categorical Analysis and the Heterogeneity Problem

Contemporary sociological and psychological theories of revolutionary movements are faced with a factual perplexity or anomaly they can neither address nor resolve.[2] The factual perplexity can be identified in every instance of revolution but it either passes unremarked in authors narratives, or it is accorded little significance. I call this factual perplexity or anomaly the heterogeneity problem. By heterogeneity I mean that every revolution has manifest a heterogeneous composition of participants on all sides of the struggle. More specifically, I mean that it can be demonstrated that participants on all sides of a revolution manifest varying psychological motivations and varying social statuses.[3]

This observation is important because most psychological and sociological approaches to revolutionary participation assume that some predispositional category, that is, a subjective psychological state or an objective social position somehow compelled participation. Thus, revolutionary participants, it is assumed, find themselves on one or another side of the struggle because of what they are or do before and carry forward to the movements in question. This logic of cause and effect in terms of "what people carry within them from place to place,"[4] or in terms of "initial states,"[5] which predispose them to certain outcomes, has dominated the social sciences.[6]

Such approaches are based on the identification of unities or universally shared categories that act as the cause of various effects. But categorical approaches to collective action are hard pressed to make sense of the heterogeneous composition of revolutionary participation. How can homogeneously predisposed people who share an initial state end up on different sides of a revolution? By the same token how can persons of different psychological and social backgrounds end up on the same side of a revolution?

S.M. Lipset's comments on the Nazi social base of support represents an unintended but typical example of the pitfalls of categorical analysis. Lipset notes that,

> The ideal-typical Nazi voter in 1932 was a middle-class self-employed Protestant who lived either on a farm or in a small community, and who had previously voted for a centrist or regionalist political party strongly opposed to the power and influence of big business and big labor.

This "ideal-typical" voter was predisposed by virtue of social location and psychological vulnerability to authoritarian consciousness. On the other hand Lipset also notes that although the core of the S.P.D. support was "employed, skilled manual workers,"

> An analysis of the sources of the vote for the Social Democratic party in 1930 estimated that 40 per cent of the SPD voters were not manual workers, that the party was backed in that year by 25 per cent of the white-collar workers, 33 per cent of the lower civil servants, and 25 per cent of the self-employed in artisan shops and retail business.[7]

Peter Lowenberg's explanation of the Nazis also illustrates the heterogeneity problem. Lowenberg attempts to show that participation by the young in the Nazi movement was determined by socialization events experienced by a particular cohort in pre-Nazi Germany. However, Lowenberg's data regarding the age composition of the Nazi movement indicate that although 42.2 percent of the Nazi party were between the ages of eighteen and thirty, nearly 20 percent of the S.P.D. were of that same age; and of course 57.8 percent who did participate were not from that age cohort.[8]

Thus, what Lipset and Lowenberg describe is a central tendency, a degree of effect produced by a predispositional category. As for the rest, those who deviate from the tendency can be explained in terms of supplemental, exigent personal and social circumstances. But even if we were willing to grant the usefulness of this slide down Occam's razor we would still be left with the factual perplexity; why can some members' participation in a social movement be described in terms of the explanatory category and some not? Clearly a coherent, consistent theory must subsume the central tendencies routinely found in social science literature while explaining the heterogeneous social and psychological composition of the movement.

Before we go forward with such a theory we should illustrate in a positive way the heterogeneous psychological and social composition of a regressive and a progressive revolution. Following these illustrations, we will demonstrate the epistemic unity and failure of both psychological and sociological categorical approaches to revolution.

Two Examples of Heterogeneous Participants in Revolution

For two reasons it is important to illustrate psychological heterogeneity in revolutions. First, some of the worst abuses of psychology in history have been those that have glossed historical reality by characterizing whole populations by a single psychological type. Second, and related, psychological heterogeneity points to an understanding of how the use of psychological categories is as removed from the subjective experience of revolution as are social statuses that purport to depict motives for participation.

An example of psychological heterogeneity in revolutionary participation has been offered by Weinstein in his work on Nazism. Weinstein writes that the Nazi activist "is typically viewed as dynamically homogeneous, predisposed to seek authoritarian solutions, having experienced psychological deterioration before the event, sharing a common motive on the basis of the threatening socialization practices in the family." Thus the typical Nazi participant is characterized as angry, envious, ignorant, intellectually and culturally impoverished. Additionally, this description is meant to "account for the most general features of the greater number of people."[9]

Drawing on three forms of data, including Henry V. Dicks's systematic psychological studies of German prisoners of war, his own investigations of the psychological and intellectual capacities of a number of professionals, artists, intellectuals, and academics who were Nazi or pro-Nazi activists, and studies of elite Nazi figures available in the psychoanalytic literature, Weinstein demonstrates that Nazi supporters were not psychologically homogeneous.

Following Dicks's work with German prisoners of war, for example, Weinstein states that there was a range, not a polarization of dynamic traits characteristic of those who scored high and low on Nazi fanaticism even in terms of the extremes of commitment. However, retrospectively judging the psychological responses of prisoners of war could be faulted because of the potential effects on conceived motivation resulting from the events interceding between the willingness to participate in whatever capacity and the time of data collection. Obviously a great deal had transpired between Hitler's rise to power and the Nazi's subsequent wartime defeats, and this could affect the memories of the prisoners of war, contaminating the reports that Dicks solicited.

In an effort to substantiate Dicks's findings, then, Weinstein turned to a traditional investigation of various biographical documents, analyzing emotional and cognitive capacities among contemporary professionals and intellectuals involved with Nazism to one degree or another, including Martin Heidegger, Gottfried Benn, Ernst Junger, Wilhelm Stapel, Rudolf Binding, and C.G. Jung. Weinstein found no evidence among these individuals of the cultural and intellectual impoverishment typically held to be characteristic of susceptibility to fascist solutions. Moreover, Weinstein noted that people participated in the movement for their own personal, idiosyncratic reasons: there was no homogeneity of motive, as this can be identified by available, extant documentation.

The so-called authoritarian personality type has been routinely invoked to explain participation in or support for the Nazi movement, but this is not the only dynamic explanation of participation. At the same time, the very diveristy of analytic conceptions, especially of Nazi leadership, underscores the case for psychological heterogeneity. Weinstein points out that Hitler has been described in the psychoanalytic literature as paranoid, paranoid-schizophrenic, sadomasochistic, and narcissistic, Himmler has been portrayed as schizoid, Goering as an aggressive narcissist, Hess as an hysteric, and so on. Heterogeneity is also the obvious conclusion to be drawn from Theodore Abel's collection of biographical data and especially of Peter Merkl's statistical reworking of the Abel data.[10]

It is possible to assume that this interpretive heterogeneity is the product of an imprecise science. But it is also reasonable to assume that such heterogeneity is a certain reflection of reality, a conclusion that is consistent with, and additional support for, the works of Dicks and Weinstein on the psychological heterogeneity extant in the Nazi movement.

The Nazi movement may be considered historically regressive. The standards orienting behavior embodied in the Nazi ideology integrated a society characterized by traditional rather than modern principles of social organization. For example, the Nazi stress on nationalism, folk relationships, and political and economic activities based on ascriptive ties such as blood and race are standards associated with traditional rather than modern society. By contrast the seventeenth-century English Civil War was historically progressive, having been directed toward the institutionalization of standards limiting monarchical rule and reducing ascriptive bases for action by increasing the importance of personal achievement, individual autonomy, and the inclusion of all productive social classes in economic and political institutions and processes. The outcomes of the English Civil War were not as widespread nor as democratic as had been hoped for in Puritan and Leveller ideologies, but expected innovations in social organization are always tempered by material and social conditions during the institutionalization phase of revolution.[11]

However, at this juncture we are less interested in outcomes than with the failed explanations of the English Civil War in terms of social class origins. There is a great deal of interpretive and historiographical controversy in the literature on the English Civil War, particularly with regards to the role played by social classes.[12] Marxist historians and historians influenced by Marxist categories have explained the conflict as the result of demands made against an exclusionary crown and aristocracy by a rising bourgeoisie, a land-owning and land-managing class, for effective political power.[13] However, the revolution has also been explained in terms of the antagonisms generated among economically threatened elements of the gentry striving to bring about changes in restrictive commercial laws governing trade and business as the means for maintaining their position against the greater aristocracy.[14] Still other historians have claimed that the paramount cause of the Civil War was the growing incapacity of the aristocracy to rule, that is, to maintain its position of power, authority, esteem, and economic advantage against a talented and aggressive gentry. In this view, however, the gentry's rise to power was not as significant as the aristocracy's fall.[15]

These several views are obviously contradictory. But even more interesting is the fact that recent historical and statistical analyses demonstrate that the contending sides in the Civil War were not simply divided along class lines. Both the Parliamentarian and Royalist factions were heterogeneous and to a significant degree shared their class composition.[16] Thus a statistical analysis of the demographic characteristics of the Long Parliament indicates that there were "no specifiable social and economic characteristics that differentiated the leadership of the Royalists from the Parliamentarians."[17] On both sides of the conflict there were peers, greater and lesser gentry, "old" and "new" families, lawyers, merchants, and yeomen.

Some historians, especially those oriented to the social sciences, continue to insist that the contradiction will be resolved with more refined categories of analysis and more rigorous statistical techniques.[18] But the numeric distributions and the size of the sample are now large enough so that it is unlikely that the heterogeneity problem would be cleared up even with better definitions of class and larger samples. The evidence for the heterogeneity of populations on both sides of the struggle appears incontrovertible and raises problems that will not prove amenable to procedural and technical refinements. However, this should not imply that such refinements have not been attempted and with some success. It has been suggested again that social class mobility, in upward and downward directions, affected Civil War loyalties.[19] But even if the trends in the latter findings are in some degree correct, and we have not heard the last on effects of class or class mobility on revolutionary participation the heterogeneity of class composition on both sides of the English revolt will not go away. We are well advised to heed the suggestion of the initiator of the modern Marxist analysis, R.H. Tawney, that the ". . . venerable legend of a conflict between, on the one side, a monarchy supported by a feudal aristocracy and, on the other, an aspiring *bourgeosie* be given . . . the short shrift that it deserves."[20]

The Epistemic Failure of Categorical Analysis

Two exemplary failures, of course, do not a convincing story make. But the failure of categorical analysis runs deep. The epistemology of categorical analysis is unequal to the task set for itself. Marx and Freud remind us that subjective experiences (motives, intentions, perceptions, interpretations, emotions, and so forth) are not bound by location in any social space. We should keep this thought in mind as we move toward an alternative explanation of revolution and a solution to the heterogeneity problem.

In one sense the heterogeneity problem is no more than a quantitative expression of the underlying situation, which Marx and Freud note. However, their insight can be more formally stated: theorists who employ categorical schemes of explanation must assume: (1) that individuals in their subjective experiences act in a manner consistent with the categories employed to describe them; (2) that people will use these categories (whether a social status or psychological type) as bases for motive, intention, perception, experience, interpretation, and feelings about objects and events in their lives; (3) that these categories will have a primary or prominent significance for the people they describe, that is, the salience of the category will shape the subject's experience without regard to the specifics of any situation; (4) that there are invariant interpretive rules embedded in the particular category to which relevant people are obliged to refer as they live out their lives.

On the one hand, the categorical mode of analysis is obviously an attempt to find bases for coordinated action, not only in objective trends but in terms of human subjectivity as well. On the other hand, the existence of unwarranted inference should be clear: without demonstrating that persons do in fact refer to, or use, these categories theorists cannot be assured that they are actually the bases for action. Moreover, the use of such categories to explain collective behavior assumes what must be proved, that is, the subjective bases for coordinated action. The use of these categories simply objectifies subjective experiences; reality is too often not being reconstructed but constructed according to the observer's inclinations. The theorists' categories objectify subjectivity by transforming that subjectivity into unexamined invariant objective states and orientations to action. The data invariably disclose that although some portion of a population may act consistently in terms of these categories, some portion also does not. Moreover, there is no basis for assuming that all persons of a particular psychological or sociological bent will subjectively relate to circumstances in the theorist's terms.[21]

In short, categorical analysis violates the subjective sense of being in the world and cannot act as the basis for coordinated action especially in such complex social circumstances as revolutionary movements. It is no surprise that the use of categories is linked to the consequent composition of revolutionary participation only by partial or statistical relationship. Additional factors must be involved in shaping the subjective experience of revolutionary participants to produce the heterogeneous composition of the combatants.

A second problem of categorical analysis is the certainty of the categories' independent causality in revolutionary events. This is especially important in historical analysis, because the assumed temporal priority of social and psychological categories, which suggests their potential for causality in revolutionary events, is an illusion. After all, historical conclusions are retrospective, and revolutionary consequences are frequently known to the investigator. Thus, categories may be selected or formulated in light of known results. Such an anachronistic procedure reverses the causal sequence, making the results the basis for identifying the cause.

This issue may be stated more concretely. The English Civil War may indeed have resulted in economic, political, and legal advantage for the bourgeoisie as conventionally understood, but this result does not constitute proof that class interest was the basis for participation, nor would this result uniquivocally point to class interests as the cause for the War.[22] Similar remarks may be made regarding the Nazis's book burning, xenophobic feelings about nonaryans, and so forth. These social-organizational arrangements do not constitute proof that they originate in paranoid, sadomasochistic, narcissistic, or other personality dynamics. One cannot infer any causal relationship from the appearance of certain results regarding class or behavioral and emotive features. The results of revolution in these terms become not only events in themselves but also the explanation for the causes of revolution and of participation in revolution. Clearly, alternative causal explanations for the same results are always possible.[23]

Categorical analysis is not adequate to the task it is meant to fulfill, except as an abstract gloss. It is certainly not enough to infer different subjectivities from the social structural arrangements that occur in a revolution. It is necessary to demonstrate the causal independence of various categories and their effects on revolutionary events. The best that can be said for the categorical approach is that some portion of revolutionary results may be caused by class or self-interested activity or certain psychological predispositions.

This problem is related further to the complexity and gravity of revolutionary events and the adequacy of their explanation in categorical terms. It is one thing to link class interests to conflict among segments of the society, identifying the freedom of trade, taxation, land enclosure, and the like as examples. But it is another thing to link these to the trial and execution of Charles I. The former activities may well have involved class conflict between competing interests. But the latter activities involved a desire for a completely changed society and the willingness to commit acts of violence and transgression in a systematic and deliberate way.[24] The difference between the two consequences is not simply one of degree. Rather, class interests may be realized in many different social contexts, which could have been organized short of the revolutionary events that characterized England in the period 1642-1649, culminating with the execution of the king.

Similarly, it is possible to characterize Hitler and the men who surrounded him as paranoid, paranoid-schizophrenic, sadomasochistic, and narcissistic. But such psychological categorizations do not immediately translate into social organizations based on race, blood, hierarchy, and violence, nor do they lead immediately to fantasies of and expressed desires for world conquest. These subjective orientations to action could have been satisfied in a number of social contexts. The leap from psychological typology to the effective military organization of the German army, or the bureaucratic-rational organization devoted to the Holocaust, is too great, the situation too complex, to be explained by psychological categories stressing psychic conflict or even mental derangement! There was much more involved in the Holocaust than the paranoia and sadomasochism depicted in the psychological categories.[25]

Such complex and grave events are only grossly explained by dispositional categories, which are too distant from the events they are supposed to inform. What is needed is a theory closer to the data, one that simultaneously explains the reasons for the revolution and revolutionary participation and the complexity of the events characterizing a particular revolution.[26] Adequate theory must satisfy the social scientist's desire for generalization and the historian's need for detail, while remaining philosophically coherent.

But why make so much of the kind of theory used to approach knowledge, why not just get on with historical research using the theories already extant? The data, the findings, the characterizations of phenomena reflect the methods by which they were obtained. Theory transforms the world, and intellectual work on revolution can be detailed and true to subjective experiences of the participants only if the methods for transforming the world are adequate to the task. We cannot bypass these problems and get on with the work of history (and psychohistory). The characterization of phenomena is inseparable from the theoretical epistemology we employ to transform the world of social and psychological events into scholarly discourse. We must therefore continue to evaluate the adequacy of our theories and to improve them when they fall short.[27]

An Alternative Theory

An alternative theoretical framework is needed that can subsume and surmount the inadequacies of categorical analysis and can explain the forces producing heterogeneous populations in revolutions while offering a detailed understanding of the complexity of revolutionary events. Such a theory would focus on individuals' subjectivities, but not in terms of preconceived categories. Rather, individuals' subjectivities would be linked to the particularities of their historical circumstance.[28]

This kind of theory is important because it remains oriented to scholarly standards of adequate description and analysis similar to categorical analysis while it generates recognizably "correct" descriptions, that is, adequate descriptions from the subjective viewpoint of the participants in revolutionary activities. This last criterion of adequacy is crucial because of the unavailability of contemporary subjects for personal and close examination. Less adequate descriptions of revolutionary actions, depictions inconsistent with the data and contrary to our empathic understanding of the individuals involved in a historical event, are no more than glosses that satisfy the theorist's, but not the participant's, version of events.

The central conceptual terms of empirically adequate theory are language, affect, cognition, and ideology. It is by linking these concepts that we can develop a subjectively adequate theory of revolution, explaining simultaneously the heterogeneous composition of revolutionary movements and the complexity of revolutionary events. A theory based on these concepts will be acceptable to historical demands for detail while fulfilling the sociological demands for generalization.

The point of departure is the link between individuals' subjectivities and social contexts organized in terms of interpretive responses to the historical circumstances. However, it is first necessary to develop theoretically interpretive specific rules employed by revolutionaries who must integrate cognitive and affective responses to real circumstances. Once we develop such rules we have a basis for understanding the shared experiences of people involved in revolutions. In addition, these rules must provide a unified conception of the ways in which individuals construct their worlds and the meanings these constructs have for them in revolutionary situations. (The means by which we develop interpretive rules are applicable to all revolutionary situations but the rules are specific to particular revolutions.)

We can discover the interpretive bases for action through language used to organize cognitive and affective processes. Language codified in revolutionary ideology, whether written or spoken, is crucial for our analysis. The ideological language allows us to know the subjective experiences of revolutionaries. This is not to substitute a one-sided idealist conception of revolution for a one-sided materialist conception. On the contrary, real individuals and groups struggle over real economic and political grievances and interests, but these can only be reconciled and reorganized in terms of coherently elaborated, believable standards to which people can become cognitively and emotionally attached and by which they can organize and orient actions.

Thus, the analysis of the language of social process is not an example of idealism. Gadamer denies "that the linguistically articulated consciousness claims to determine all the material being of life-practice." Rather, as Gadamer has claimed in his debate with Habermas,

> It only suggests that there is no societal reality, with all its concrete forces, that does not bring itself to representation in a—consciousness that is linguistically articulated. Reality does not happen "behind the back" of language; it happens rather behind the backs of those who live in the subjective opinion that they have understood "the world" (or can no longer understand it); that is, reality happened precisely *within* language.[29]

Additionally, I should note that a subsection of British Marxists are aware, and have been aware, of the need to integrate language and social process to the material base. It is the contemporary American political economists still wed to American positivism that have reified the material base into a mechanistic determinant of process, class consciousness, language, ideology, and so on. In contrast to this attitude, Coward and Ellis wrote:

> For Marxism, the question of language posed the problem of subject in two ways. First, Marxism asked whether the role of language in the social totality is determined or determining, whether language is superstructural or not. In admitting—as linguists seemed to insist—that it is neither of these oppositions, Marxism had also to admit the possibility that the theoretical opposition base/superstructure were inadequate and that analysis of language was not possible within a rigid and false distinction between objective (mode of production) and subjective (individual identity).[30]

In short, the different contending ideological positions, the codified images of the past, present, and future worlds are the repositories of the principles by which revolutionaries orient themselves to action. Ideology therefore, is not the cause of action, but rather a mode through which action is made subjectively meaningful. And ideology is the mechanism by which diverse populations are bound together.

Although more can and will be said of the role of language and ideology in revolutionary situations, affective and cognitive processes are more fundamental to action. At one point Weinstein and I suggested that aggressive impulses released by moral transgressions served as the basis for revolutionary activities, particularly as this occurred in traditional societies.[31] At a later point we generalized this position, suggesting that experiences of loss in real social circumstances generated affective responses mobilized in the service of revolutionary action, a notion that stemmed from Freud's conception of signal affect.[32] That is, affective experiences in the face of threatened or actual external social losses (for example, the failure of the economy, the incapacity of the political system to integrate divergent political interests, and so on) are reactive responses to failed or failing aspects of society. Affective states of depression, anxiety, anger, and so on caused by societal failures threaten the personal sense of continuity and act motivationally to produce collective action rectifying the social failures. However, although these formulations are generally correct, they must not reify society on the one hand nor anthropomorphize affect on the other.

What after all, can affect signal? And what do we mean when we speak of societal failures and a sense of loss accruing from such failures? Externally or internally provoked arousal is by itself meaningless. An interpretive theory of collective action must give meaning to and integrate affect to the intersubjective experience of constructing reality. Societal failures, loss, affect, personal continuity, and the production of conceptions of society are inseparable in an interpretive theory stressing the subjective construction of meaningful social action.

Every aspect of social action is viewed in an emotional context, and every social setting demands a certain experience of emotion.[33] To be sure, this is not reflected on or in awareness when interactions are routinized, that is, conceived as consistent with familiar past experiences. However, the disruption of routine interactions results in heightened physiological arousal.[34] Meaning placed on such arousal, or emotional labeling, is achieved through socially evaluative cognitive processes.

This relation of cognition to emotion is spelled out by Schachter as follows: "The cognition, in a sense, exerts a steering function. Cognitions arising from the immediate situation as interpreted by past experience provide the framework within which one understands and labels his feelings. It is the cognition which determines whether the state of physiological arousal will be labeled "anger," "joy," or whatever."[35] Schachter's notions regarding cognition, and emotion stem from his laboratory studies. It is necessary, however, to generalize these notions to all forms of situated action.

We can begin by suggesting that meaningless action never occurs. Action and meaning are associated by definition. Thus people are continuously engaged in producing meaning in their lives, in making sense of their activities and their situations, interpreting the conditions in which their activities occur, rendering meaningful their feelings and the activities of others and so on. People will not and cannot live in chaotic meaningless worlds, as Susanne Langer observed.[36] People are constantly involved in constructing their worlds, employing several devices for providing meaning to activities. (It is impossible to present an exhaustive list of devices or sources persons employ in conceiving their worlds.)

In the widest sense biographical and social history provide people with cognitive standards for organizing experiences in particular settings. Individuals may also rely on some cognitive features of their categorical identities (that is, class, age, sex, religion, and so on) to bring situated experiences to coherent closure. People derive private or idiosyncratic cognitive standards in various ways; moreover situations require the emergent shaping of standards.[37] However, there is no way to suggest what portion of any population will employ various combinations of sources to construct their experiences. Nevertheless, it can be said with some certainty that it is in the routine "sense making" of daily life, in providing for one's sense of membership and worth, in giving meaning to everyday emotions, and in giving the commonplace world a sense of meaningful social order that the language of culture, class, situations, and so forth offer standards to organize experience. It is in the organization of the routine sense of everyday life that such sources for cognition play a paramount role.

We may then say that revolutionary activities follow from perceived interferences with routine attempts to construct a familiar world. Economic unemployment, productive reorganization, geographic and social mobility, changes in the distribution of wealth, redistribution of resources, changes in spending and purchasing power, inflation and deflation, political disenfranchisement, redistribution of power, arbitrary uses of power, failure of effective political authority, illegitimate decision making, and so on, all constitute shared disruptive situational conditions that interfere with constructive processes. Prolonged and/or severe and rapid forms of change inhibit the capacity to construct images consistent with familiar personal and social experiences. The routine modes of organizing the world cannot be managed under these conditions, the result being a world that is inconsistent with previous experiences.

Loss is experienced when the familiar modes of cognizing and experiencing the world, and familiar forms of action, are no longer available. Loss is experienced when the routine sources, including the familiar ways of integrating the material aspects of social action, become ineffective in constructing meaningful orders and one's place in them. What is lost, then, is the experience of a familiar social order and one's place in it, or the capacity to rely on the routinized sources of belief and action to produce familiar social situations. This type of experience has ramifications in several directions.

The loss of familiar social orders and one's place in them is potentially chaotic. People who cannot sustain a biographically achieved sense of personal identity, continuity, feelings of worthiness, self-esteem, membership in a community, and so on, are easily overwhelmed by affective experiences. When these conditions are widespread the society is undergoing a sense-making crisis.[38]

In the face of a sense-making crisis, of course, different people perceive the situation differently; there will not be a single response to the crisis throughout the population. For private reasons people may be capable of denying the disorder or of perceiving the disorder and not responding to it. Other persons in the society may continue to use the routine sources for sense making despite their ineffectiveness and the personal and social discomfort experienced with producing variant and even deviant forms of familiar world views. These individuals attempt to normalize the experience of chaos by retrospectively reviewing their accomplishments as only temporary variants on traditional and familiar experience. Another class of people may use its categorical identities for making sense of the chaotic situational conditions. These people interpret the world, even disruptive economic and political events, in terms of class, religion, age, psychological disposition, and so on, make the events meaningful and thus cognitively and emotively organized according to subjective interpretive principles embedded in the categorical identities.

This last type reaction is most important and consistent with expectations derived from categorical subjectivities. However, we cannot expect, and the evidence indicates, that not all people in any category will be so affected and will employ their identities to make sense of the world and their place in it. And further, there is no way to predict which of the many categories a person holds or identifies with will act as the basis for action and therefore will be effective in these terms. A Catholic man of working-class background with "authoritarian" tendencies in pre-Nazi Germany could employ any of these identities singly or in combination to make sense of the world and his place in it. The result being that such a man could account for and experience the world in terms of religion, class, "authoritarianism," and so on, thus making sense of the world in a variety of ways including pro- or anti-Nazi affiliation.

A substantial portion of the population whose relation to material conditions, to their place in the world and their relations to others is undermined by these circumstances; that portion of the population who experience these circumstances as enduring unendingly, unresolvable in traditional terms, experiences a sense-making crisis. Those individuals cannot continue to employ routine sources of sense making to organize their meaningful actions and they experience bewilderment and loss. They cannot make sense of the emotional arousal they experience. They cannot harness and give direction to the emotional arousal. Once the familiar sources are inapplicable, unavailable, or disrupted individuals experiencing this cannot resolve and make meaningful the sources of arousal in constructive directions.

It is at this point that situationally produced chaos leads to the search for new situated rules for interpreting the world; that is, the search for new methods for cognizing and experiencing the world and making sense of the emotional arousal. These situated rules of interpretation provide meaning to the experienced chaos by providing for alternate world views. They harness emotional arousal and they guide persons to a renewed sense of meaning in the world. The emerging interpretive rules accomplish this by informing their adherents of the meaning of chaotic experiences, pointing to the modes for resolving such experiences.

However, the system of rules which arises is characterized by an intermingling of the traditional with the new interpretive sources. A population thus is being offered simultaneously both an explanation of the failure and a reason for hope. A temporal relationship exists between the routine sources of meaning and the new interpretive rules. The latter slowly emerge from and are dialectically related to the former. The new system incorporates parts of the old systems as the new rules are being institutionalized in a significant portion of the population. This evolution permits a transition to the new sources of meaning, a new mode of constructing meaning without a total abdication of the past. As the dialectical interplay between the failing and rising modes of construction of the new system is sharpened, the population becomes attuned to the failures of the traditional sources and the effectiveness of the new interpretive procedures. Finally, a leadership for the new sources arises in society either expressing or simply codifying the new rules of interpretation. And if this leadership gains access to sources of power it makes attempts at superimposing the new interpretive system upon broad ranges of the society's population.

The new interpretive system is codified in the language of ideology, determining the meaning of emotional arousal, suggesting the reestablishment of a coherent world and one's place in it. The language of ideology points to new modes of cognizing and making sense of the material circumstances, past failures, present circumstances, future hopes, and the meaning of the whole society.

Thus, it is in the language of ideology that the meaning of the social senses of a failing society are formulated. It is the language of ideology that the experiences of chaos and emotional arousal are harnessed and the sense of loss resolved. Moreover, personality and social order are formulated as inseparable in this theoretical context. There is no duality of self and society, rather they are unified. Cognition, emotion and the sense of society and one's place in it are all features of the social process.

Of course, ideology does not serve all people equally in a society during a sense-making crisis. Portions of the population are not drawn into the new system but remain attached to other sources of morality, other sources for constructing the world. Additionally, ideology itself is not the same to all people who accept it. Rather, ideological language is itself a complex fabric of social rules of interpretation, which draws together different persons for different reasons. In no sense is the language of ideology a coherent logical statement. Further, the language of ideology is itself situationally interpreted so that its meaning changes with changing private and/or collective interests of its use, with changing time and social space of its application and so forth.[39]

Engels has formulated ideology as, ". . . a process accomplished by the so-called thinker consciously, it is true, but with a false consciousness. The real motive forces impelling him remain unknown to him; otherwise it would simply not be an ideological process."[40] If we are to fit Engels definition of ideology to collective action it must be elaborated in terms of its purposes for sense making, that is, for organizing personal and social events in a sense-making crisis. First, we accept Engels implicit distinction between the conscious sense-making experience and unconscious interpretive rules embedded in ideology for producing sense making. Although the latter constructive methods are never entirely beyond the ideological adherent's reflexive comprehension such effort at understanding is without purpose, for ideological adherence necessitates that certain interpretive rules are intractably part of the adherent's ideological sense-making process. The sense of the world and methods of production are tied to one another; world views are dependent for their sense on their methods of production.[41] Thus, in a sense-making crisis, it is not only the ideological conception of the world that adherents accept but also the methods for its production. And it is the latter that are transferable from situation to situation. It is the latter rules of interpretation that lend the ideology whatever degree of coherence it may have in different social settings of its application.

These interpretive rules in ideology may be likened to Chomskian deep structures but not simply native language rules. Rather they are social rules interpretively fitted to situational exigencies in the manner similar to that suggested by Cicourel's investigation of rule use.[42] That is, ideological language rule use is accomplished through social interpretive procedures fitted to situated sense making. We may extend these thoughts in another direction especially pertinent to our analysis. For example, it is possible to think of psychoanalytic defense mechanisms, situationally employed, as a lexicon of interpretive rules for sense making. Such a formulation generalizes defenses from personal modes for controlling internal drives and external information to shared interpretive rules for patterning experience and social content. It is from such a perspective that we can come to understand the ways in which movements take on particular dynamic appearances. However, such accomplished appearances are not forms of mental illness but rather the expression of particularly institutionalized defenses as methods in the constructive process.

Thus, an ideological orientation that allows for the construction of the meaning of the world in terms of external factors may give a movement the appearance of being "paranoid." Such an interpretive orientation could produce a movement resembling, for example, the paranoid-aggressive style of the Nazis, but it could also produce certain movements among Diaspora Jews characterized by a paranoid-passive appearance. The interpretive lexicon of ideology is not constituted by a simple system of rules but rather by a complex of interconnected interpretive language rules comprising the total rule set embedded in the ideology. Thus, characteristic appearances of movements, perhaps dominated by a particular practice, will appear as more than the product of a single rule always supplemented in its production by the work of other rules. The result is that even movements with dominant social characteristics are always many-sided.

There are advantages to formulating defenses in terms of a lexicon of language rules. On the one hand, this formulation is consistent with Anna Freud's use of defenses; on the other hand, it also incorporates recent interpretive approaches to psychoanalytic theory, approaches that are more readily articulated to sociological analysis.[43] Additionally, this formulation of defenses ties them to all aspects of the constructive process, whether the reference is to dream work, the construction of daily life, pathological life, or revolutionary movements. It is in this sense that defenses are generalized to all social processes.

But the most significant analytic point presented here is that through an empirical investigation of ideology we may develop a set of language rules that act as orienting principles for ideological adherents in constructing a viable world in the face of a sense-making crisis. Neither the scope of such interpretive rules nor the particular rules can be worked out without turning to a specific revolution. For while the particular rules may be transferable from situation to situation in a particular revolution, they are not transferable from revolution to revolution.

The subjective experience of revolutionary situations, thus, is tied to a particular dominant ideology. We become intimately acquainted with the revolutionary experience through an investigation of the interpretive rules embedded in that ideology. Although this is a general approach to revolutionary experience, the specifics of the subjective orientation to and experience of revolution must be reworked in each historical setting.

I should stress that the analytic development of these rules and the ideological content are situationally accomplished rather than deduced from generalized abstractions about revolution. Thus, Engels is correct in suggesting that the real circumstances that persons face are inseparable from their developing ideology. But we must supplement Engels's thinking in three ways. First, we should note that social conditions sufficient to produce such an ideology for collective action do not arise from a failure of sense making in a single societal dimension. Rather, ideologies that can mobilize collective revolutionary activities arise from the real failures in multiple dimensions of society. Ideology directed to revolutionary action builds on the experiences of sense-making failures in several dimensions of society. The result is that revolutionary ideology becomes a total fabric regarding the total society, one that draws together multiple issues and populations. The characterizations of the specific real problems the society faces are integrated in the language of ideology. The ideology offers formulas for making sense of the experiences being felt and offers methods for their solution. The ideology becomes a composite of the heterogeneous issues that plague the society. And a composite ideology is the medium through which the many events confronting society are interpreted.

The second point by which we should amend Engels's definition is that real circumstances cannot interpret themselves. The objective character of social events offer no unequivocal conception of themselves and of their meaning. Evaluated events in the world such as the inequitable distribution of power, the unjust allocation of resources, the exploitation of labor, the oppression of religious factions, the discrimination against classes of persons, and so on, are so experienced because the interpretive rules embedded in ideology inform its adherents that particular activiites in the world should be ascribed with such meanings.

In addition, although ideological adherents' ordering of interactions in society is accomplished according to the interpretive rules embedded in the ideology, these interpretive rules are bound not only to sense making in the present but also to the achievement of future circumstances, that is, the manner in which the real events should proceed in the society in light of the ways in which past and future worlds are envisioned.

Finally, while adherents experience a sense of unity and solidarity in their ideologies, in a strict sense ideologies do not enjoy such coherence. Different aspects of an ideology serve different purposes and not all aspects of an ideological fabric are important to all adherents. Particular members are drawn to particular subfeatures of the ideological interpretive system of rules. Frequently this is an outgrowth of people's interests or the result of a segment's need to resolve a sense of crisis confined to less than the total array of issues falling within the perview of the ideological fabric. The result is that different segments of an ideological movement construct shared but incongruent views of the world while appearing to be committed to, and not questioning the commitment of others to, the ideological whole. An ideology therefore, appears as shared and held in common by all adherents, giving the illusion of welding its heterogeneous members together for a single purpose or for all purposes in common.

Thus, it is the ideology that appears to hold together the heterogeneous populations but does so not for a single purpose. Ideological adherents are really oriented to and by multiple moralities.[44] Each adherent constructs from his circumscribed commitment to and conception of the ideology his particular conception of the movement. And yet from the point of view of the ideological whole adherents can envision themselves as members unified into a single movement. Similarly, outsiders may envision a unified movement although it is only at the surface. Finally, it is because ideology is so many things to so many people that it can be situationally and practically interpreted, and thus it can draw together such diverse sociological and psychological populations.

A significant analytic feature of treating ideology in this fashion is that it turns ideology from the theorists' formulation about the ways in which persons proceed in the world to the ways in which ideological adherents conduct their own lives in their worlds and the ways in which ideology affects that performance. This formulation removes ideology from an objective category of analysis, which the analyst superimposes on persons, describing the ways in which actors may or may not be motivated to action, and focuses on the subjective uses of ideological rules that persons in collective movements use to interpret the real interests of their lives, to evaluate the actions of others, to construct meaning, and to give sense to their emotions. It is through ideology that real worlds are experienced and made cognitively and emotively meaningful for revolutionary activities.

This approach calls for special research strategies. How people decide which way they must identify themselves in a revolutionary struggle can in part be explained in terms of the traditional sociological and psychological categories such as class, religion, age, and so forth, as stated. As for the rest, it is necessary to proceed by analyzing their subjective experiences, feelings, conceptions of the world, and so on as these are spelled out in a multidimensional ideology. From this perspective, the revolutionary process is not conceived in crass political, economic, or social terms but in terms of standards for organizing life, including the yearnings and moralities as well as expressions of interest. A second methodological refinement then follows from this position, one that requires the analyst to start with the given ideology working backward to the individuals and the groups that develop these statements to understand how, why, and the ways in which heterogeneous populations become committed to them. This involves something quite different from the traditional technique of distinguishing people according to the social locations and particular social and psychological spaces and then assuming shared interests and shared yearnings because of shared location and disposition. It is precisely this assumption that has led to the contradictory positions noted and particularly to the inability to explain the heterogeneity of participants in revolutionary action in any comprehensive or parsimonious way.

Notes

1. I want to thank my friend Tom Cottle for his unfailing support of my theoretical efforts over the years. I should also note that my thinking is always influenced by my friend and colleague Fred Weinstein. Weinstein and I continually discuss our work, and I am sure that his published and unpublished thoughts have shaped the contents of this chapter. More specifically, however, the point I am about to make regarding the heterogeneity of the composition of revolutionary participants was part of a lecture I gave to a faculty and graduate student history seminar at Johns Hopkins University in the fall of 1973. This point was in some initial sense stated in our *Psychoanalytic Sociology*, Baltimore, Johns Hopkins University Press, 1973. However, it was not until the seminar at Johns Hopkins that I saw its generality and its implications for other theories of revolutionary action. The points with regard to affect were initially made by Weinstein in his "Events and Affects: Aspects of the Psychoanalytic Study of Groups," published in *The Group for the Use of Psychology in History Newsletter* 4 (March 1976):8-17. Weinstein has elaborated the issues discussed in this article, and they are included, along with those on the psychological heterogeneity of the composition of revolutionary participants, in his forthcoming *Germany's Discontents, Hitler's Visions: The Claims of Leadership and Ideology in the National Socialist Movement* (New York: Academic Press, 1980). Some of the remaining issues discussed in this chapter were parts of talks given at the first and second annual psychohistory conferences held at Stockton College and later Adelphi University and to the Sociology Board, the University of California, Santa Cruz. However, the contents of these talks have been considerably changed and elaborated. Finally, Fred Weinstein needs to be thanked again for his editorial work on the first draft of this chapter.

2. In my discussion of social movements I will focus on revolutions. By revolutionary movements I mean any struggle over the organizing principles of a society or organizing principles of any subsection of the society such as the standards organizing political, economic, family, religious and other institutions. More specifically then, these struggles are directed toward change in the organizing principles of any activity among persons in society, but they are especially focused on those principles that govern the social organization of particular institutions and the ways institutional resources such as power, wealth, prestige, and so forth are distributed in

society. Although this definition is worded specifically for the language analysis that forms the center of the alternative theory, it is consistent with those definitions employed in the recent literature on revolution. Charles Tilly, *From Mobilization to Revolution* (Reading, Mass.: Addison-Wesley, 1978), see especially chap. 3; Theda Skocpol, "France, Russia, China: A Structural Analysis of Social Revolutions," *Comparative Studies in Society and History* 18 (April 1976):175-210, see especially p. 175; Elbaki Hermassi, "Toward a Comparative Study of Revolutions," *Comparative Studies in Society and History* 18 (April 1976):211-235, see especially 232-233; Jeffery M. Paige, *Agrarian Revolution, Social Movements and Export Agriculture in the Underdeveloped World* (New York: The Free Press, 1975), see especially chap. 1, pp. 1-71. Finally, for a most explicit effort at reaching a definition for revolution see Perez Zagorin, "Prolegomena to the Comparative History of Revolution in Early Modern Europe," *Comparative Studies in Society and History* 18 (April 1976):151-174, especially p. 165.

3. A typical example of the way heterogeneous composition in collective action is dealt with in the narrative is offered by Tilly in his discussion of seventeenth-century French peasant rebellions. Tilly observes, "Although (as Bercé himself concedes) the scheme homogenizes unduly the participants and motives in the older forms of conflict, it captures an essential contrast." See Tilly, *From Mobilization to Revolution*, p. 147.

Another way authors deal with the problem of categorized heterogeneity is to describe these in terms of alliances among persons of different classes suggesting ad hoc reasons for the alliance usually explained by temporarily shared interests as the basis for the coalition. However, none of these explanations, to my knowledge, suggest systematic theoretical rationale for why and how such categorically heterogeneous segments of the population achieve solidarity even for relatively short periods of time.

4. Murray Melbin, "Behavior Rhythms in Mental Hospitals," *American Journal of Sociology* 74 (May 1969):650-665.

5. Albert K. Cohen, "The Sociology of the Deviant Act," *American Sociology Review* 30 (February 1965):5-14.

6. Exceptions to this model of categorical or predispositional variables that cause expected outcomes can be found among a small number of recent works in the social scientific literature of collective behavior. However, none of these works have attempted to integrate psychoanalytic and language theories in their approaches to collective behavior. However, in connection with these approaches see such as Clark McPhail's "Civil Disorder Participation: A Critical Examination of Recent Research," *American Sociological Review* 36 (December 1971):1058-1073. McPhail also points to the failure of categorical analysis, and some of my thoughts are stimulated from his "Civil Disorder Participation" article. See also McPhail's article with Miller, Clark McPhail and David L. Miller, "The

Assembling Process: A Theoretical and Empirical Examination,"
American Sociological Review 38 (December 1973):721-735. We should also
note here the symbolic interactionist point of view to collective behavior, a
framework with focuses on the interaction itself as the source for collective
activities. See in this connection the works of Ralph H. Runer and Lewis
Killian, *Collective Behavior*, 2nd ed. (Englewood Cliffs, N.J.: Prentice-
Hall, 1972), and Ralph H. Turner, "Collective Behavior," in the *Handbook of Modern Sociology*, Robert E.L. Faris (ed.) (Chicago: Rand-
McNally, 1964), pp. 382-425.

7. Seymour Martin Lipset, *Political Man, the Social Bases of Politics*
(Garden City, N.Y.: Anchor Books, Doubleday and Company, 1963); the
quotes are from p. 148, and fn. 29, p. 148.

8. Peter Lowenberg, "The Psychohistorical Origins of the Nazi Youth
Cohort," *American Historical Review* 75 (December 1971):1457-1502.

9. Weinstein, *Germany's Discontents*, chap. 1.

10. Weinstein, *Germany's Discontents*.

11. Fred Weinstein and Gerald M. Platt, *The Wish to Be Free: Society,
Psyche and Value Change* (Berkeley and Los Angeles: University of
California Press, 1969).

12. A summary of interpretive and historiographic controversies regarding the English Revolution is given in chap. 2, "The Social Origins of
the English Revolution," of Lawrence Stone's *The Causes of the English
Revolution, 1529-1642* (London: Routledge and Kegan Paul, 1972), pp.
26-43. See also Stone's anthology on the English Civil War, *Social Change and
Revolution in England 1540-1640* (London: Longmans, 1965).

13. R.H. Tawney, "The Rise of the Gentry, 1558-1640," *The Economic
Review* 11, no. 1 (1974):1-38. Christopher Hill maintains Tawney's inter-
pretation, J.E.C. Hill, *Society and Puritanism in Pre-Revolutionary
England* (New York: Schocken Books, 1964).

14. H.R. Trevor-Roper, "The Elizabethan Aristocracy, an Anatomy
Anatomized," *The Economic History Review* 3, no. 3 (1951):279-298. H.R.
Trevor-Roper, *The Gentry 1540-1640* (London: Cambridge University
Press, 1953).

15. Lawrence Stone, *The Crisis of the Aristocracy 1558-1641* (London:
Oxford, 1965).

16. R.H. Tawney, "Introduction," in *Members of the Long Parliament*
ed. Douglas Brunton and Donald Pennington (Cambridge, Mass.: Harvard University Press, 1954); Perez Zagorin, *The Court and Country* (London: Routledge and Kegan Paul, 1969), see especially pp. 329-331; Robert
Ashton, *The English Civil War, Conservatism and Revolution, 1603-1649*
(London: Weidenfeld and Nicolson, 1978), see especially chap. 4.

17. Brunton and Pennington, *Members of the Long Parliament*, pp.
19-20.

18. Stone, *English Revolution*.

19. Steven Antler, "Quantitative Analysis of the Long Parliament," *Past and Present* 56 (August 1972):154-157; R.S. Schofield, "Quantitative Analysis of the Long Parliament," *Past and Present* 68 (August 1975):124-129.

20. Tawney, in Brunton and Pennington, *Members of the Long Parliament*, p. XIX. Friedrich Engles was the initiator of this approach to the English Civil War.

The evidence for heterogeneous composition in progressive and regressive collective movements is copious. However, I find a recent, unpublished study of the Parisian Mobile Guard especially interesting. Mark Traugott in an intensive historical-statistical analysis of the occupational composition of the Parisian Mobile Guard (1848) in six *arrondissements*—found that the Guard was from a variety of social classes, and it was not different in class background from the insurrectionists. In addition, the Guard was not drawn disproportionately from the *Lumpenproletariat* as Marx had suggested. This work is important because it vividly demonstrates the heterogeneity problem and further because it illustrates that progressive and regressive orientations in the same collective action can be unrelated to a particular social status. Further, this is real, hard data and not the typical sociological-historical narrative regarding statistical distributions that interprets for the reader the numeric trends. See Mark Traugott, "The Parisian Mobile Guard in 1848: Test of the Lumpenproletariat Thesis, Parts I and II," unpublished manuscript. From a different perspective Faye Crosby is struggling with a similar problem regarding the validity of psychohistorical explanations in her "Evaluating Psychohistorical Explanations," *The Psychohistory Review* 7 (Spring 1979):6-16.

21. Alfred Schutz, *The Phenomenology of the Social World*, trans. G. Walsh and F. Lehnert (Evanston, Ill.: Northwestern University Press, 1967); Gerald M. Platt, "Recent Issues in Interpretive Sociology: The Case of Ethnomethodology," unpublished manuscript.

22. Wallerstein used this approach in his analysis of the English Civil War, see chap. 5, "The Strong Core States: Class-Formation and International Commerce," in *The Modern World System; Capitalist Agriculture and the Origins of European World-Economy* ed. Immanuel M. Wallerstein (New York: Academic Press, 1974).

23. For example, Charles Tilly points out that the consequences of revolution that favor a particular sense may result from political machinations during and after the revolt by one class among the several who participated in the conflict rather than a product of class interest favoring those who initiated the conflict in the first place. Writing on the American Revolution, Tilly notes, "and the middle class members of the revolutionary coalitions wielded exceptional power in the shaping of our new policy." *From Mobilization to Revolution*, p. 227.

24. Michael Walzer, *The Revolution of the Saints, a Study in the Origins of Radical Politics* (New York: Atheneum, 1968), see chap. 1.

25. Weinstein, *Germany's Discontents*.

26. Clifford Geertz, *The Interpretation of Cultures, Selected Essays* (New York: Basic Books, 1973), see chap. 1.

27. Gerald M. Platt, *Theorizing in Sociology* (Englewood Cliffs, N.J.: Prentice-Hall, forthcoming), chap. 1.

28. We asserted this point in both *The Wish to Be Free* (1969) and in *Psychoanalytic Sociology* (1973); that is, revolution arises out of realistic circumstances beyond the control of individual wishes. However, this does not imply that revolutionary events arise outside the formulating processes of individuals. Recently a similar point regarding social structure in revolution was suggested by Skocpol and Trimberger, "We have a different conception from Marx about what creates objectively revolutionary crises, but our analysis, like his, hinges on discerning how revolutionary situations arise out of structural relations and historical processes outside of the deliberate control of acting groups." See Theda Skocpol and Ellen Kay Trimberger, "Revolutions and the World-Historical Development of Capitalism," *Berkeley Journal of Sociology* 22 (1977-1978):101-103.

29. Hans-Georg Gadamar, "On the Scope and Function of Hermeneutical Reflection," in *Philosophical Hermeneutics*, trans. and ed. David E. Linge (Berkeley and Los Angeles: University of California Press, 1976), p. 35.

30. Rosalind Coward and John Ellis, *Language and Materialism, Developments in Semiology and the Theory of the Subject* (London: Routledge and Kegan Paul, 1977), p. 154. E.P. Thompson also has correctly insisted that class and class consciousness are not determined by objectified class positions but rather in terms of historical and social process. Thompson's Marxism integrates base and superstructure in a manner that is absent from the works of his American counterparts. Recently, Thompson reasserted this formulation in his polemic against Althusser. See E.P. Thompson, *The Making of the English Working Class* (York: Vintage Books, 1963), pp. 9-14; also see, E.P. Thompson, *The Poverty of Theory and Other Essays* (New York and London: Monthly Review Press, 1978), pp. 56-57, pp. 103ff. I am indebted to Rick Fantasia for calling these points to my attention.

31. Weinstein and Platt, *The Wish to Be Free*, chap. 1, "The Sociology of Value Change," pp. 20-44; recently Barrington Moore, Jr. made a similar point in his, *Injustice: The Social Bases of Obedience and Revolt* (New York: Pantheon Books, 1978).

32. Fred Weinstein and Gerald M. Platt, *Psychoanalytic Sociology, An Essay on the Interpretation of Historical Data and the Phenomena of Collective Data* (Baltimore: Johns Hopkins University Press, 1973), see especially chaps. 3 and 4. Weinstein, "Events and Affects"; and *Germany's Discontents*, chap. 2.

33. Parsons made this point in 1951. See Talcott Parsons, "The Super-ego and the Theory of Social Systems," reprinted in his *Social Structure and Personality* (New York: Free Press of Glencoe, 1964), reprinted from *Psychiatry*, February 1952.

34. Garfinkel demonstrated this in his paper, "Studies of the Routine Grounds of Everyday Activities," reprinted in his *Studies in Ethnomethodology* (Englewood Cliffs, N.J.: Prentice-Hall, 1967). Reprinted from *Social Problems*, Winter 1964.

35. Stanley Schachter and Jerome E. Singer, "Cognitive, Social and Physiological Determinants of Emotional State," *Psychological Review* 69 (September 1962):379-399; Stanley Schachter, "The Interaction of Cognitive and Physiological Determinants of Emotional State," in *Advances in Experimental Social Psychology*, ed. L. Berkowitz, vol. 1 (New York: Academic Press, 1964), pp. 49-80, quote from p. 51. Schachter's work on cognition and emotion has influenced my thinking on this issue. Most studies indicate that physiological states of arousal are indistinguishable when described by such diverse emotional terms as joy, anxiety, depression, anger. The very terms of emotion have social connotations. To be happy or anxious implies deviation from standard levels of societal emotions in the direction of excessive positive and negative excitation. The language of emotion is socialized in individuals and is socially produced. We are made happy by joyful events, by social successes, by the warmth and concern of friends and kin. We are angered and depressed by contrary circumstances, by the perceived hostilities of others, by death of friends and loved ones, by social failures. Persons who profess such arousal without apparent social cause are deemed simpletons, deviants, and insane.

36. Susanne K. Langer, *Philosophy in a New Key* (New York: Mentor, 1951), p. 241.

37. Ralph H. Turner formulated this type of emergent norm devised by people in exigent situations; see his "Collective Behavior" pp. 394ff. We should also note Peter McHugh's work, which demonstrates people's use of similar emergent cognitive devises; see his *Defining the Situation, the Organization of Meaning in Social Interaction* (Indianapolis, Ind. and New York: Bobbs-Merrill Company, 1968), chap. 4.

38. Tom Juravich suggested this metaphor.

39. Karl Mannheim, *Ideology and Utopia, an Introduction to the Sociology of Knowledge*, trans. L. Wirth and E. Shils (New York: A Harvest Books, Harcourt Brace and World, 1936), pp. 68, 83.

40. Karl Marx and Friedrich Engels, *Selected Correspondence* (Moscow: International Publishers, 1954), p. 541.

41. Garfinkel, "What is Ethnomethodology?" *Studies in Ethnomethodology*, pp. 1-34.

42. Aaron V. Cicourel, "Cross-Modal Communication: The Representational Context of Sociolinguistic Information Processing," in his

Cognitive Sociology, Language and Meaning in Social Interaction (New York: Free Press, 1974), p. 141-171, especially pp. 164-171.

43. Anna Freud, *The Ego and the Mechanisms of Defense*, C. Baines (trans.) (New York: International Universities Press, 1946); Paul Ricoeur, *Freud and Philosophy, an Essay on Interpretation* (New Haven, Conn.: Yale University Press, 1976).

44. Mannheim, *Ideology and Utopia*, p. 58; Alfred Schutz, "On Multiple Realities," in his *Collected Papers*, vol. 1, *The Problem of Social Reality*, ed. M. Natanson (The Hague: Martinus Nijhoff, 1962), pp. 207-259.

**Part II
Psychohistory: Literature,
Biography, and Social
History**

8

Psyche, Clio, and the Artist

Cushing Strout

In mythology Psyche is a rather equivocal figure. Apollo tells her that for all her beauty she is grimly destined to marry a terrible winged serpent; in the end instead, she happily marries Cupid and becomes immortal. The prospects for psychoanalytic thought also seem to point in two directions. Either it is seen as subversive of true historical and literary understanding, or it is championed by a few as the ultimate oracle for all interpretation of history and art. Witness *The Journal of Psychohistory*, committed to reducing all history to the psychic story of the effects of child-rearing practices, while among historians and literary critics dominant tendencies disdainfully ignore psychology for the more impersonal truths of quantitative or structural analysis.

It is difficult to insist on both the uses and the abuses of psychological interpretation without alienating those who have already chosen sides. But I think a restoration of humanistic critical and historical understanding requires both a sharper and a more ironic assessment of the issues. When Erik H. Erikson twenty years ago introduced the term "psycho-history" in *Young Man Luther*, the inverted commas and the hyphen stood for his own modest sense of the provisional nature of the enterprise. Even in 1973, when both the qualifying marks had disappeared from common usage, he looked forward to the day when history would "simply be history again, but now a history aware of the fact that it has always indulged in a covert and circuitous traffic with psychology which can now be direct, overt, and aware," just as "psychoanalysis will have become conscious of its own historical determinants, and *case history* and *life history* will no longer be manners of speaking."[1] I honor him, above all, for this ideal, which informs my remarks on psychological interpretation even when they sometimes criticize him.

Literature, history, and psychoanalysis belong to a common family, perhaps even to a somewhat incestuous one. The historian Hayden White has pointed out how histories may be organized by the literary categories of comedy, romance, irony, or tragedy; and the clinician Roy Schaffer has translated Freud's scientific language of force, energy, and apparatus into "a historical, experimental, intentionalistic model."[2] In all three disciplines, moreover, the favored mode of explaining is telling a story. For all three the original data are interpretations, whether they are documents, texts, or dreams. Their facts are not like pebbles on a beach; they are acts of mind. A crucial difference among them, however, is that neither historian nor critic can benefit from the evidence-creating feedback produced by the clinical encounter in transference, resistance, and free association, nor can their interpretations be tested by therapeutic results; on the other hand, scholars usually have a wealth of documentary evidence denied to the clinician.

Freud's genius, like some of his follies, lay in reading between the lines. The same may be said of historians, biographers, and critics, but they have a prior, greater obligation first to read the lines as scrupulously as possible. The humanistic scholar has to try to understand historical persons as they see themselves before he can see them in terms that may account for the mistakes they may have made about themselves. Even Freud thought that people sometimes said what they meant: "people make no mistake when *they are all there*, as the saying goes."[3] His examples—speaking to the king, making a love declaration, or defending one's honor before a jury—reflect his preference for the seemingly casual as the locus of betrayal, rather than our most committed acts. No doubt, they sometimes might refute him, but his point stands that our acts do not always betray our inner conflicts. For that reason I think it is a wise procedural rule to recognize that even when the covert speaks its message louder than the overt message, we still need much overt evidence to interpret it. Let me use an example from my own research. William James in his old age recorded a dream as supposed evidence for a mystical experience. "It seemed thus to belong to three different dream-systems at once," he wrote, "no one of which would connect itself either with the others or with my waking life."[4] But the dream speaks more eloquently about the dreamer's identity conflict than it does about a transcendent world, pointing back to the time of his youth when he was divided in anguish by his conflicting ambitions to be a painter, a scientist-doctor, and a philosopher.[5] Erikson cites the dream as being revelatory of "an acute identity confusion," resolved in the reinstatement of the dreamer's mature professional identity by an exercise of the psychologist's "'objective' empathy and systematic compassion" in recording it; but he does so against the necessary, implied background of the "prolonged identity crisis" of James's youth and also in the light of the necessary hint about its source, noting that the son's later philosophy was "a continuation and an abrogation of his father's creed."[6] The covert message of the disturbing dream makes sense only in the light of a much larger context that includes many overt and covert messages of his youth and his old age.

My methodological moral, therefore, is that before unconscious conflict can be reliably inferred and interpreted as a covert message in a text with a different overt message, we should first locate the conflict firmly in a documentable crisis of the author's life. Otherwise the richness and convenience of theory substitute illicitly for the poverty and untidiness of the data. Erikson in *Young Man Luther* relies heavily on Luther's supposed fit in the choir, an event that is dubiously derived from testimony by an enemy of Luther's, given some four decades after it was supposed to have taken place, and never mentioned (as Erikson notes) by Luther himself.[7] "We are thus obliged to accept half-legend as half-history," Erikson concludes, "provided only that a reported episode does not contradict other well-established facts; persists in having a ring of truth; and yields a meaning consistent with psychological theory."[8] It is a standard well suited to a historical novelist, who must often supply motives for which the record speaks either too softly or not at all; but a historian cannot take the same license without producing a suppositious history of surmises.

Fawn Brodie has written a book on the supposition that the legend about Jefferson's liaison with a young slave girl actually happened, as his enemies claimed. She can show that, being present nine months before Sally's pregnancies, Jefferson might have fathered her children, but even this hypothesis does not warrant the literary gothic of Brodie's romantic supposition that Sally Hemings, like Maria Cosway, actually *was* one of Jefferson's "tragic secret loves."[9] Whereas Victorian biographers were tempted to veil or suppress scandalous evidence of sexuality, Brodie is typically modern in celebrating her scandal as proof of her hero's continuing sexual vitality. If he were not sexually involved with Sally and Maria, she concludes, "Jefferson is made out to be something less than a man, and Alexander Hamilton's ancient canard that Jefferson was 'feminine' is perpetuated even in our own time."[10] One might call this standard "the Norman Mailer test" for historical truth. Even if this argument were convincing, however, since she justly shows that "from the beginning of Jefferson's life as a political man and as a lawyer he was caught up not only in the slavery problem but also in the psychological complexities and ambivalences provoked by the issue of miscegenation," there is no evidence at all that the alleged liaison made any difference to Jefferson's social ideas and political actions.[11] The point of paying attenton to the presence of deep-seated emotional conflicts, after all, is to connect them with their agent's historically influential thoughts and actions so that we can understand them better.

Michael Paul Rogin in *Fathers and Children* spins out a psychoanalytical tale about Andrew Jackson, as an explanation of American Indian policy, an account bristling with references to "oral introjection" fantasies of regaining the "primal infant-mother connection," the "death instinct," an insane "oral rage," and the "anal stage" of development, all supposedly showing "a logic of the psyche" that "led from children to mothers, from debt to the bank, from Indian removal to removal of the federal deposits."[12] But if we do not abandon our skepticism in the face of all this facile generalizing, mixing Freud, Erikson, and Melanie

Klein in a strange brew, we must ask what sort of biographical evidence are we dealing with? Rogin's answer is: "We have, of course, no clinical evidence to root Jackson's rages in early childhood experience." Instead we have what are called "suggestive facts," which mainly turn out to be theories: "Problems in infancy, involving feeding, weaning, or holding the child, often intensify infantile rage and accentuate later difficulties in the struggle of the child to break securely free of the mother. . . . Speech difficulties often indicate a problematic oral relationship. . . . Disturbances in the parasympathetic nervous system, like slobbering, commonly derive from tension in the early maternal tie."[13] In this litany of generalities a few facts are visible: Jackson was a posthumous child who suffered recurrently from a laundry list of medically unspecific symptoms, often expressing anger and occasionally feeling deep depression. Rogin himself admits that the illnesses may not have been psychosomatic at all, but even if they were, he never puts this material into a datable context by which we could decode the sufferings in relation to specific conflicts in a pattern of development, as Erikson seeks to do with Luther. Rogin's type of argument, too common in "psychohistory," perhaps should be called "poor but honest," like the parents of a nineteenth-century rags-to-riches hero.

My second methodological moral is summed up in this quotation: "To learn to say 'I don't know' is the beginning of intellectual integrity."[14] Psychohistorians should paste this remark of Freud's in their hats, remembering, alas, that he said it with William C. Bullitt in their tendentious, dogmatic, and denigrating biography of Woodrow Wilson, which actually admitted ignorance only on the question of the strength of Wilson's libido, an issue they then rejected as being unimportant. Very much more in the true spirit of the remark is Erikson's measured observation that the data about Jefferson's alleged liaison with the slave girl "oscillate between conveying something that seems possible to something even probable."[15] The first thing to go in much psychohistory, however, like truth in wartime, is the willingness to take seriously the Scotch verdict of "not proven." Robert Frost once compared free verse to playing tennis without a net. Too much psychohistory is like jumping over the net before the match has been played out.

Too many interpretations are also monistic, like a player who always runs around his backhand. Oedipus reigns with a heavy hand. Erikson's schedule for growth departed from Freud, however, and anticipated current interest in the problems of the aged by alluding to adult crises of personality with their own emotional issues. Freud pointed out that the creative writers had dramatized the oedipal crisis before he ever analyzed it, and in Willa Cather's *The Professor's House* or Lionel Trilling's *The Middle of the Journey*, for example, Erikson could have found novelistic evidence for his own concept of a mid-life crisis of "generativity," threatened by stagnation and self-indulgence. Yet the hold of earlier psychoanalytic concepts is tenacious, and some biographers use them even when they have better evidence for Erikson's point. Thus a recent biographer of the historian Frederick Jackson Turner thoroughly documents his extravagance in smoking, eating, buying, and contracting for books that he never wrote; his interest in popularizing his ideas on the lecture circuit, rather than refining them professionally; and his hoarding and underlining of all favorable references to his work, while covering every available surface with his large flowing signature. The author either sees these traits as the charm of "a hedonist in a Victorian world" or as the sign of "a life-size inferiority complex." But the biographer himself records the crucial fact: "the most tragic year" of Turner's life was when two of his three children died when he was thirty-eight.[16] Yet rather than explore this crisis as an explanatory source for Turner's treating of himself in such a self-indulgent way, he interprets it instead as a way-station on the path to maturity, despite the fact that the Turners went into debt permanently on their recuperative European vacation after the death of their children.

If the rule of licensing one's explanations by starting out from a specific disturbed moment in the career of the subject might help to keep us from fixating on the familiar Freudian categories, it also would tend to free us from their causal reference to infancy, where the historian and biographer seldom have any evidence. It is all very well in the name of realism to bring the bedroom, the bathroom, and the nursery back into our historical awareness, but the problem of evidence cannot be solved simply by relying on the abstractions of theory, which is itself continuously under critical revision. Causal knowingness always tends to promote the imperialism of theory and to disguise moral judgments in scientific lingo. Rogin tips his hand to show the moral in his linkage of American expansionism with Jacksonian "oral rage" when the book ends by tying Jacksonianism to the coming "Leviathan" of "corporate power, worldly acquisitiveness, and bureaucratic order."[17]

The psychologically sensitive biographer can focus, if the surviving record includes it, on his subject's conflict of relatively obscured intentions and conscious aims as an explanation for his career and thematic intent. A clinician has recently argued that psychoanalysis itself is only the redescription of an action in narrative terms that points to hidden reasons, rather than a causal explanation of it in terms of conditions.[18] The novelistic form of Freud's case studies is certainly the novel part of psychoanalysis in terms of his innovative break with the organic disease models for hysteria; but psychoanalytic theory is also traditionally engaged with asserting genetic and causal propositions about psychosexual development, not merely with decoding language and symptoms in terms of unrecognized and conflicting wishes. It is precisely this scientific part of the legacy that has led an English literary scholar to believe that "the notion of causality in the emotional life of the individual" must give psychoanalysis the useful function not "to deepen or subtilize the complexities of life or literature, but rather to devise simplifying formulae that make all things clear."[19]

Every narrative is a balance between particulars and generalizations. If it is easy to lose the individual in the role of illustration, which happens in case histories, it is also necessary to look for recurring themes in a biographical subject to see it as a life and not "a happening." But these generalizations define patterns, rather than causal mechanisms. Peter Shaw's study, *The Character of John Adams*, for example, is refreshingly free of all clinical jargon, yet he presents Adams in terms that reflect familiarity with psychoanalytic ideas. He shows Adams to be more prostrated by success than by failure, suggests in a footnote that "the common element among Adams's collapses may have been defiance of figures in authority," and points to a recurring pattern by which "in common with his other revolts, once Adams had defeated an individual in authority, he acted to legitimate the principles underlying his opponent's position."[20]

Shaw's note cites "Freud's essay on "Those Wrecked by Success," which highlights the way in which the forces of conscience may forbid a person to gain the hoped-for enjoyment brought about by a change in reality, but he does not draw Freud's conclusion. Freud disarms us at first by confessing, after several stabs at explaining why Lady Macbeth should collapse after her success, that he cannot penetrate "the triple obscurity of the bad preservation of the text, the unknown intention of the dramatist, and the hidden purport of the legend." But he abandons this agnosticism when he turns to Ibsen's Rebecca West and finds that "everything that befell her at Rosmersholm, the passion for Rosmer and the enmity towards his wife, was from the first a consequence of the Oedipus-complex, a compulsive replica of her relations with her mother and Dr. West."[21] Freud's literary detour finally returns him to the certainty of his clinical diagnosis that illness-inducing conscience is always connected with the Oedipus complex. Shaw, on the other hand, as a historian, wants to situate Adams in the village life of eighteenth-century Massachusetts with its Puritan tradition, and he convincingly presents Adam's "anxious uncertainty arising from self-examination" as a translation of "the Puritan concern over salvation into the question of his worthiness for success."[22] Freudian confidence in the universality of the oedipal theory of guilt would blot out this historical context.

Shaw does not tell us why Adams legitimated his opponents, but there is a clue in Erikson's remark about Luther's conservatism: "psychological dialectics" must assume it to be "even probable" that "a great revolutionary's psyche may also harbor a great reactionary."[23] The remark exploits the psychoanalytic idea of ambivalence, one of its most useful concepts, which has entered into our way of interpreting thoughts and actions, quite without respect to the psychosexual etiology that Freud developed for it. The clinical encounter has distinct advantages for turning up evidence about fantasies derived from our feelings as children, and the quest for them is conducted not for theoretical reasons but to find a therapeutic remedy for the patient's problem. The biographer has no such advantage or purpose. It is appropriate therefore to look elsewhere in tracking down Adam's ambivalence. We might find it, for example, in his querulous Puritanism, a political religion that provided him with a double legacy, justifying both revolt against authority and submission to it.

Psychoanalytic therapy is notable as a modern mode of understanding that takes the individual seriously. Inevitably, its impact on historiography has been to sponsor studies of what used to be called "great men" in politics, science, philosophy, and art. But Freud's theory also highlighted the matrix of the family and the weight of cultural norms as they are mediated by parental voices. From this point of view psychohistory has looked to common child-rearing practices or shared childhood experiences in the hope of finding explanatory keys. "The history of childhood and of the family, collective biography and prosopography," Peter Loewenberg observes, "are now moving to the forefront of historical interest."[24] Erikson's *Childhood and Society* (1950, 1964) had pointed the way. Biography of children or a movement's followers is often empirically hard to come by, and the temptation is great to rely on theory to fill the gaps, or to turn every property of an individual life-cycle into a property of the community. Rogin cites Erikson's authority, for example, in taking Jackson, whose mother died when he was an adolescent, "to represent antebellum America," because by definition the leader "experiences widely shared social tensions as personal trauma."[25] It is true that Erikson did see Luther as one of those rare individuals who "lift his individual patienthood to the level of a universal one" by trying "to solve for all what he could not solve for himself alone."[26] But it is one thing to show the hero using his struggle with his conflicts to develop universal statements of religion or philosophy; it is quite another to identify his psychological conflicts with those of his followers. The issues that the hero defines may, indeed, be shared with his followers; the specific psychological biography that led to them may be very different, precisely because similar conflicts do not produce necessarily similar responses.

The language of identity has become the common coin of current ethnic, national, and ideological movements without their having any indebtedness to psychoanalytic ideas, which they usually scorn. But a psychology that emphasizes how a person becomes individuated through conflict in the family ought to be able to appreciate how other groups also

achieve definition in extrafamilial conflicts; but to do so it has to transcend
the Freudian emphasis on family-centered issues. Erikson has expanded the
tradition by taking vocational ambitions as seriously as Freud took sexual
wishes, and the departure itself comports with Freud's famous remark
about the sign of health being the capacity to love and work. But Erikson
has also usefully emphasized the developmental need for ideological orientation as part of the identity-making process, thus taking more seriously
what Freudians have always been inclined to unmask as mere rationalization of deeper instinctual issues. As a historian and a sociologist have justly
emphasized, the sense of identity and self-esteem are always vulnerable to
historical events and keyed to social mandates that are not necessarily
located in the family context.[27] The point ought to constitute a third
methodological moral—there are more things in heaven and earth than are
dreamed of in our family life.

Like biography and history, novels are narratives that tell stories of
change, often imitating their ancestors by a show of presumed documentary
validity. For psychological interpreters the text is a disguised
autobiographical document. Freudianism assumes that the function of the
interpreter of a text is "to reveal significances of which the poet himself was
unaware and which (at least in the first instance) he might even strenuously
deny."[28] D.H. Lawrence has greatly influenced the interpretation of
American literature, for example, by his formula, enunciated in *Studies in
Classic American Literature*, that we should always "trust the tale and not
the teller." This path, however, is booby-trapped. By interpreting Cooper's
Leatherstocking saga as "a wish fulfillment vision" of "the nucleus of a
new society" as "a stark, stripped human relationship of two men, deeper
than the deeps of sex," Lawrence also projected on Cooper his own romantic wishes for America, and he ignored Cooper's deep fascination with
the realistic problem of law and justice in a frontier society.[29] The moral is
that a theme does not have to turn on love or death to have an obsessive appeal in a writer's work.

Moreover, messages in a text may be covert to us for historical, rather
than psychological, reasons precisely because of our distance from the time-
laden concerns of the author and his audience. Today, for example, in
reading Hawthorne we are not likely to be tuned into the extraordinary
density of his historical imagination, nurtured by a close reading of colonial
sources that only professional historians now read. We readily see that "My
Kinsman, Major Molineux," for example, with its disturbing dream-
sequence about a boy's witnessing of the tarring and feathering of his
wished-for patron, says something about the ambivalent growing pains of

the youth, as well as of his country, caught up in the crisis of the Revolution. But we are not likely to appreciate fully the multitude of highly condensed and disguised historical allusions to English May Day riots, Masonry, the Boston tea-party mob, the raid on the lieutenant governor's house, the political idiom of the conflict between the "country party" and the "court party," and the familial imagery about the mother country's imperial policy. Instead, psychoanalytic critics are inclined to see in young Robin Molineux, whose names conflate two colonial political references, merely a stand-in for "what every young man does and must do" in "destroying an image of paternal authority so that, freed from its restraining influence, he can begin life as an adult."[30] But Hawthorne's best short stories are powerful precisely because they overlap the psychological and historical levels, as if he were himself an unusually subtle psychohistorian. Roy Harvey Pearce, who has done much to unravel this tale, appropriately decodes Hawthorne's historically oriented symbolism as declaring that "man has no nature, except in his history."[31] One must add, however, that Hawthorne himself used the term "psychological romance" in reference to his stories, and the psychological interest always points to recurrent features of our mental life, to transhistorical issues, however much they are grounded in our historical existence.

One virtue of the psychologically oriented critic is to remind us that texts are not anonymous. Nor are they merely verbal patterns. The "most essential event, the dominant category of experience" for reader and writer alike of a Hemingway novel, declares Frederic Jameson, is "the process of writing."[32] This formalism, surprising in a Marxist critic, offers little guidance to the reading of *For Whom the Bell Tolls*. The trouble is that it incorporates not only Hemingway's political experiences, but also his obsession with death. It is not merely hindsight but insight that ought to make us notice the deeply felt quality of Robert Jordan's final dialogue with himself about his father's suicide and his own fear of reenacting it, a theme that led Hemingway to think first of calling his novel *The Undiscovered Country*, that fatal territory from which, as Hamlet said, "no traveller returns." The first title usefully reminds us of how isolated the hero really is in spite of the second title's affirmation about human solidarity. The shadow cast on the novel by the earlier title affects our reading of the hero's final claim that he is "completely integrated now," just as the claim itself distinguishes the hero from his author, who died in a sick despair.

A closer look at another writer may clarify this problem of distinguishing author and character. I shall choose a much-admired and discussed story by Henry James, because he has misled some critics by sponsoring the modern idea of the artist as a god-like impersonal creator, who does not intervene in his story except to tell it, letting his protagonist instead be the central intelligence on whom nothing is lost. In fact, James is often profoundly autobiographical in his fiction and never more so than in "The Jolly Corner," written in 1908 when he was sixty-five, thirty-three years after he had left for Europe to make his career abroad. Freud, with his interest in the psychological significance of numbers, would surely not have been surprised to discover that the hero of James's story, also an expatriate returning to America after thirty-three years, had left when he was twenty-three and returned when he was fifty-six, thus exactly reversing the digits in his creator's case. This numerical mirror image is very appropriate to a story about a man confronting his alter ego in the form of a ghost haunting his family mansion. Dismayed by the rampant commericalism of a city that has overwhelmed his fond memories of an earlier New York, the hero's feelings resonate with those James would soon express in *The American Scene*, a travel book recording his mixture of painful nostalgia and shock about his country.

The central situation of the story is a psychoanalyst's gold mine, for it is described in terms similar to those James used in the travel book and in his memoir, *A Small Boy and Others*, where he records his nightmare of confronting a ghost. As a returned expatriate, who was himself the grandson of an immigrant, James had been troubled at Ellis Island by the vast flood of new immigrants, who seemed to invade "the intimacy of his American patriotism," and he spoke of himself as a "questionably privileged person who has had an apparition, seen a ghost in his supposedly safe old house," just as his story's hero has done.[33] The story is also full of details derived from the author's family situation. The hero's girlfriend, Alice, bears the first name of the author's sister and his sister-in-law; the ravaged ghost is afflicted with eye-trouble, which the author's psychologist-brother had suffered, and with two amputated fingers, perhaps suggesting the wound suffered by another of the author's brothers in the Civil War, or perhaps his own back injury experienced at the outbreak of the war. In revisiting his birth place in 1905 to find it blocked out by a high-rise building, James complains of "having been amputated of half my history" and indulges himself in the "free fantasy of the hypothetic rescued identity" of his family mansion.[34] Finally, to cap the connections, the fictional hero experiences a sort of second birth as a result of his troubled fantasies, just as the author's father and brother had done in the disturbing "vastations" and "visitations" that had marked their vocational crises. Seen in this light, the formalist's notion of the text as something detachable from its author seems absurd.

Yet what at first looks a gold mine for the analyst is also a quagmire. This dream-adventure and the story differ in one important respect: in the actual nightmare the dreamer turned the tables on the ghost, frightening him away, whereas in the story the ghost overwhelms the hero, who blacks out in horror at this vision of his possible other self.[35] Furthermore, the haunted man is presented to us as an egocentric hypocrite who, as a frivolous expatriate, has been living off his leasing of an American skyscraper while sentimentally keeping up the old house of his boyhood with the profits from his rent. In the story he awakes from his nightmare in the embrace of the girl who represents his congenial American past; but in reality James returned to Rye to resume his bachelor-expatriate life.

The biographer is entitled to make what he legitimately can out of the relation of this intriguing story to the working out of James's complex feelings, which are as much involved with the different appeals of America and Europe as they are with family feelings. But the story still is also detachable from them, insofar as we can appreciate the irony of Spencer Brydon's experience without knowing about the many possible correspondences between the story and the author's life. These correspondences are richer than the conventional Freudian categories take account of. In the forties Saul Rosenzweig's psychoanalytic account of the ghost reduced him, in accordance with the formula of "the return of the repressed" to a symbol of James's "unlived life," itself the product of "castration anxiety" arising from the identification of his own back injury with that of his one-legged father in the context of an unconscious sense of guilt for not having participated in the Civil War.[36] In this view James finally laid the ghost only by his feverish war-work in England, when he overcompensatedly identified himself with the Allied cause. This interpretation, however, would be more plausible if William James had suffered the back injury, for the evidence is overwhelming that he (not Henry) did have a long, troubled, overidentification with his father, an eccentric and original theologian. Furthermore, as Peter Buitenhuis has remarked, by emphasizing the theme of the unlived life, this Freudian interpretation distorts the nature of the story's hero, who confesses that far from missing out on experience, he has been living a "scandalous" life. There are Jamesian heroes who have an unlived life, yet Brydon has lived; the point is that he has not lived "edifyingly," but has "followed strange paths and worshipped strange gods."[37]

In the next decade Leon Edel brought to bear another Freudian category in interpreting Henry James's dream-adventure. Edel noticed that James had been provoked in 1911 to discuss the nightmare, whose setting was the Louvre, by recalling his youthful visits to the museum with William James. In those early days the elder brother, unlike Henry, spoke French with assurance and moved confidently in the world of painting. Read in this light, the younger brother's nightmare expressed a persistent sibling rivalry by imagining the elder as a routed ghost, more fearful than frightening. The dream incorporated this wish fulfillment, as well as Henry's mingled fear and love of the past. He has simply been bolder in his dream than in his short story, where the hero succumbed to his horror of the ravaged ghost. Not surprisingly, Edel reads the tale as a vehicle for Henry "laying the ghost of his old rivalry with William."[38]

Edel's theory of the dream is plausible enough, but on Edel's own showing the novelist may have dreamed his dream in 1910, a year before he wrote
about it, as part of his recovery from a disabling breakdown of self-
confidence, occasioned by the meager response to his collected edition of
his works. If true, then the story antedated the dream rather than reflected
it, and life then imitated art. Furthermore, sibling rivalry with William
James as a theme needs to be more plausibly translated from oedipal terms
into a larger identity issue, involving the different choice of country each of
the brothers made, a decision connected with their work as well as with their
much-debated cultural attitudes. Henry James was, in fact, his mother's
"darling," and he chose to live in the mother country. "The Jolly Corner"
most obviously has to do, as Edel himself puts it, with the author's ambivalent feelings about his "Americano-European legend," arising from his
act of expatriation. In the decade that remained to him, Edel asserts, "all
that he did from this time on was intimately related to his American past."[39]
Yet if this fact seems to imitate his hero's posture in recognizing his love for
the girl, James (as Edel himself shows) would still suffer a few years later in
1910 from a deep depression in which he burned forty years of accumulated
papers. Spencer Brydon and Henry James cannot be merged.

Moving back and forth between the life and the text is essential footwork for the critic and the biographer, but one moral of this example is that
the journey is as hazardous as Eliza's crossing the ice in escaping slavery.
Edel's foot slips, tumbling him into the water, at a critical point when he
blurs the hero of "The Jolly Corner" with the subject of the biography.
"He sees at last his own dual nature," Edel asserts, "the self of intellect and
power and the self of imagination and art; the self that for so long had tried
to live in his brother's skin but could now shed it, and the self that reflected
his creativity."[40]

But these assertions merge the hero and his creator at the price of
obscuring the irony of the story. Spencer Brydon never does see himself in
the frightening specter of a maimed capitalist. On the contrary, he rejects
the creature absolutely: "He's none of *me*, even as I *might* have been,
Brydon sturdily declared," assuming he was supposed to have known
himself. "You couldn't!" his girlfriend rightly remarks, recognizing his
blindness, which is symbolically reflected in the specter's "poor ruined
sight."[41] Edel assumes that the character, like a patient having his inner
conflicts explained by his psychoanalyst, comes to a liberating self-
recognition, but James portrays him instead as a man who never does learn
to see himself quite straight and must be rescued instead by the more discerning love of a woman. She too has dreamed of his American alter ego,
but she has always been ready to accept it out of pity, for she knows the
specter is also his past self, as well as his alternative self.

Wayne Booth has sensitized modern critics to the difference between the author as a historical person and the author as an implied narrator of his story. Yet the question of their relationship can still be raised. I suggest paradoxically that when the links between author and character are obvious, the differences may usually be more significant. Similarly, when the links are not evident, the similarities may be more important. Edel's footwork in negotiating the hazardous ice floes of psychological criticism is more convincing, for example, in his treatment of Willa Cather's *The Professor's House* where he shows in detail how a correlated study of a life and a work can deepen our understanding of both.

Cather's official biographer leaves us with something of a mystery. He notes that the artist's study in the elegant Pittsburgh home of her patron, Isabelle McClung, was a former sewing room, like the professor's study in the novel. He notes as well that the fifty-two-year-old hero is the same age as the author was when the novel was published in 1925, revealing in her a new, surprising attitude "more desolate by far than any fear of the price that worldly success tries to impose, or a disapproval of new forces in American life." He also suggests helpfully that "it is by a scrutiny of the approach to houses that the deepest meaning in the novel will disclose itself," and he even inadvertently provides a further clue by recording that when Willa Cather visited the French house of her recently married patron in 1923, she sadly found herself unable to work there.[42] He does not, however, bring any of these details into relation to each other or to his reading of the story. They remain inert items of fact.

Edel's psychoanalytic curiosity enables him instead to illuminate the professor's mysterious despair, as well as his regressive nostalgia for an idyllic past, by connecting this character's outlook to the author's feelings after her displacement from the security of her patron's home.[43] Edel's analysis by accounting for the pressure of Cather's sense of personal loss on the novel explains not only a neurotic strain in her hero but also the novelist's own mysterious remark that "the world broke in two in 1922 or thereabout." That was the year in which she wrote a story called "A Lost Lady."[44] Surely the psychobiographer is helpful in connecting the implied author of this story with the actual writer. The methodological point of Edel's demonstration of how correlating life and text can illuminate both is his use of it to show that *The Professor's House* is "an unsymmetrical and unrealized novel because Willa Cather could not bring the two parts of her broken world together again."[45] The biographer has thus joined together the critic and the psychoanalyst.

This same merger is the high merit, for example, of Justin Kaplan's biography, *Mr. Clemens and Mark Twain*. The novelist lived in Vienna at the same time that Freud was developing psychoanalysis, and the American writer was also fascinated with what he called his "dream self" and with the presence in man of a Dr. Jekyll and Mr. Hyde, who, he felt, were "wholly unknown to each other.''[46] The biographer was prepared for his work by having spent ''a number of rewarding years in psychoanalysis,'' at the same time sharply critical of ''doctrinaire Freudianism'' with its insensitivity to social history and its ''numbing sense of predestination, and inexorable chain of neurotic cause and effect reaching all the way back to earliest childhood.'' For Twain's biographer, Erikson was ''an even greater liberator for the writing of biography,'' but because of his recognition of ''the possibilities for change at every stage of life,'' rather than for his ''complex schematics.''[47] Kaplan's biography is distinguished by its artful rendering of the novelist's multiple conflicts in his sense of himself, as he set out at thirty-one to explore ''the literary and psychological options of a new, created identity called Mark Twain,'' who found ''fulfillment and crushing disillusionments'' in his engagement with the post-Civil War period that he labeled ''the Gilded Age.''[48]

Kaplan's perspective enables him to see that no sharp distinction can be drawn between autobiography and fiction in Mark Twain's work, and he brings to the surface the rich tangle of emotional ties between ''The Private History of a Campaign that Failed,'' the author's satirical novel, and *The Connecticut Yankee in King Arthur's Court*, written shortly afterward. The memoir records the author's remorseful participation in the killing of an innocent stranger in civilian clothes, who was mistaken for a Yankee scout. At the time he wrote it, Twain idealized General Grant and was reading proof of the General's memoirs in which he wrote of being accidentally wounded while wearing civilian clothes as a stranger in Missouri. Later, in 1887, the novelist read aloud ''A Campaign that Failed'' to a Union veterans group and added a satirical remark about the incident being the only battle in the history of the world where the opposing force was ''utterly exterminated.'' Kaplan points out that this phrase precisely describes the conclusion of the novel, when the Yankee destroys his Arthurian enemies with gatling guns and electric fences. The novel thus translates ''the unresolved tensions of his uncomfortable role as Confederate irregular and deserter'' into ''the major conflicts of the book itself.''[49]

Making this connection between the two texts, Kaplan more easily can call our attention to the implicit parallels in the novel between Arthur's England and the American South, between the Yankee's republican, industrial ''new deal'' program and the ideology of the victorious North, between the two civil wars, which, both in history and in the fiction, destroy an old order, thus linking up the Rebel's encounter with the Yankee scout and the Yankee's battle with the enemies of his Republic. Kaplan's correlations tell us not only about Mark Twain's feelings about his postwar friendship with Grant but also about the raging ambivalence in the novelist's southern and northern loyalties, a conflict that turned his novel into a ''curse on both parts of the 'contrast' and ended his battle of ancients and moderns with a double defeat.''[50]

Critics have fallen out over interpreting the strange switch in tone from comedy to tragic apocalypse in the novel, and any close reader must be puzzled by the Yankee's final expression of a yearning nostalgia for the very order he has been ridiculing and subverting throughout the story. To clarify these issues in the light of the comparisons Kaplan has made, we can go even further by noting a neglected analogy between the memoir and the novel: both documents end exactly the same way with a Yankee in the arms of Mark Twain and each dying man is mumbling about his wife and children. Having seen the biographer read between the lines, we can now, as it were, notice this similarity in the "lines" themselves, a parallel we can then take as further confirmation of the biographer's analysis and a clue to the incoherences of the novel.

Is there a summary moral we can legitimately draw from these examples? Let me suggest one: in reading any single work from a critical perspective on its artistic meaning for us, we use biographical insight by subordinating it to the service of textual interpretation and evaluation. In reading any life, however, we see all its texts, fictional and documentary, as historical actions within a context of artistic craft, social milieu, and private life. Every text is then part of a continuing story not only of a canon but also of a person's self-definition. Neither perspective can ignore or rule out the other. Speaking of Henry Adams's two novels, R.P. Blackmur says that "unlike those of a professional novelist," they do not "show their full significance except in connection with his life."[51] Certainly they are illuminated by his life and are inferior to the works of major novelists, but how do we know that biography can add nothing to the significance of even the best novels? Aesthetic evaluation and genetic analysis are logically different, but understanding of genesis not only may influence our understanding of the nature of successful art, it may illuminate failures of art as well and so locate points of development and decline in the artist's canon.

John Cheever in a recent interview protests that "any confusion between autobiography and fiction debases fiction." He suggests, however, that "the role autobiography plays in fiction is precisely the role that reality plays in a dream." There is a "not capricious but quite mysterious union of fact and imagination" in both. This is an odd analogy, however, for Cheever to use, because from the analyst's point of view the mysterious union of fact and imagination in the dream always speaks covertly about the autobiography, linking up the deeper emotional themes of both. Cheever does not clarify the distinction he wishes to preserve by going on to speak of his "morbidly close" relationship to his brother following on the separation of his parents and the persistent recurrence in his work of "the brother theme."[52]

Similarly, Rene Wellek and Austin Warren in *The Theory of Literature* rightly warn that a work of art has "a quite different relation to reality than a book of memoirs, a diary, or a letter." They also observe that "a work of art may rather embody the 'dream' of an author than his actual life.'' But the dream of an author, as a wish or an ideal, is itself a deeply personal matter of autobiography, and this fact must qualify the validity of their assertion that ''even when a work of art contains elements which can be surely identified as biographical, these elements will be so rearranged and transformed in a work that they lose all their specifically personal meaning and become simply concrete human material, integral elements of a work.''[53] The word *all* corrects the distortions of merging life and work at the price of producing the distortions of an absolute separation, as if the true work were anonymous, signed merely ''artist.'' No doubt, E.M. Forster was right to suggest that in some sense a work of art wants not to be signed; but it usually is signed because its creator also wants to declare his responsibility. On this issue I share the view of a German Marxist critic who suggests that criticism ought to find ''its most rewarding task in discovering and interpreting the very crossing-points and links between the two aspects—the real author and the fictional narrator.[54]

In this task a heuristic, noncanonical, self-critical use of elements in the psychoanalytic tradition may help us to preserve the human concreteness of history, biography, and fiction, while freeing us as well from the prison house of mere language, whether it be structuralist or metapsychological. But it will also require that virtue that Santayana once defined as a skepticism that is ''the chastity of the intellect.'' Erikson can be an ally in this humanism because, as Roy Schafer has observed, although he ''retains Freudian drives, defenses, identifications, superego dictates, and stages of development as components of the concept of identity, he tends to view them in the context of life themes and to explain them by reference to these themes. Thus, like the existentialists, he reverses the Freudian priorities which require explanations to move from content to formalistic concepts.''[55] It remains to be seen whether psychoanalysis can succeed in reformulating its conflicted tradition in a style more congenial to historical and literary understanding. We need to see Erikson's achievement not as a definitive resting place, but as a crucial step forward in that direction.

Contemporary influential literary movements, however, are virulently antihistorical, preferring the ''synchronic'' to the ''diachronic,'' formal structure to temporal sequence, ''codes'' to biographies, archetypes to history. ''Indeed,'' an English critic has remarked, ''one of Levi-Strauss's aphorisms might be nailed to the mast of the entire structuralist enterprise as a message and a warning to the rest of us: 'to reach reality we must first repudiate experience.'''[56] But whatever differences divide them, historians, critics, and psychoanalysts are all engaged in imaginative participation in other people's experience. If as an intellectual historian I have surprised myself during the last decade by becoming interested in ego psychology, it is not only out of the awareness of life's stages that middle-age usually stirs up. It is also because I have looked to it as a way of keeping alive the sense of historiography and literary analysis as forms of reflection on experience, actual or vicarious, forms that incorporate and revise our own experience—incorporate, because the historian must draw on his own experience to interpret the experience of others, whether in documents or texts, and revise because every written history, biography, or literary interpretation organizes experience in shapes that did not previously exist. Responding to them, we also add to our experience and examine our lives.

Notes

1. Erik H. Erikson, *Dimensions of a New Identity* (New York: Norton, 1974), p. 13.

2. Hayden White, "The Historical Text as Literary Artifact," *Clio* 3, no. 3 (1974):277-303; Roy Schafer, *A New Language for Psychoanalysis* (New Haven, Conn.: Yale University Press, 1976), p. 192.

3. Sigmund Freud, *Psychopathology of Everyday Life*, in *The Basic Writings of Sigmund Freud* trans. and ed. A.A. Brill (New York: Modern Library, 1938), p. 86.

4. William James, "A Suggestion about Mysticism," in *A William James Reader* ed. Gay Wilson Allen (Boston, Mass.: Houghton Mifflin, 1971), p. 208.

5. Cushing Strout, "The Pluralistic Identity of William James," *American Quarterly* 23 (May 1971):135-152; see also Strout, "William James and the Twice Born Sick Soul," *Daedalus* (Summer 1968):1062-1082.

6. Erik H. Erikson, *Identity: Youth and Crisis* (New York: Norton, 1968), p. 151.

7. Lewis W. Spitz, "Psychohistory and History: The Case of Young Man Luther," *Soundings* 56 (Spring 1973):182-209.

8. *Young Man Luther* (New York: Norton, 1958), p. 37.

9. Fawn M. Brodie, *Thomas Jefferson: An Intimate History* (New York: Norton, 1974), p. 470.

10. Ibid., p. 30.

11. Ibid., pp. 92-93.

12. Michael Paul Rogin, *Fathers and Children: Andrew Jackson and the Subjugation of the American Indian* (New York: Alfred A. Knopf, 1975), p. 280.

13. Ibid., p. 45.

14. Sigmund Freud and William C. Bullitt, *Thomas Woodrow Wilson: A Psychological Study* (Boston: Houghton Mifflin, 1967), p. 67.

15. *Dimensions of a New Identity*, p. 58.

16. Ray Allen Billington, *Frederick Jackson Turner: Historian, Scholar,*

Teacher (New York: Oxford University Press, 1973), pp. 430, 423, 159. See my review essay, *History and Theory* 13, no. 3 (1974):315-325.

17. *Fathers and Children*, p. 313.

18. *A New Language for Psychoanalysis*, pp. 210-211. His analysis is consistent with my own in "Ego Psychology and the Historian," *History and Theory* 7, no. 3 (1968):281-289, especially, which stresses the descriptive rather than causal nature of the identity-crisis concept. See also my bibliographical essay, "The Uses and Abuses of Psychology in American History," *American Quarterly* 28, no. 3 (1976):324-342, for the mixture of intentional and causal modes in Freud and his historian followers.

19. George Watson, *The Study of Literature: A New Rationale of Literary History* (New York: Scribners, 1969), pp. 163-164.

20. Peter Shaw, *The Character of John Adams* (Chapel Hill, N.C.: University of North Carolina Press, 1976), pp. 66, 129-130.

21. "Those Wrecked by Success," in Sigmund Freud, *Character and Culture*, ed. Philip Rieff, (New York: Collier Books, 1963), pp. 170, 178.

22. *The Character of John Adams*, p. 65.

23. *Young Man Luther*, p. 231.

24. Peter Loewenberg, "History and Psychoanalysis," *International Encyclopaedia of Psychiatry, Psychology, Psychoanalysis, and Neurology*, vol. 5 (New York: Aesculapius Pub. Co., 1977), p. 373.

25. *Fathers and Children*, p. 14.

26. *Young Man Luther*, p. 67.

27. Fred Weinstein and Gerald M. Platt, *Psychoanalytic Sociology: An Essay on the Interpretation of Historical Data and the Phenomena of Collective Behavior* (Baltimore, Md.: Johns Hopkins University Press, 1973), pp. 82-84.

28. *The Study of Literature*, p. 160.

29. D.H. Lawrence, "Studies in Classic American Literature," in *The Shock of Recognition*, ed. Edmund Wilson (Garden City, N.Y.: Doubleday and Co., 1943), pp. 953, 956-957.

30. Simon O. Lesser, "Hawthorne and Anderson: Conscious and Unconscious Perception," in *Psychoanalysis and American Fiction* ed. Irving Malin (New York: E.P. Dutton, 1965), p. 98. For the historical allusions see Peter Shaw, "Fathers, Sons, and the Ambiguities of Revolution, in 'My Kinsman, Major Molineux,'" *New England Quarterly* 49 (December 1976):559-576.

31. Roy Harvey Pearce, "Hawthorne and the Sense of the Past; or the Immortality of Major Molineux," *Historicism Once More: Problems and Occasions for the American Scholar*, ed. R.H. Pearce (Princeton, N.J.: Princeton University Press, 1969), p. 162.

32. Frederic Jameson, *Marxism and Form: Twentieth Century Dialectical Theories of Literature* (Princeton, N.J.: Princeton University Press, 1971), p. 411.

33. Henry James, *The American Scene* (New York: Charles Scribner's Sons, 1946), p. 85.

34. Ibid., p. 91.

35. Leon Edel (ed.), *The Ghostly Tales of Henry James* (New Brunswick, N.J.: Rutgers University Press, 1948), p. 724.

36. Saul Rosenzweig, "The Ghost of Henry James," *Partisan Review* 11 (Fall 1944):436-455.

37. Peter Buitenhuis, *The Grasping Imagination: The American Writings of Henry James* (Toronto: University of Toronto Press, 1970), p. 217.

38. Leon Edel, *Henry James: The Untried Years 1843-1870* (New York: Lippincott, 1953), pp. 79, 313.

39. Ibid., pp. 315-317.

40. Ibid., p. 315.

41. "The Jolly Corner," in *Americans and Europe: Selected Tales of Henry James*, ed. Napier Wilt and John Lucas (Boston: Houghton Mifflin, 1965), pp. 439-441.

42. E.K. Brown, *Willa Cather: A Critical Biography* (New York: Alfred A. Knopf, 1953), pp. 97, 239, 240, 236.

43. "Willa Cather and *The Professor's House*," in *Psychoanalysis and American Fiction*, pp. 217-221.

44. "Willa Cather", p. 44.

45. "Willa Cather and *The Professor's House*," p. 221.

46. Justin Kaplan, *Mr. Clemens and Mark Twain*, (New York: Simon and Schuster, 1966), p. 341.

47. Justin Kaplan, Letter to Albert Stone, 7 March 1977.

48. *Mr. Clemens and Mark Twain*, p. 9.

49. Ibid., pp. 274-277, 296.

50. Ibid., p. 297.

51. R.P. Blackmur, "The Novels of Henry Adams," *A Primer of Ignorance*, (New York: Harcourt, Brace, 1967), p. 201. For a psychological-biographical interpretation of Adams's *Esther* see my "Personality and Cultural History in the Novel: Two American Examples," *New Literary History* 1 (1970):423-437.

52. John Hersey, "John Cheever, Boy and Man," *The New York Times Book Review*, 26 March 1978, pp. 31-32.

53. Rene Wellek and Austin Warren, *Theory of Literature* (New York: Harcourt, Brace, 1949), pp. 71-72.

54. Robert Weinman, *Studies in the History and Theory of Historical Criticism* (Charlottesville, Virg.: University of Virginia Press, 1976), p. 241.

55. *A New Language for Psychoanalysis*, p. 114.

56. David Lodge, *The Modes of Modern Writing: Metaphor, Metonymy, and the Typology of Modern Literature* (Ithaca, N.Y.: Cornell University Press, 1977), p. 64.

9 Continuity across Generations: The Adams Family Myth

David F. Musto

I will define "familial continuity" as a resemblance between parents and children in their personal style, outlook on people and institutions outside the family, and the special meaning they attribute to the family's past and anticipated destiny. That an individual or a family bestows a special meaning on the past or future does not imply, of course, a positive or optimistic interpretation, but rather that this special significance is the possession of a particular family, an important part of one family's or one individual's identity. Although familial continuity might also be defined as physical similarity, like the Hapsburg jaw, I will confine myself to the inner sense of common identity which often, particularly to those outside the family, seems equally singular. For those within a family, their shared sense of the past, their common understanding of the family's place in society now, and their similar way of interpreting and filtering out the myriad events every day brings, is as natural and imperceptible as breathing.

The selective and arbitrary character of any one family's way of looking at itself and the world is most easily seen by an outsider—who, in turn, may have absorbed without the least doubt an equally arbitrary familial identity. The powerful persistence of familial continuity can be observed among poor or wealthy, distinguished or anonymous, mobile or sedentary families. The tendency toward continuity may be seen at times as unfortunate or advantageous. It has been praised and condemned but, however regarded, the yearning by a family—and other groups as well—to make sense out of life's confusion by clinging to an identity—a psychological map on which is marked everything seen by the mind's eye—is a profound, primeval human trait.

Continuity of identity across generations is one of life's commonplace observations, so obvious that its expression in proverbs has become the tritest among a stale lot: "a chip off the old block"; "like father, like son." This continuity seems such a simple truth that close examination may be justified not only on grounds of its elemental interest to us all, but also

Reprinted by permission of the Smithsonian Institution Press from *Kin and Communities: Families in America*, edited by Allan J. Lichtman and Joan R. Challinor, "Continuity across Generations: The Adams Family Myth," David F. Musto: pp. 77-94. Washington, D.C.: © 1979, Smithsonian Institution.

because "simple truths" which influence some of society's gravest decisions have occasionally proven neither simple nor true. Certainly the subject of this talk is near the center of social policies in the United States, to look no farther, regarding rehabilitation of criminals, treatment of the mentally ill, childcare, campaigns against poverty and unemployment, mental retardation, and immigration quotas. These social questions underlie the search for a stable, predictable environment; answers to them would ensure a desirable social community, failure would mean descent into chaos.

Common sense and social science have regularly placed both the origin and the remedy for society's ills in that humble demographic unit, the family. Therefore, beliefs about familial continuity, how continuity is achieved or missed, whether it is closely linked to heredity or contact with family members, how tenaciously identity is grasped, and whether a new, improved identity can be created by altering family structure, giving psychotherapy, medication or some other intervention—these beliefs guide far-reaching reform movements.

For about a half-century students of familial and individual identity have stressed the malleability and correctability of that self-perception. Continuity began to appear weaker than the instruments of intervention which could, and ought to, be used to remold or break an undesirable continuity. But before this era of faith in intervention and rehabilitation, society was just as firmly assured that mental illness was as much the result of heredity as was genius and that social improvement would come by letting the weak fall in life's competition. I would like to illustrate this earlier confidence in familial continuity by two statements. The first is taken from an eminent and kindly physician, dean of Harvard Medical School, and a major literary figure of the last century, Dr. Oliver Wendell Holmes. The Autocrat of the Breakfast Table advised that:

> I go (always, other things being equal) for the man who inherits family traditions and the cumulative humanities of at least four or five generations.[1]

Here we have a positive outlook on family traditions, an appreciation of what good values they can encourage.

The other quotation is neither cheerful nor advisory. It is rather the law of the land, which approved sterilization for defects claimed to be hereditary for reasons now known to be specious. The source is the Supreme Court's decision in *Buck* v. *Bell*. There is a double appropriateness to this second excerpt, for not only does it express the darker side of familial continuity, the author is Dr. Holmes' son, Justice Oliver Wendell Holmes, Jr. Carrie Buck was a feebleminded teenager whose mother had been committed as feebleminded and who had a six-month-old baby "supposed to be mentally defective." A eugenics expert testified in 1925 that feeblemindedness was a simple mendelian recessive. Two years later—fifty years ago—Justice Holmes wittily supposed that "the principle that sustains compulsory vaccination is broad enough to cover cutting the Fallopian tubes." He concluded with the stirring affirmation of hereditarian doctrine: "Three generations of imbeciles are enough."[2] I mention the public policy aspect of our topic not because I believe such simple answers as sketched above can be given, but to point out that an assumption, "like father, like son," can become a justification for more than a casual observation or a subject for curious reflection.

Certainly one of the disadvantages of explaining individual differences on the basis of biological constitution is that, in the absence of any biological remedy, the end result can be a paralyzing hopelessness. The physician falls into a therapeutic nihilism. Society at large adopts what George Orwell warned would be "the revival of pessimism" characterized by the conviction that "man is non-perfectible, merely political changes can effect nothing, progress is an illusion." Since the burgeoning interest in family history and search for stabilizing links or "roots" to our American and ancestral origins may be one sign of a return to an earlier confidence in heredity as an explanation for behavior, we should be aware of over-simplification at the end of the path. Although Orwell conceded that, "So long as one thinks in short periods it is wise not to be hopeful about the future," he was able to maintain his faith in gradual, hard-won progress toward a "better," not a "perfect," society and not to be thrown into pessimism by the failure of utopian programs.[3]

How can we account for these pendular swings between an almost total hereditarian explanation for family continuity and an equally strong belief that family similarity is due to childhood experiences in that family? Of the possible factors driving the pendulum, I would like to consider just one before passing on to some of the themes which appear when a family is studied over several generations. That factor is the obscurity, invisibility even, of that process responsible for similarity, or continuity, or familial identity. No one has located a genetic element which is a personality-carrier or reproducer. On the other hand, there is no general agreement about which child-rearing practice is responsible for a given specific adult character-type. Child psychiatrists are often hesitant to predict adult character even after study of children and their families; the effects of future events are too complex to permit a confident judgment. I grant that it would be easy to locate environmental and biological adherents who would make predictions or explain the past on one or the other strongly held premise, but the broad trend of family research in the past decade has revealed how difficult it is to separate the two familiar categories, nurture and nature, in any one instance. It is still risky to offer a formula or attempt a detailed explanation of how continuity in a family is achieved.

That so many respected observers of behavior, such as Freud and Jung, have needed to postulate some carrier of continuity across generations in addition to the effect of child-rearing practices suggests at least some good students have been puzzled by the existence of traits they could not attribute only to environmental experiences. In their recognition of some special problem in explaining continuity across generations, Freud and Jung were anticipated somewhat by Aristotle, who rejected the simple material explanation for inheritance in favor of a transmission of immaterial form or essence. This Aristotelian form transmits two categories of characteristics: those appropriate for the species, and those peculiar to the individual parent and, with less force, those of the parent's ancestors. His theory of generation does not reveal how the transmission is effected. Aristotle's closest approach to the conjectures formed more than two millennia later by Freud and Jung is a hierarchical ranking of influences, giving the greatest likelihood of transmission to those traits most primary and widespread among humans.[4]

We could take one further observation from ancient philosophy. Three centuries after Aristotle, the Roman philosopher-poet Lucretius presented a materialist description of the world which included some ingenious speculation on inheritance. Asking his readers to consider what the world would be like if the seeds of any flora or fauna were randomly patterned, he postulated the existence of genetic material which inevitably led to production of similar animals and plants. He reminds us of two facts often overlooked: the dominant characteristic of life is not change, but continuity; second, the continuity extends over time, but not across the full range of conceivable types of living beings—there are gaps in the spectrum of species.[5] This last observation of Lucretius may be applicable to the kinds of human personalities, families, and cultures. When one considers the full range of human expression and interaction that could possibly exist, there seems to be a rather limited number of personality styles, family styles, and cultural styles. An absolute and unexamined assumption that the microcosm of the family—at least in the case of children—and the macrocosm of a culture—in the case of adults—reflects correctly that the real world may offer powerful aid to the survival of the human species, for the assumption has been common in history and over the globe.

Praise for stable families and fear of the effect of broken homes and inconsistent childrearing rest on the comfort and social orientation provided by a family or family-surrogate. As we consider the world-view established in families and transmitted by whatever process, though, we might well question how much the good effects of the family's socialization is related to some universal human "truths" inculcated, and how much to an arbitrary, even singular, perception of the world, which could be preserved by a family's psychological defenses against the many subverting challenges a lifetime will offer. The closer the family's world view approximates its society's norm, the more easily is it preserved.

Freud and Jung shared an interest in how the mind could create its own world and successfully defend even the most exposed salients against the attack of reality. Freud has been thought of as explaining the origins of each personal mental world in the traumata of childhood. Anecdotes abound about his ability to discern quickly the probable existence of some specific event in a patient's childhood which the doubting sufferer would then discover, by checking with parents or governess, to be true. Gustav Mahler is said to have had a block in his ability to compose removed when, after an afternoon's consultation, Freud pointed out to him a conflict over the name Mary. Such a simple and popularized understanding of great psychologists does injustice to their work. Here I will concern myself with just one category when I take exception to the oversimplified impression that they considered childhood experiences to be the determinants for adult character. That exception is the reliance of both Freud and Jung on the inheritance of ancient attitudes and modes of thought. I would like to draw your attention to a few statements by them on this less well known element in their psychologies for this reason: the necessity these two observers felt to postulate a sort of psychological inheritance over many generations illustrates the mysterious and fascinating difficulties encountered in studying family continuity. Both Freud and Jung came up against human characteristics which they could not fully explain even after they had taken into account a patient's life experiences.

There is something odd about their hypotheses—we just do not know how specific mental sets or styles of perception could be transmitted by heredity. Their reasoning, however, is analogous to that employed in one of the most astounding discoveries during the nineteenth century. I am reminded of the discovery of Neptune by the Smithsonian Institution; for the discovery of Neptune and the establishment of the Smithsonian both occurred in the late summer of 1846. Leverrier of Paris calculated that irregularities in the orbit of Uranus were greater than could be explained by influence of the known planets. He then hypothesized the existence of a more distant planet and predicted its location. On the first night of observation, the astronomer Galle discovered the planet less than a degree from Leverrier's calculation. This is a good point at which to say again that no biological analogue to Neptune has been discovered in humans which could explain the attraction across generations of primeval memories. But a frustration like Leverrier's does exist, that a sufficient explanation for family continuity still eludes the investigator.

Jung's "unknown planet," the archetype, derived from "repeated observation that, for instance, the myths and fairy-tales of world literature contain definite motifs which crop up everywhere." He found "these same motifs in the fantasies, dreams, deliria, and delusions of individuals living today." These repeated images and associations he called "archetypal ideas." Jung was neither as systematic nor as consistent as one would like in his definition of archetype. Early on he termed them "primordial images,"

not specific ideas with detailed content but rather a "possibility of representation" of "congenital conditions of intuition" in the unconscious. Only if
the archetype rises to consciousness, elicited perhaps by cultural stimuli,
does it become clothed as it were in language and image. The archetypes are
present in everyone and therefore are part of the "collective unconscious."[6]

At times archetypes are large abstract concepts, such as "self"; at other
times Jung found evidence for archetypes in very detailed myths. Jung convinced himself that the archetypes were universal after coming to St.
Elizabeth's Hospital in Washington, D.C., shortly before World War I. He
studied the dreams of black patients in which he detected the same
archetypes he had found in the dreams of white European patients and in
Babylonian myths. He could only conclude that the archetypes are a common heritage.[7]

Although recently a resurgence of interest in Jung's theories has joined
other signs of weakened faith in scientific determinism, Jung's concepts and
terminology have never achieved the acceptance of Freud's. Freud never rejected his youthful faith in an ultimate organic or biochemical explanation
for human behavior; psychoanalytic theory discussed the conscious and unconscious, gave rules for their interaction and suggested ways to modify
them as a necessary simplification awaiting a complete neuro-physiological
explanation.

Freud relied until about World War I on a theory of inborn instinctual
drives. These unfolded as the child developed; events in the environment
were mere occasions for revealing instinctual vicissitudes. This "id-
psychology" evolved into the "ego-psychology" of the 1920s and 1930s and
extends to our own time in the studies of Anna Freud and Heinz Hartmann.
Freud, like his younger colleague Jung, tried to discover what were universal characteristics of the human mind as well as the reasons why each
personality was unique. He believed the answers lay in a complex interaction between heredity and environment. Further, he suspected that some apparently universal human characteristics such as the incest taboo had an
origin in the early experiences of mankind. He was fascinated with conjec-
tured prehistoric human groups like Darwin's "primal horde" ruled over by
a powerful father. From these early social and family experiences, Freud
believed, certain attitudes and styles of thought were inherited, somewhat
like Jung's archetypes.

In the 1920s Freud postulated a more powerful role for environmental
experiences. The child would incorporate the family's expectations, standards, and culture into what Freud called the "superego," thereby providing for each generation a psychological means of transmitting culture.
Yet Freud did not find the family's enculturation of children a sufficient explanation for certain deep elements of continuity.

In 1937 Freud argued that "it does not imply a mystical overevaluation
of heredity if we think it credible that, even before the ego exists, its subse-

quent lines of development, tendencies and reactions are already determined. The psychological peculiarities of families, races, and
nations . . . admit no other explanation. Indeed, analytic experience con-
vinces us that particular psychical contents, such as symbolism, have no
other source than hereditary transmission."[8] In an essay published in 1939,
the year of his death, Freud was more specific:

> The behavior of a neurotic child to his parents when under the influence of
> an Oedipus and castration complex . . . seems unreasonable in the in-
> dividual and can only be understood phylogenetically, in relation to the ex-
> periences of earlier generations. . . . In fact it seems convincing enough to
> allow me to venture further and assert that the archaic heritage of mankind
> includes not only dispositions, but also ideational contents, memory traces
> of the experiences of former generations.[9]

When Freud wrote this he was not relying on the theories of heredity
taught him in the nineteenth century, oblivious of new knowledge and attitudes based on mendelian genetics. He frankly states that he knows his
position is made difficult "by the present attitude of biological science,
which rejects the idea of acquired qualities being transmitted to descen-
dants." His students were embarrassed by this neo-lamarckism. I quote
Freud's acknowledgment that his conjectures on heredity were outmoded to
show the awkward position to which one of the most creative and perceptive
psychological investigators was driven by a lifetime of observing the
remarkable strength of transgenerational identity. He showed his deter-
mination to theorize, however tentatively, by "admit[ting] that in spite of
this [rejection by biologists] I cannot picture biological development pro-
ceeding without taking this factor of [inheriting acquired qualities] into account."[10]
So much remains to be learned about the brain, genetics, physiology,
the effects of social relations on the body, and the body's ability to alter
perception and mood, that we can easily sympathize with Freud's or
anyone's attempt to map out even in large scale a terrain still in shadows.
My own effort has been at a lower altitude. I have been studying the private and public documents left by four generations of a family begun by
Abigail Smith and John Adams in 1764. Following one trail in the dark
forest does permit a pretty close inspection: if we are careful not to over-
generalize or to build elaborate theories from experience on one path,
possibly study of one reflective, well-documented family will reveal
something about continuity. Although an unusual family, the extraordinary
accomplishments of some of the Adams family do not remove them from
the human condition. Therapeutic work with families in New England and
Appalachia has convinced me that the role and endurance of family continuity as well as its dynamics are a common heritage of both noted and
anonymous families.

The Adams family in the four generations to which I will refer evolved early a rather unusual perception of itself which dominated the second generation including John Quincy Adams, then the next generation, that of John Quincy Adams's sons, chiefly Charles Francis Adams, Sr., and finally the early years of the fourth generation, until its members gradually and painfully became aware that their household was under the influence of an inappropriate view of the world and their role in it. I would like to borrow a term from family therapists and call this internal stream of identity flowing from one generation to the next a "family myth."[11] If the family myth approximates the norm of the surrounding culture, it will probably continue to bridge generations until dislodged by another way of looking at the world. A family myth seems to follow some psychological equivalent of Newton's First Law of Motion: once established, it tends to continue its course through succeeding generations.

A shared family identity defining and giving significance to what the family does, has done, and will do in its society, and what is the nature of that society is an eagerly sought psychological foundation. People have an imperative need to know where they are on the map. With this knowledge, the famiy group is united against an often hostile world, filtering the innumerable stimuli flooding in, and thereby maintaining a stable environment. It is not unreasonable to assume that a family or other group could have an increased chance of survival if they reinforced one another's shared perception of themselves and the outside world.

A family's tendency to coalesce around a myth is easily triggered; if the shared myth coincides with what others might call "the real world" in only a few essential points so as to assure food and shelter it still may be firmly held. I say this because families exhibit an astounding tenacity in holding their mutual outlook in the face of contradictory information or events. In families where an atypical shared myth has been established, clinicians have often been witness to the group's stubborn defense of a self-perception of little apparent social value or even one destructive to family members. Could the Adams family, the four generations just mentioned, illustrate, at least partially, these observations? The answer appears to be "yes," although a full statement of evidence is here impossible. Since the microfilms of the Adams papers stretch over five miles, more space is obviously needed for a thorough analysis. Meanwhile, let me provide some examples of the power of a family myth in those four generations.

The Adams family myth crystallized during the American War of Independence and was transmitted by Abigail Adams to her children Nabby, John Quincy, Charles, and Thomas Boylston. The myth was compounded with John Adams's enormous ambition to guide nations and to receive a justified admiration for his talents. Abigail and John shared a hope that their children would rise to eminent positions in an ordered society.

Abigail created this new myth not with design, but out of a desperate need to justify loneliness and hardships she suffered in wartime Massachusetts while her husband rose to fame in Philadelphia and Europe. At first, in the spring of 1776, she resented his ridicule of equal rights for women. She chafed at his irritation when he learned she was allowing their eldest child and only daughter, Nabby, to study Latin. Nabby received a letter from her father in April 1776—while he was urging adoption of a Declaration of Independence upon Congress—warning her about the impropriety of a girl studying Latin, the key to the masculine political world. "You must not tell many people of it," he wrote his ten-year-old daughter, "for it is scarcely reputable for young ladies to understand Latin and Greek."[12]

Abigail's eventual response to the hopelessness of her own cause was not unusual: she justified her sacrifice by glorifying her husband and the cause for which he fought until, as the years of his absence accumulated, her children began to picture a stern, perfectionist father who was the key figure in American independence. Further, she overlooked John's gratification of his personal ambition at her expense as he achieved the very style of life he had thirsted after since at least his nineteenth year. His rise was the reward of merit, she felt, and his work a patriotic responsibility. She began to portray them both as under the same burden of ardent patriotism. She wrote him, "All domestic pleasures and enjoyments are absorbed in the great and important duty you owe your country, 'for our country is as it were a secondary God, and the first and greatest parent. It is to be preferred to parents, wives, children, friends. . . .'"[13]

Her own ambition was transferred to her children, as well as to John. They would achieve greatness under her guidance. For example, she cajoled John Quincy, then twelve and tearfully begging to stay in America, to ask his father for permission to join him on a trip to Europe. John Adams took him through the British blockade so that the boy might benefit in his adolescence from a European education. This was preparation, Abigail told her son, for a "hero and statesman."[14] She conspired with the dashing and romantic Colonel William Stephen Smith in his pursuit of Nabby's hand, for she was sure that he would be another Washington leading his country's defense (but instead he "did more injury to me and my administration," John Adams later wrote, "than any other man"); these were the variegated fruits of her transferred ambitions.[15] She believed that the just, educated, moral, and ideologically pure Adams children would receive merited reward from the great republic, cleansed of European monarchy and social preferment. An important addition to this myth was that merited reward should never be sought by political maneuvers but rather should be awaited patiently and confidently. The bind in which this placed a family member who fully accepted the myth and acted upon it in the American political maelstrom can be readily imagined, and that few family members bore up under the burden, is not surprising.

Into the second generation, Nabby did not marry happily or well—the primary life task she had accepted. Nevertheless, she did not complain. The second son, Charles, died of alcoholism at the age of twenty-nine, deep in debt from land speculation, the myth's very antithesis of proper behavior. The youngest son, Thomas Boylston, did not succeed at the literary life he tried to establish in Philadelphia and returned to rusticate in Quincy, an increasingly bitter man. Only the eldest son, John Quincy, stayed the course and became the only child of a president to attain the same office. He had three children who lived to adulthood, George Washington, John II, and Charles Francis.

Until nearly his tenth year, Charles Francis was raised as an only son, although in fact he was the youngest. Just a baby when his father accepted appointment at the Court of the Czar, he was taken along while his brothers stayed home to go to school. Charles proved to be at least as independent and aloof as John Quincy Adams had been in his adolescence and youth. He did not admire his brothers' talents, nor did he feel as loved as they by his parents. One day in June 1824, after a family row with his Uncle Thomas, Charles went upstairs to read to his illustrious grandfather, then aged eighty-eight. John Adams uncharacteristically chose to discuss with his austere grandson the failures of the young man's uncles, Charles and Thomas, and the blazing success of John Quincy. What the ex-president told Charles Francis is a classic example of defending the family's myth in the face of evidence that its overall effect on the family members was tragic rather than glorious. Charles Francis's *Diary* carries the message:

> He [John Adams] laments the fate which has thrown so much gloom over our house, [but] something was necessary to check our pride and we have suffered bitterly. We should have been crushed, had the Sons all been distinguished, but now while the World respects us, it at the same [time] pities our misfortune and this pity destroys the envy which would other-wise arise.[16]

John Adams saw no problem about the family's goals except the understandable envy of others. The failed sons were fodder for pursuing wolves of public envy, allowing John Quincy to escape.

Charles Francis's generation suffered equal destruction, but he survived. George Washington Adams could not fulfill the eldest son's responsibility to carry on the political tradition. Neither could he release himself from the myth's grip. In April 1829, he fearfully started for Washington to help ex-President John Quincy Adams's return to Quincy and presumed retirement after defeat by Andrew Jackson. George became convinced that a conspiracy against him existed on board the steamer *Benjamin Franklin*. In the early morning hours, leaving his cloak and hat on the deck, George leapt into Long Island Sound and brought an end to his pain. He had just turned twenty-eight.[17]

John Quincy's second son, John, disliked politics and abandoned plans for a legal career. He had "deserted the State," as Charles Francis put it. John preferred to operate—without ability or success—his father's debt ridden grist mill in Rock Creek Park. John Adams II died after a lingering illness in 1834 at the age of thirty. The youngest son reflected on his two brothers' early deaths:

> I may be called cold in heart, and I have often thought with possible justice, but I cannot regard the loss of either of my brothers as calamity either to their families or to themselves.[18]

Charles Francis lived to the age of seventy-nine, a year short of his father's lifespan. The survival of the fittest, but by whose standards?

Charles Francis, of course, represented the United States to Great Britain during the Civil War. He was thought by contemporaries to come close to the presidential nomination, especially in 1872. Six of his children lived to adulthood, confronting the unusual family role and perception of society they had, as it were, inherited. In his mid-sixties Henry Adams reviewed his life and found his education sadly deficient: the world did not work the way he had been taught. "For some remote reason," Henry Adams mused, "he was born an eighteenth century child."[19] John Adams had set out in the eighteenth century with a youthful ambition to establish the rules of political science and to help—at least help—establish a great North American nation. The remarkable Abigail educated their children to believe the family destiny was to guide what John had established. Shortly before becoming president, John wrote Abigail on a note of youthful fantasies achieved, "I have often told you laughing, what may become a real truth, that 'I shall be the great Legislator of Nations and that Nations must learn of me or cut one another's throat.'"[20] In the early twentieth century, Henry Adams recalled a youth in which John's ambition was no longer a laughing matter: he describes in his *Education* a memorable encounter as a child with the family's Irish gardener. He recalled the gardener saying to him, "You'll be thinkin' you'll be President too!" It was not the possibility of such high office that struck him; it was the disturbing element of uncertainty in the man's voice. Henry wrote in the third person: "This made so strong an impression on his mind that he never forgot it. He could not remember ever to have thought on the subject; to him, that there should be a doubt of his being President was a new idea. What had been would continue to be."[21] This was another classic statement of family myth, recalled only decades later when the series of family presidents had without doubt ended.

The fourth generation eventually settled down into a more conventional, less demanding, vision of themselves and their destiny. Less exciting, perhaps, than past power struggles, but also favoring an improved average lifespan. Henry's volatile brother Brooks thought of preparing a book on heredity, demonstrating that personal characteristics persist while the world changes. "It is seldom," he wrote in 1919, "that a single family can stay adjusted through three generations. . . . It is now full four generations since John Adams wrote the Constitution of Massachusetts. It is time we perished. The world is tired of us.''[22] Charles Francis, Jr., a one-time president of the Union Pacific, looked back in his autobiography upon his failure to prove the family's ability to guide a great empire of business, the new location of power. The Robber Barons outsmarted him. Reviewing his life, he closed with a humble consolation: he had enjoyed some days of "pure happiness," perhaps not many, "but, more or less, I am very confident they exceed in number those of anyone of my forbears.''[23]

In a more primitive world, the myth's intolerance could have survival value. Unquestioning acceptance of the family myth gave tenacity to those who had the extraordinary ability required to approach the myth's standards. In the face of the most bitter personal and political hostility, they held to the myth. John Adams's ambition, Abigail's need to justify her lonely distress, and their faith in a revolutionary promise of a purified society were fused with a certainty and sense of purpose that would have sustained one of Darwin's primal hordes through an ice age.

This family's experiences illustrate some of the intriguing questions which have arisen in our century over the nature of family continuity. They suggest that a family myth can be forged in a stressful period, continue for several generations almost as an inherited set of attitudes, and, eventually, may be restructured under the impact of an incongruous environment.

Notes

1. O.W. Holmes, *Autocrat of the Breakfast-Table* (New York: Sagamore Press, 1957), p. 23.

2. *Buck* v. *Bell,* 274 US 200 (1927).

3. George Orwell, in *Collected Essays, Journalism and Letters*, vol. 3, ed. Sonia Orwell and Ian Angus (New York: Harcourt, Brace Jovanovich, 1968), pp. 63-64.

4. Cf. *De generatione animalium*, Book I, 1, pp. 159ff.

5. *De rerum natura*, Book I, 1, pp. 159ff.

6. C.G. Jung, *Memories, Dreams, Reflections*, ed. Aniela Jaffe (New York: Vintage Books, 1965), pp. 380-381. Cf. M.L. von Franz: *C.G. Jung* (Boston: Little, Brown, 1975), pp. 125ff.

7. C.G. Jung, "Psychological Types," in *Collected Works*, vol. 6 (Princeton, N.J.: Princeton University Press, 1971), p. 443.

8. Sigmund Freud, "Analysis Terminable and Interminable," in *Collected Papers*, vol. 5 (London: Hogarth Press, 1950), pp. 343-344.

9. Sigmund Freud, *Moses and Monotheism* (New York: Vintage Books, 1955), p. 127.

10. Ibid., p. 128.

11. D.F. Musto, "Youth of John Quincy Adams," *Proceedings of the American Philosophical Society* 113 (1969):269-282.

12. *Adams Family Correspondence*, vol. 2, ed. L.H. Butterfield and others (Cambridge, Mass.: Harvard University Press, 1963), pp. 387-388 (18 April 1776).

13. Ibid., pp. 401-403 (7 May 1776).

14. Ibid., vol. 3, pp. 268-269 (19 January 1780).

15. John Adams to John Quincy Adams, 26 June 1816, *Adams Papers, Microfilm Edition*, Reel 432. Quotations from the Adams Papers Microfilm Edition are by permission of the Massachusetts Historical Society.

16. Charles Francis Adams, *Diary of Charles Francis Adams*, vols. 1-2, Aida DiPace Donald and David Donald (eds.), vols. 3-4, ed. Marc Friedlander and L.H. Butterfield (Cambridge, Mass.: Harvard University Press, 1964), vol. 1, p. 164 (2 June 1964). Words in brackets supplied.

17. Cf. S.F. Bemis, *John Quincy Adams and the Union* (New York: A.A. Knopf, 1965), pp. 178-184.

18. C.F. Adams, *Diary*, vol. 5, p. 411 (28 October 1834).

19. Henry Adams, *Education of Henry Adams* ed. Ernest Samuels (Boston: Houghton Mifflin, 1974), p. 11.

20. John Adams to Abigail Adams, 2 January 1796, *Adams Papers, Microfilm Edition*, reel 381.

21. H. Adams, *Education*, p. 16.

22. Brooks Adams, "Heritage of Henry Adams," Introduction to *Henry Adams: Degradation of the Democratic Dogma* (New York: Mac-Millan, 1919), p. 93.

23. Charles Francis Adams, Jr., *An Autobiography* (Cambridge, Mass.: Houghton Mifflin, 1916), p. 211.

10 Words and Work: A Dialectical Analysis of Value Transmission between Three Generations of the Family of William James

Howard Feinstein

Introduction

I first had contact with Erik Erikson through reading *Childhood and Society* when I was in medical school in the early 1950s. I didn't understand much of what I read, particularly the sections on the life cycle. Since then my own life experience, analysis, clinical practice, and historical research have made his poetic construct of ego development more accessible to me. In the fall of 1967, I was a participant in his psychohistory seminar at Harvard. It is fitting that my work benefited from the critique of an early formulation in that seminar. This chapter is concerned with the transmission of ideas between generations, between father and son, between teacher and student. In this regard I will attempt to extend Erikson's ideas by putting them to a test that he himself has hinted at but not yet attempted. Whether my efforts clarify, creatively misunderstand, or transform the work that eluded me as a man in my twenties, I leave to the judgment of others.

I intend to focus my remarks on the generational transmission of values regarding work and vocational choice in the family of William James. Erikson has demonstrated the importance of this issue for identity formation in his biographical and theoretical works.[1] My aim will be to elucidate the process in which William James engaged with his father over this significant life decision. Biography is not my foremost concern in this discussion. Rather, I wish to use James family materials to demonstrate a method for uncovering the integenerational exchange.

It is tempting for a historian to describe the transmission of values as a linear sequence between cohesive, stable entities. Henry James Senior believed that scientific work was appropriate for his eldest son. William became a scientist, ultimately concerning himself with the philosophic aspects of that subject. But such a view is far too simplistic. It fails to capture the complexity implied by Erikson's developmental psychology and the flux of social history. Henry James Senior, born in 1811, was not a monolith but a man who was vital and developing throughout his life. We cannot talk of him as the possessor of an inert block of ideas that he simply handed over to his son, however convenient this may be for literary clarity. Nor can we look at William James as the passive recipient of those values which, once in hand, were borne through a lifetime, hermetically sealed from his own changing experience. To do justice to our subject, we must talk not about the transmission of values, but value exchange between persons who are alive, as we are alive, and whose inner worlds may move to the rhythms of Erikson's developmental chronology, as our own seem to do.

Before turning to the James family intergenerational exchange, I would like to emphasize the methodological problem that we face by calling your attention to figure 10-1, borrowed from Klaus F. Riegel. It illustrates the nature of dialogue.[2] This figure represents the simplest kind of dialogue, but, as Riegel has pointed out, it is useful as a model for other types of exchange. Each of two speakers is shown relating his statements to those of the other and to his own previous statements. At A_1 a statement is made to B_1, but that is not the end of it, as a linear view would imply. A_1 is also directing his statement to the next step in his thought as well at to B_1, and that next step is shaped in response to B_1's answer, so that it becomes a new nodal point in the process, or A_2. A_2 is also an anticipation of the next stages of the exchange as well as a reaction to previous stages. In this simplest exchange, A_2 is a thesis to which B_1 is the antithesis, and A_1 is the synthesis that completes the first unit of dialogue. To be sure, this simple case implies a level on consistency and attentiveness that is unfortunately rare when fathers and sons exchange words. But it will suffice to show the goal toward which we need to aspire if we are to reconstruct what happened in a value exchange.

This representation serves equally well for any interaction that involves two temporal sequences. I would like to adapt it for an exchange between father and son, where each of the nodal points represents that person at a different point in the life cycle. In other words, each point for A represents

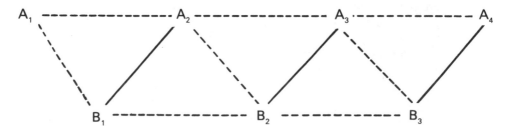

Figure 10-1. Diagram of the Nature of Dialogue.

an anticipated or past self of Henry James Senior in relation to each point in the temporal sequence B that represents an anticipated or past self for his son William. Obviously, the very same diagram could represent either father or son in interaction with society or his historical moment (the state of development of a particular field, and so on). Each of the elements in this paradigm is constantly changing in relation to itself and the other. Although I have utilized a simpler diagram for this discussion, the paradigm is implicit in Erikson's epigenetic model.[3]

To bring this diagram to bear on the James family values regarding work choice, the problem can be formulated as follows: We want to reconstruct the dialogue between young Henry James Senior becoming middle-aged Henry James Senior becoming elderly Henry James Senior in relation to young William James becoming middle-aged William James becoming elderly William James. As if our task were not complicated enough, we have to keep in mind that young Henry James Senior developed his work values in relation to his father. Our work choice exchange thus becomes a trialogue engaging three generations.

Although our paradigm is simply diagrammed, the historical research required is complex and the literary task of reporting that interaction is very difficult, if not impossible, within the constraints of historical narrative. Film or music are media better adapted to the recreation of elements that are both synchronically and diachronically related. We are left with the option of retelling the same story over and over again, returning to enrich the context and shift the perspective so that the reader can appreciate the dialectical flux we have uncovered.

William James of Albany, an immigrant from Northern Ireland, amassed a huge fortune before his death in 1832. His son Henry refused to prepare himself for a career in the law as his father demanded. He was virtually cut out of his father's will as an unrepentant prodigal. The will was broken, but Henry smarted under the rejection. He avoided work and lived on his inheritance as his father had feared. When his son William chose his vocation, he did so in the shadow of his father's battle with his grandfather. One way that we can tap into this intergenerational exchange is by examining the shifting meanings of the words Henry used to map the world of work for himself and his son.

Work

The twelve years from 1860 to 1872 marked the period of William James's initial vocational floundering. Beginning as an eighteen-year-old student, he made transient forays into painting, natural science, and medicine. He completed a medical degree but never practiced. His studies were frequently interrupted by trips abroad to recover from recurrent depressions that plagued, yet guided, his search for work. Belatedly, in 1873, he began teaching at Harvard, first anatomy and physiology, then psychology, and finally philosophy.

Henry James Senior wrote extensively, particularly during his Fourierest phase (1847-1855), about the nature of work. By the time his son considered a career as an artist, scientist, or philosopher, Henry had commented on each of these fields of endeavor—and he continued to develop his ideas about them throughout his life. The shifting language of vocation provides a map of the work world, as Henry James saw it. By studying the transformation of the father's specific meanings for the language of vocation, we can appreciate the difficulty William had in finding his way.

Had he been alive to read *The Harbinger* in 1848, William James of Albany would have been shocked to read his son Henry's declaration that, "No man dislikes labor." He would have been pleased, perhaps, that his son had finally come to his own conclusion that "it is in every man a divine inspiration which he can no more resist, than he can resist the attraction of the earth."[4] Work as a law of nature was close enough to work as a divine duty. But that apparent shift in Henry's thinking was illusory.

If he read on, William James of Albany would have discovered that his son Henry had not changed as much as he might have liked: "We repeat it: no man dislikes labor, free labor, labor which is the outgrowth of his own spirit, and expresses himself. But every man dislikes to labor for his *living*." The notion of force was anathema to James. "This is what disgusts him, *compulsory* labor in which the heart is not, labor which is dictated and enforced solely by the demands of bodily subsistence, or of social position." Work was an expression of the God within, an act of self creation, or it was branded infernal labor. Writing on such an issue was always a personally significant act for Henry, and we can easily see how this deviation from the traditional Calvinist view suited his position as an independently wealthy man of letters who was freed of the necessity of earning a living because his father had labored so well.

Judging from his hortatory writings and humorous asides, Henry James never overcame a feeling of discomfort over not working successfully for money. His judgment became more severe as he grew older culminating in a flood of vituperation that could only signify deep self-loathing. Sixteen years after the *Harbinger* articles he declared, "No one of my readers is capable of feeling the least respect for an idle God anymore than for an idle man. Everyone respects labor; everyone respects the man who does something more to vindicate his human quality, *than just live upon his ancestral fat*" (my italics).[5] Henry James was in his fifties by then and still without gainful employment. William James of Albany had been dead for over thirty years; and this son that he had warned, and threatened, and finally punished, had come to pronounce his father's judgment on himself.

Henry James's view of work held contradictions within it that he never resolved. That failed resolution complicated his son's vocational development. He placed a high value on work that was self-expressive. Judging by his own example, work of this design required wealth and leisure. Yet he condemned those who lived on ancestral fat when others lacked the bare necessities of life. If a son wanted to follow his admired father's map of the work world, which way was he to go? Was it permissible (or admirable?) to use his grandfather's resources as his father had done, for a prolonged search for vocation? What was to be the test of its value? Utility? Self-expansion? Should an eldest son make his forays brief to make way for the younger children? That might make way for others who lacked what was necessary for them, but why follow such worldly sign posts when the quest for authentic labor beckoned him down yet one more tantilizing path?

Henry James was not a methodical thinker. But it would be a mistake to conclude that he was unaware of the tension between his individualistic faith and his increasingly renaissant Calvinism. He was painfully torn between the push of desire to have his own way and the pull of social demands for productive work. His utopian solution was to assume that conflict would disappear in a properly organized society in which "man will work no longer to life but only from it, no longer with a servile but only with a filial spirit."[6] Ideally, a man would want to do what he had to do, but as he knew all too well, this was not yet true. William James was about to discover this for himself. The lectures and books and table talk of a father, who seemed to urge both self-expression and religious duty with conviction on his son, compounded his dilemma. What if he did not want to do society's bidding? What if work performed in a filial spirit turned him to stone? What if he wanted to be like his father and avoid any lawful calling? As he approached each of his choices—art, science, and philosophy—William had to find his way through a labyrinth of contradictory paternal injunctions.

Art

For a brief period in his late thirties, Henry James thought art was the expression of divinity within man, and the artist was a hero grandly enthroned on the pinnacle of his hierarchy of spiritual development. The artist was the quintessential spontaneous man. Yet when William decided to be a painter in 1859, he met vigorous resistance from his father. This apparent contradiction becomes a little less mysterious when we examine Henry James's usage. It is perfectly clear from his essays that he did not have painters or sculptors in mind. It is also obvious that he believed his *Harbinger* articles were art, and he himself was an artist in the pure (that is, his) sense of the term.

Art does not refer to any particular occupation but to a quality of spiritual relationship to work. "The sphere of Art properly so called, is the sphere of man's spontaneous productivity." Negatively stated, it was to be distinguished "on the one hand from his *natural* productivity, or that which is promoted by his physical necessities, and on the other by his moral productivity, or that which is prompted by his obligations to other men." In short, "Art embraces all those products of human genius, which do not confess the parentage either of necessity or duty."[7]

A painter was not necessarily excluded from the sphere of art. He might be an artist in James's sense if he did not have to paint to support himself. If a painter had always been "Beyond the reach of want," and had been well educated "to ensure a comparatively free development of his faculty," and was devoted to his art, then James allowed that "the very highest happiness he is capable of lies in the untrammelled exercise of his calling."[8] By the time William was eighteen (1860) and had decided to launch himself in a painter's career, he fulfilled the criteria of his father's ideal case. He had never known want. He had been the subject of many experimental forays into the best schools his father could find in Europe and America. He had considerable talent for drawing, and this faculty had been developed under the guidance of his teachers. And he frankly described moments of artistic creation as high points of happiness for his inmost self. Yet his father balked, in 1860, at a plan that seemed to match his ideal itinerary of 1848. By the time William was old enough to fulfill that promise, his father's conception of the vocational world had changed.

Henry's paeon to art was orchestrated to his own vocational needs. To be sure he copied from Swedenborg, and Schopenhauer, and Shelling; but he was using them to make sense of his own life.[9] He offered himself as an example of the artist to his *Harbinger* audience. "Take for example, my present employment. It does not spring from any necessity of the natural life, for I have bread for all my physical wants. Nor does it spring from any sense of obligation to my neighbor, for being addressed to the universal reason of man, it is not fitted to promote any specific or individual interests. It is exclusively the offspring of my own delight or attraction towards this kind of labor."[10] If his journalism was art, then he was an artist in the grand sense. Rather than an unemployed writer without position in a work-oriented society, he was ensconced on the romantic heights where admiration was his due. Thus enthroned, Henry James could see himself as a prince rather than a failure.

The period of Henry James's enthusiasm for art and the artist covered William James's early school years. From the time when he was six until the time he was eleven or twelve, praise of aesthetic man flowed from his father's pen. We can only imagine how father's praise of the artist sounded to a boy with a talent for drawing. He was too young to be concerned with the question of his future vocation, although, in boyish fashion, he might have wanted to emulate Mr. Coe, his drawing teacher. It is doubtful that

William was able to follow his father's philosophical view of art. What would have made an impression on him was the aura of excitement and parental approbation surrounding the word in his admired father's discussions. To be free, spontaneous, and creative was mysterious, grand, and admirable. To be an artist was something fine that might do some day.

In the next thirty years Henry James rarely wrote of art or the artist, except in minor asides to compare the work of the artist unfavorably with the handiwork of God. In the scale of Henry James's adult life, this was a brief moment, a transient experiment in his own search for vocation. But as an artistically talented boy, with a strong affinity for his father, it was more important for William who was of an age when young people are eager to learn about the work world of adults as they imaginatively prepare themselves for the life that awaits them beyond childhood.[11] Career choice was not a real question but a playful possibility. Such is the disparity between time sense and ability to comprehend the adult world, that an ephermeral paternal experiment may become fossilized in an impressionable son's mind. What parent has not had the experience of having his own ideas recited back to him by a child who had made them his own, with an intensity that belies their source, and content that no longer represents the parent's current beliefs? Uneasily, one views a caricature encased in time—recognizable but no longer oneself. As Henry James struggled with his demons, the concept of aesthetic man was temporarily useful. When it came time for William to choose a career and he wanted to be a painter, he used his father's arguments. Henry did not make any note of recognition. He may have been too involved in the struggle to notice his old weapons being turned against him.

Science

In Henry James's map of the world of work, art was not a territory discrete from science. His earliest usage blended the two concepts. Science could be encompassed by art, and a scientist could be an artist. The bridging idea that linked art and science in his early *Harbinger* formulation was technology. Henry James looked upon technological advance as art, since it was expressive of "the actual life of God in man." He was convinced that this particular expression of the "perfect marriage between Creator and creature" had important theological implications. He claimed that, "every railroad refutes Calvinism, and the electric telegraph stultifies Apostolic succession." Technology authorized a new theology because it could bring about two important changes in man's condition: subjugation of nature, and through that subjugation, a solution of the problem of evil.

He reminded his fellow associationists that "science has at last brilliantly solved the problem of human destiny, and demonstrated in a thousand superb and palpable forms the truth of immemorial prophecies, that destiny involves the complete subjugation of nature." And he underscored the implications of that achievement, that radiant hope. "We find that science makes no advance but in the ceaseless direction of human welfare, in the ceaseless vindication of man's essential dignity; we find that the things which we have all along called evil and noxious, have at bottom a heart of the tenderest love to man, and exist only for the purpose of developing the otherwise inconceivable resources of his divine and omnipotent genius."[12] Thus rendered, a scientist was a worthy peer to share the pinnacle of James's spiritual hierarchy.

Henry used science in yet another sense. This second meaning found in his Fourierist writings also had theological implications. By science, he meant a rational program for political and social reorganization. A social program on the model of Fourier's phalanxes would overcome man's natural depravity and undermine this basic Calvinist tenet about human condition. Thus broadly conceived, science was a covering term for many different reform movements from temperance to antislavery. It held the promise of a society based on spiritual community rather than police, or convention, or legislation by men. And the movements of reform were sure signs that the promise would be fulfilled.

The advance of science authorized a new theology because it showed that the Calvinist vision of God was incorrect. Man was not evil, and God had not created an evil world. It was this view of science that made it natural for Henry James to welcome the scientist as an ally in his war on orthodoxy. He was happy to fight alongside fellow scientists (his affiliation with the associationist movement qualified him as a scientist) clearing vestiges of an outworn Calvinism (William of Albany was Presbyterean) from the American scene. He was also prepared to annoint his scientist ally into the priesthood of the new age. In an 1851 lecture, he actually suggested that professional ministers resign from their posts in favor of the priesthood of science. "Then at least *we* shall be well off: that is to say, we shall stand a chance at last of getting a capable or real priesthood of men of science, who ask no tithes, but are yet amply able to instruct us in all the conditions necessary to inaugurate the divine life on earth."[13] In Mr. James's confusing lexicon, a painter might not be an artist, and a scientist might be an artist or a priest.

As he moved beyond his Fourierist enthusiasm toward systematic speculation, Henry James changed the meaning of "science." Science became one element in his theory of knowledge. Briefly, he delineated three realms of human life: body, mind, and spirit. Each realm followed its own principle of organization. The organizing principle for body is sense. The principle for mind is science, and for spirit it is philosophy. In addition to having a separate principle of organization, each of the three realms is illuminated by its own unique light. The light of sense is the sun, for science it is reason, and for philosophy it is revelation. The three realms form a three-tiered hierarchy, building in ascending order from body-sense-sun, to mind-science-reason, to culminate in spirit-revelation-philosophy. Each level in the hierarchy builds on the knowledge of the one below but is not bound by the limitations of the inferior realm. Henry outlined this theory in the 1860s, and it demonstrates how much science had declined in his estimation. Before, the scientist was hailed as a priest. By the 1860s the scientist had given ground to the philosopher, who James now thought was the only man who could be trusted to speak authoritatively on matters of the spirit. Science was now placed in an ambiguous position. He appreciated its potency but insisted on the limitations of that power. As he grew older, there were still occasions when James emphasized the importance of science for the spiritual development of mankind with as much conviction as he had in the 1840s. But he more often reserved his enthusiasm for philosophy as the highest form of truth.

When he was enthusiastic about science, Henry James encouraged his son's scientific studies. He persisted in his preference for science over art, and William ultimately abandoned painting and entered the Lawrence Scientific School at Harvard in 1861. Even as William entered to halfheartedly prepare for a scientific career, Henry's high opinion of science had begun to wane. The hierarchy of knowledge that he explicated the year his son entered Harvard to become a scientist unseated science from its elevated position. At the outset, the shift was one of emphasis and left much that was admirable to science and the scientist. But the trend gathered momentum culminating in his frank declaration, in 1879 (six years after William began teaching science at Harvard), that "if a man's mind determine itself towards science or the senses, the result to one's spiritual understanding cannot help being disastrous in the extreme."[14] The priesthood of science was a glorious career, as Henry James mapped the work world in the 1850s. By the time his son gave in to his father and actually became a scientist, the lustre had tarnished. Indeed, rather than a glorious vocation, it had actually become dangerous for the soul.

Philosophy

Henry's usage of the term "philosophy" changed through his adult life along with the transformations in meaning of art and science. In the late 1840s it meant abstract thinking that "perpetually balks the intellect instead of satisfying it."[15] In the context of his Fourierist years, it was a term of opprobrium. In the 1860s, as he elaborated his formal doctrine of spiritual knowledge, philosophy became a field of the utmost importance, and it was transformed into a term of approbation. Philosophy was the most profound discipline that synthesized the lesser realms of science and sense into a reconciling form of truth. He contrasted it more and more with the narrowness of science. "Philosophy deals only with the essence of things, that is with the spiritual realm, . . . where science never penetrates—to which indeed she is incapable of lifting an eye."[16] There can be little doubt that as he reworked and expanded his doctrine of spiritual creation in his later years, Henry James thought of himself as a philosopher in the highest (his own) sense of the term.

Conclusions

When we place Henry James's writing on art, science, and philosophy in dialectical context, it is clear that he was intent on dramatizing his own vocational search and vindicating himself with his father. When he was most enthusiastic about art, it was because he could conceive of himself as an artist. He praised science when he considered himself one of the elect band publicizing Fourier's program of social science. He was happy to embrace the scientist as an admired ally laying waste the pretensions of conventional religion. He devalued science as he abandoned Fourier and directed his speculative efforts to his theory of spiritual creation. Then he admired philosophy and thought of himself as a practitioner of that elevated vocation. Each step along the way, William James had to cope with his father's confusing map of the world of work. He must have found it disheartening to discover that he could never catch his mercurial sire. When he aspired to be an artist, a heroic personage depicted by his beloved father in glorious hues, Mr. James was unhappy. When he shifted toward science, his father was no longer enthusiastic about scientists. When he changed from science to philosophy, it was merely technical philosophy that Mr. James considered inferior to his own spiritual doctrine. In effect, no matter how much acclaim the world would give William James, the development of his father's ideas kept him kneeling before him as the elder Henry gazed heavenward.

It would have been possible to present this as a history of ideas tracing Henry James Senior's participation in the currents of his times from Calvinism through Romanticism and Transcendentalism to Swedenborgianism. It would also have been possible to retell it, as many others have, as biography with the issue of work choice placed in the temporal sequence of a single life. Each has its merits, but if we are to recover the flux of value exchange between generations, the dialectical paradigm is closer to experience. Having undertaken this three generational, synchronic approach, I am painfully aware of all that has been left out. I appreciate the wisdom of Henry James's remark about his own literary omissions: "Really, universally, relations stop nowhere, and the exquisite problem of the artist is eternally but to draw, by a geometry of his own, the circle within which they shall happily appear to do so."[17]

Notes

1. Erik Erikson, *Childhood and Society* (New York: W.W. Norton, 1950); *Young Man Luther: A Study in Psychoanalysis and History* (New York: W.W. Norton, 1958); *Gandhi's Truth: On the Origins of Militant Nonviolence* (New York: W.W. Norton, 1969).

2. Klaus F. Riegel, "Labor and Love: Some Dialectical Commentaries," unpublished manuscript; K.F. Riegel, "From traits and equilibrium toward developmental dialectics," in *1974-1975 Nebraska Symposium on Motivation*, ed. W.J. Arnold and J.K. Cole (Lincoln, Neb.; University of Nebraska Press, 1976), pp. 349-407; K.F. Riegel, "The dialectics of time," in *Life-Span Developmental Psychology; Dialectical Perspectives of Experimental Research*, ed. H.W. Reece and N. Datan (New York: Academic Press, 1977).

3. Erikson, *Childhood and Society*, pp. 219-235.

4. Henry James, "Theological Differences in Association," *The Harbinger* 6 (1848):26.

5. Henry James, *Substance and Shadow; Or Morality and Religion in Their Relation to Life: An Essay upon the Physics of Creation* (New York: AMS Press 1977 reprint of 1863 ed.), p. 74.

6. Henry James, *The Church of Christ Not an Ecclesiasticism; A Letter of Remonstrance to a Member of the Soi-Disant New Church* (New York: AMS Press, 1977 reprint of 1854 ed.), p. 4.

7. Henry James, *Lectures and Miscellanies* (New York: 1852), p. 102.

8. Henry James, "The Divine Life in Man," *The Harbinger* 7 (1848):9.

9. Frederic Harold Young, *The Philosophy of Henry James, Sr.* (New York: College and University Press, 1951).

10. Henry James, "The Divine Life in Man," *The Harbinger* 8 (1848):9.

11. Erickson, *Childhood and Society*, pp. 226-227.

12. Henry James, "Theological Differences in Association," *The Harbinger* 6 (1848):26.

13. James, *Lectures and Miscellanies,* pp. 242-243.

14. Ibid., p. 314.

15. Henry James, *Society, the Redeemed Form of Man, and the Earnest of God's Omnipotence in Human Nature* (New York: Johnson Reprint, 1971 reprint of 1879 ed.), pp. 296-297.

16. Henry James, "On the Philosophical Tendencies of the Age—J.D. Morell," *The Harbinger* 7 (1848):3.

17. James, *Substance and Shadow*, p. 305.

11 Authority and the Transmission of Values in the Rajput Joint Family

Susanne Hoeber Rudolph and
Lloyd I. Rudolph

Introduction

Psychohistorians face certain handicaps that psychoanalysts do not: they must rely on "secondary" data, they are more than usually affected by the observer-actor dualism, and they are often separated from their subjects by historical and cultural differences. Psychoanalysts by contrast have access, in the clinical setting of the psychoanalytic interview, to primary data whose immediacy and intensity are meant to transcend or dissolve the observer-actor duality. They can rely on the tacit knowledge of a common historical and cultural context that they share with their subjects to minimize if not entirely eliminate these forms of separation. The psychoanalyst's use of theory and application of concepts is disciplined and "corrected" by the free associations and explications of contextual meanings that occur in diadic, clinical encounters with his subjects. The psychohistorian must rely on evidence that happens to be available and on inference and deduction uninformed, and in this sense uncorrected, by direct observation much less by direct access to an actor's motives and meanings. The collaborative construction of motive and meaning by analyst and analysand in psychoanalysis becomes in psychohistory a solo performance by an observer whose tacit historical and cultural knowledge is more likely to impede than facilitate his understanding of the forces that shaped his subject's orientations to action.

The pyschohistorian attempts to reconstruct imaginatively a good deal that the psychoanalyst can learn from his subject and from the era they share. When these tasks of reconstruction are not well done, psychohistorical analysis and explanation can fall victim to projections that fill the vacuum created by the absence of shared knowledge and acquired scholarly understanding. Erik H. Erikson's exemplary capacity to bridge the observer-actor dualism and to enter the worlds of subjects from bygone eras, distant places, and exotic cultures has established that psychohistory can be psychoanalytic without engaging in ahistorical and culturally insensitive Freudian reification and reductionism.

The family is a critical context for psychoanalysis and psychohistory because it is unique in joining and merging the psychic and historical forces that shape personality. We cannot assume that the family circumstances of Freud's time and the European and American family of the late nineteenth and early twentieth centuries speak to family circumstances of other times and places. "Exotic" (that is, non-European) family circumstances must be reconstructed and their consequences for members examined rather than assumed, a task we address in this chapter. It is no accident that when Malinowski tried to apply Freudian concepts to an exotic setting, he was immediately struck by the array of roles and their consequences for norms and behavior that were absent from the European and American haute bourgeois families with which Freud was familiar. We may not wish to embrace Malinowski's nonpsychological and affect-insensitive interpretation of Trobriand island life, but his "discovery" was surely vital. In trying to reconstruct affectively and historically the psychological environment of a turn-of-the-century north Indian nobleman, the diarist Amar Singh (1872-1942), we have found ourselves engaged in an effort to reconstruct an exotic family context. Our own nuclear family experience, tacit and scholarly knowledge about it, and scholarly knowledge about "traditional" and/or "oriental" joint or extended families (which we found more often than not mirror image projections of what "we" were not, ought not to be, but once were) were of little help. Understanding and explaining alien psyches, including how and why they acquire values, entails in our view the historical and cultural reconstruction of the families that established the parameters and shaped the psychic space and energy within which or against which affective forces move.

The generational transmission of values involves different and sometimes opposed strategic dispositions, conservation, and adaptation. There is, on the one hand a propensity to generational narcissism in the attempt to recreate the self and its social setting; on the other, there is species inventiveness that seeks to provide, or to accommodate to, futures for sons and daughters that are better adapted, more appropriate, to changed family and/or historical circumstances. The literature and conventional opinion seem to hold that the traditional joint family is oriented to conservation, the modern nuclear family to adaptation, the first inhibiting or retarding modernization, the second a necessary condition, even a cause, for it. A good deal of doubt, which we share, has now been raised about this simple distinction and its consequences for change. In any case, evidence from the Amar Singh diary about the north Indian joint family circa 1890-1910 reveals both conservative and adaptive propensities at work, both an interest in shaping offspring to live in and to perpetuate the social character and setting that parents or lineage elders have known and an interest in or an ability to allow or encourage the formation of character, the acquisition of knowledge and skills, and the affirmation of values that will fit the young to new environments that are visible or anticipated.

The traditional joint family as exemplified by Amar Singh's kin is sufficiently alien to require cultural and historical reconstruction if the forces that shape the transmission of values are to be validly interpreted and explained. Our work on Amar Singh's life history as revealed in his eighty-seven-volume diary has led us to the view that the extended family and the nuclear family differ markedly over the way affect and authority are organized and distributed. Neither a minioriental despotism nor a tradition-bound primary group, Amar Singh's family was more open, conflictual, and flexible than these two faces of the traditional family suggest. We have stressed elsewhere the importance of the human context of the joint family: the presence in the big house of a hundred souls, of a variety of significant others spread over several generations, of persons of high and low degree encompassing fictive and parafamily members. We argued that this human context contributed to the separation of affect and authority, to the diffusion and dilution of affect, and to the relative impersonality and powerlessness of an authority often pictured as all-powerful. By contrast, we found affect and authority congruent in the fathers and mothers of the nuclear family, affective relationships diadic and intense, and authority relationships laden with affect. We have likened affective relationships in the joint family to a polyhedron, because they are shared by so many and those in a nuclear family to a triad because they are concentrated in the mother-father-child relationship. The contrast between the polyhedron and the triad has implications for authority as well as affect, because the multiplicity of relationships in the joint family creates situations in which those who are most important for affect are not necessarily most important for authority. The charged atmosphere of the nuclear family in which affect and authority are confined to a triad and the relationships involved are played out diadically are in marked contrast to what we have found in the joint family as it is portrayed in the Amar Singh diary. Relationships there, positive and negative, are more often than not played out in shifting alliances and coalitions that align the generations, the sexes, and the social ranks (for example, grand-uncle, aunt, cousin, and maid-servant) on different sides of an issue. Whether the family features a polyhedron or a triad, separation or congruence in the location of authority and affect, dilute or intense affect, and impersonal or personal authority, all these have consequences for superego and ego formation and the forms and fate of noncompliance, evasion, and rebellion.[1]

We are particularly interested in authority and authority relations in the family, joint and nuclear, because we find that they have received inadequate attention given their importance for family life and psychic development. We identify authority with the roles and rules recognized by members of the family (or participants in an organization) as normatively (or legally) sanctioned to direct and control the affairs of the family (or organization). We contrast authority with power by pointing out that those with authority often are powerless; they can lack the power to gain or enforce compliance to their directives or to sanctioned rules, and those subject to authority can, by the withdrawal of affect or efficiency, or by manipulation, evasion, or rebellion bargain with those in authority over the substance and form of their compliance. Power in the joint family like power in formal organizations is not automatically available to those who exercise authority. Zorawar Singh, Amar Singh's grandfather and the head of the joint family, is honored and respected, but his decisions and directives are usually subject to attempts by coalitions and alliances to countermand or modify them. By contrast, authority in the nuclear family is much more likely to be powerful because it commands affective resources and sanctions. The oligopolistic or monopolistic control by both parents or one over love and recognition, including the threat of their withdrawal, gives them the means to enforce their will as well as to enforce "the rules." Because authority and power are more likely to be joined in the nuclear than in the joint family, authority in the nuclear family is at once more effective and more vulnerable to explosions and rebellions. Authority in the joint family is akin to authority in bureaucracies: at the operative level it is impersonal. Paradoxically, it is in the joint family that rules, not masters, are likely to orient social action.

The ambiguity of cultural norms in the joint family promotes openness, flexibility, even freedom, in a variety of ways. First, it is rarely self-evident which rule applies or, more often, takes priority. Deliberation, negotiation, or bargaining are often required before the matter can be "settled"; those with the power of noncompliance or resistance can influence the decisions of those with authority. Second, a rule once chosen must be interpreted at the general and at the specific level: what does it mean in this factual situation? How does specific context—persons, events, consequences—affect its meaning and application?

Internal differentiation and adaptive striving also promote openness in the value transmissions of the joint family. The family that Amar Singh describes in such intimate detail is constrained by the parameters established by Rajput (warrior-ruler caste) culture and rank as it is defined in the princely states of Rajasthan in the late nineteenth and early twentieth centuries. The one-hundred-odd person family that lives in the *haveli* (mansion or big house), however, is not only a large but also a complex, remarkably differentiated social organism. Its activities include many carried on in specialized secondary organizations and institutions, including financial and production enterprises, schools, the performing and creative arts, even the mass media and churches. The household was an *oikos*, an elaborate system of administration and accounting, which serviced and controlled its multifarious functions and purposes as well as the personal activities of its members. Among the many distinctions made on the basis of age, sex, and lineage, one that was a particularly critical test of the family's adaptive capacity was the distinction between the eldest and the younger sons. For a family like Amar Singh's, with an estate, a title, and a standing at court, it was the eldest son who would, under the rules of primogeniture that prevailed, inherit the patrimony and the responsibility for maintaining and enhancing the family's fortune. Amar Singh was not only the eldest son of a Rajput *jagirdar* (feudal nobleman) but also the descendant of a service family of bureaucratic lineage whose continued good fortune depended as a necessary but not sufficient condition that he, his brothers, and other male members of the family be prepared to give loyal and effective service at home in Jaipur state, at some other princely state, or even, as Amar Singh's career in the Indian Army attests, in British India.[2] Heads of bureaucratic lineages that meant to survive and prosper and younger sons that meant to avoid the dependence entailed in negotiating a living from the senior member of their families had to be adventuresome and entrepreneurial; they could not rely on merit examinations or the tenure and seniority rules of a career service to protect them from being initially and continuously judged by the quality of their performance.

The last element that we find significant for the extended family's adaptive capacity is its plasticity, its protean nature. Among the means used to do the many things extended families have managed to do and, often, to do well, is the creation of family statuses and bonds. Fictive family members, surrogate fathers such as Sir Pratap Singh, the regent of Jodhpur, and able family retainers such as Bharat Ram Nath jee, the bard and teacher-turned-historian, not only gave Amar Singh's family a remarkable reach and range that enhanced its capacity to survive in an often hostile environment but also the values, knowledge, and skills needed to adapt to changing times.

Explaining value transmission not as a mechanical process that transfers or an organic one that hereditarily imparts values from one generation to the next but as an open, adaptive encounter between a family and its historical environment seems the more appropriate to us because Erik Erikson founded psychohistory with a study that featured a break in the transmission of values. Luther, although ultimately obedient to his "father," rebelled in a variety of ways and levels against the values provided by his family circumstances and historical setting. Erikson's founding study has encouraged us to emphasize modes of explanation that feature ambiguity and uncertainty. In the account that follows we try to avoid the static and deductive message that can be read in the phrase, "generational transmissions of values," by featuring the dilemmas associated with leaning toward conservation or adaptation.

The Effect of Scale and Complexity
on Authority and Affect

The joint family that forms the basis of our investigation is a large and complex unit. A simple description of it suggests that analytic categories appropriate to the study of politics and large-scale organization can supplement the ordinary categories of family analysis. Amar Singh the diarist is grandson and heir in a three-generation household headed by Thakur Zorawar Singh of Kanota, his grandfather. Kanota encompasses a ten-village estate in the princely state of Jaipur, associated properties, including a country fort in the midst of the revenue-bearing estate, urban and suburban mansions, and a hundred-person household that includes the families of sons in three generations and the appropriate staff. Kanota in turn is part of a larger unit, the Champawat lineage at Jaipur, consisting of three sublineages, Gondher, Kanota, and Naila, the other two similar in size and wealth to Kanota and acting for many purposes—property, politics, marriages—as a unit. The big house, in which the life of the Kanota lineage is staged, features groupings that use strategic calculation, manipulation, and bargaining to achieve their purposes.

Because psychohistory relates problems of historical change to the affective underpinnings of the individual psyche as they emerge in the family, we are encouraged to couple individual compliance, resistance, and rebellion to cultural values with compliance, resistance, and rebellion in the family. Most emphatically to the fore is the theoretical perspective that locates crises involving affect and authority in the oedipal relationship; indeed, such a perspective is central in Erikson's exemplary Luther book. It is difficult in the joint family setting to locate and identify comparable oedipal crises. Because authority and affect tend to be separate in the joint family, rebelling against a particular person and against culturally, historically, and even divinely given demands is not the same (integrated) experience. Such demands are usually located in a family authority figure who is affectively distant. Such was the case with respect to Zorawar Singh's relationship to his grandson and heir, Amar Singh. In the years of Amar Singh's adolescence and early adulthood Zorawar Singh was in his late seventies and early eighties. His orders, as often as not, dealt with permission to travel, to spend money, to issue or accept invitations, and so on. They were issued through the medium of personal servants or the family priest, emissaries from the large first-floor room in a thirty-room *haveli* (mansion). Authority with respect to broad cultural injunctions tended to be diffused in the lineage as a whole, which in turn shared the cultural values of the Champawat subclan of the Rathore clan of Rajputs, in classical *varna* terms, the caste of warrior-rulers. These categories lacked both an authoritative spokesman and affective specificity but carried nevertheless a great affective and normative load. The Rajput's concern for honor, including its manifestation in martial valor, provides dramatic evidence.

In this setting, compliance and rebellion take on aspects of relationships to impersonal authority that characterize large-scale formal organizations or even those associated with—natural forces. Rebellions against the values of the lineage or the caste may be at once less and more difficult than rebellion against a specific, affectively intimate and powerful authority. On the one hand, the psychic penalties are diffuse because they lack intensity and specificity. But the consequences of such rebellions are more generalized and inescapable, so that rebellion takes on aspects of opposition to natural forces.

The Authority System of the Joint Family

What, then, is the authority system of the joint family in the context of which the generational transmission of values takes place? Our empirical referent is the joint family among warrior-ruler caste landed nobility in North India at the end of the nineteenth century, a context that entails different attributes from Indian families located in the other status groups and classes, regions and eras. The scope and penetration of the Indian joint family in the transmission of values defined for the moment as education and socialization is likely to be greater than that of nuclear families in the industrial societies of the West. The joint family tends to occupy more of its members' time and to loom larger in all their activities than would be the case for nuclear families in industrial settings. In the nineteenth and early twentieth centuries, gerontocratic and patriarchal elements were certainly strong. Although the arbitrary qualities that nineteenth-century social theory led us to expect ultimately provide an invalid account, for reasons we will suggest, generational priority looms large in the ceremonial and spatial manifestations of authority in the family.

Amar Singh is quite explicit about the norm of obedience to patriarchal authority, a norm he recognizes even while he articulates the irrationality of the commands at issue. Reporting sympathetically his father's efforts to buy peace at the cost of efficiency, he writes in his diary:

> My father is very clever and wants everything to go on smoothly and with affection. He one day told me all about the restrictions that my grandfather has put to our expenses. His purport to tell me was that I must be feeling the restriction and may not some day resent it . . . my father told me that my grandfather has curtailed the expenses of old age. It is naturally so that when a man gets old he thinks of his children and does not spend much. . . . This much my father admitted, that sometime his father was more strict than he ought to be, but he himself was quite prepared for anything of the sort. There have been instances in which my father has never spoken a word even though he knew the work was being spoiled. There is the garden being ruined for want of water and yet this was a thing of his creation and one which he loved. . . . My father does not go against

the wishes of his parents. He considers it to be the first duty to obey his father.[3]

We have the architect's plan of the three floors of Kanota *haveli*, the thirty-room mansion of the Kanota joint family in the old city of Jaipur. Space there is allocated according to the two cultural principles most significant for the family, male and female (*mardana* and *zenana*) and generational priority. Lower floors are more desirable than upper, large rooms better than small, and courtyard rooms better than interior. Space diminishes and is located at higher levels as status in the family declines. The first and second floors devote the rearmost portions to the *zenana*, and the third floor is entirely *zenana*. The generational principle in the allocation of space is consistently applied among the women, but not among the men, for reasons that cast light on the relative importance of status as against practical considerations.

The location of Zorawar Singh, the grandfather and patriarch, in the largest, most central ground floor room is what we would expect. But when Zorawar Singh dies the lineal heirs to his positions as *Thakur* of the estate of Kanota, his eldest son Narain Singh and his eldest grandson, Amar Singh, each move in turn not into Zorawar Singh's quarters, but into the best second-floor room. The reason? Both men are away from home, in service elsewhere, for most of their lives, more "visitors" than residents of the Kanota *haveli*. The first-floor *mardana* rooms are given over to Amar Singh's brothers who stay at home. But the women, including wives of the absent Narain Singh and Amar Singh, are arranged according to seniority. Patriarch Zorawar Singh's wife occupies the first floor *zenana* so long as she lives. The second generation, the wife of Narain Singh, Zorawar Singh's eldest son and heir, and Narain Singh's younger brothers, have first priority on the second floor. The third generation, wives of Narain Singh's sons, follow in descending order of seniority. The most recent wives (where there are several) of the younger brothers have least space and are on the third or top floor, an arrangement that makes access for their husbands more inconvenient because of the restrictions that must be observed when visiting one's wife.

There is one significant breach in the seniority allocation of space to women, and it is the occasion for endless commentary in the Amar Singh diary. There is a "best room" on the second floor, large, with a courtyard, and centrally located. It is clearly the senior woman's room on that floor and should by strict seniority go to the wife of Narain Singh, Zorawar Singh's eldest son and next *thakur*. But Narain Singh's brother, Gambhir Singh, dies and his widow pleads with her father-in-law, Zorawar Singh, to compensate her for the misery of widowhood by allowing her to occupy this room. Although Zorawar Singh grants her request there is continual resistance to his decision, resistance that takes the form of quarrels over many years between the two senior women.

In addition to these spatial manifestations of the high status accorded to generational priority, numerous ceremonial acts bear witness to it. The most significant of these psychologically is the injunction against showing affection, or, more broadly, against expressive behavior before elders. Sons do not drink or smoke before their fathers—or grandfather. They are not to be seen going to their wives, an injunction that makes for elaborate rituals of avoidance in a household where people tend to be aware of each other's movements and means that sons do not join their wives until elders have retired. It makes, for example, the location of Amar Singh's room at the foot of stairs leading to his wife's room highly desirable because it enables him to visit her without passing through courtyards or rooms where he can be seen. Generational precedence is expressed in elaborate body language, daughters and daughters-in-law touching the feet of parents when entering their presence, sons showing similar submission and respect. Juniors stand in the presence of their elders, except when special leave has been given. But even when it is given, and urged, it is rarely availed of: it is an even greater test of respect not to accept an exemption than it is to observe the rule routinely.

Elders expect to regulate closely the conduct of juniors, including their movements. When Amar Singh's wife's brother dies, and both wish to go to Jodhpur for a condolence visit, grandfather intervenes:

> My grandfather would not send me or my wife. We ought to have gone, and my father thrice sent word to his parent that we ought to be sent, but my grandfather would not give his permission. . . . His idea was that I come so seldom [from the army] that I must enjoy myself and not run about. . . . When my grandfather refused the third time father too got a bit annoyed, as I could plainly see by his countenance. All that he said to Umaid Ram jee [family priest, and grandfather's emissary to the household] was that "I have done what I could . . . tell them (meaning me and my wife) that my *vakilat* [agency—from vakil, agent] has been unsuccessful. . . . [My wife] was very much put out. . . . She knows that my father had tried but he as well as I were powerless to send her unless my grandfather had ordered.[4]

Amar Singh persists, finally coming up with a plan that allows him, and later, his wife, to visit her family at Satheen in Jodhpur. We will deal later with the contrast between the refusal and the eventual visits.

The regulation of behavior is minute, reaching into the most private details of life. Thus cousin Bhoj Raj Singh, Amar Singh's cousin and heir to the related estate of Gondher, has no children by his first wife. Despite his objections, he is married to a second wife so that he might have an heir. His mother takes over the training of the new wife: "The new arrangement now is that Bhoj Raj Singh jee's new wife is not allowed to speak to any of the

other ladies. . . . This is to prevent her from being spoiled by any one."
Mother also insists that her son go to his wives by turns, and that he do his
best to bring the intent of the new marriage to fruition: "The worst of it is
that his mother keeps her maid servants constantly at the doors of the room
and that every morning they report exactly what happened during the
night."[5]

If generational and male priority are the dominant and official principles of intrafamily authority, formal and informal constraints greatly
temper their operation. Among the formal constraints, lineage intervention
is the most important. Amar Singh's family is one of four related
sublineages, of which the seniormost is the family at Peelva, the estate in
Jodhpur state from which the founders of three additional estates, Gondher, Kanota, and Naila, left in the nineteenth century to seek their fortune
in Jaipur state. The lineages think of themselves as having certain corporate
existence, as indeed they do, because the political circumstances of one affects the circumstances of the others. The elders of each house exercise some
restraint on each other, mutually enforcing certain norms, a context that
allows clever younger members to advance their objectives by manipulating
differences among the elders. Amar Singh, who thinks grandfather
Zorawar Singh stingy, is able to take advantage of uncle Roop Singh of
Naila's more generous view of family expenditure, and his fondness for the
prestige and pleasures of conspicous consumption, to promote the enhancement of his female cousin's dowry. Uncle Sooltan Singh of Peelva, who has
no sons and must adopt one to the Peevla succession, would like to ignore
his nearest brother's sons, whom he should conventionally adopt, and go to
another branch that he favors more. Amar Singh's grandfather intervenes:
"My grandfather once wanted him to sign [a document] that no one was to
adopt anyone from the other houses while there were children in his own
house."

The most important means for informally constraining generational
and male authority and avoiding compliance with it was evasion and
manipulation by lower participants of a sort familiar to students of large
organizations. Juniors and women did not passively accept the efforts at
close control by male elders. While the onstage performance of family
ceremony enacted an elaborate drama of respectful, even worshipful, compliance, the actors found ways, offstage, for strategic pursuit of their own
purposes, for the inventive interpretation of accepted rules, and for choice
when several rules might apply. Amar Singh regularly evades Zorawar
Singh's close control over his movements by invoking "worthwhile" purposes for trips that have another objective, as eventually proved to be the
case in his effort to visit his wife's family in Jodhpur. Knowing that
Zorawar Singh does not like bloodsports—contrary to dominant Rajput
values—he avoids him on days that he has been hunting so that he will

not have to give an account of himself. It is easy to disappear in the big house, unless emissaries are explicitly sent.

The women excel at subterfuge that frees them from compliance. Mahatma Gandhi's understanding of women as specialists in nonviolent resistance is an insight born in the joint family household. Among the means for advancing a cause that is contrary to the will of the patriarch are alliance and coalition, a search for backers with whom one can confront authority. In the Kanota household, uncle Bhim Singh was known to be influential with grandfather, and one worked to have him on one's side:

> Thakur Bahadoor Singh jee of Nawalgarh had come to Jaipur and was living at his own house. My aunt [whose daughter was married to the *thakur*] used to send dinners for him. My grandfather did not like the idea and got angry several times but my aunt would not listen. She even went so far as to ask permission to ask the Nawalgarh Thakoor to come to our house one day. My grandfather absolutely refused but my aunt prevailed on Bheem Singh jee [her brother-in-law, Amar Singh's uncle, grandfather's son] to invite Bahadoor Singh jee. The thakoor was invited and we had breakfast . . . it was not right for my aunt to go against my grandfather's wish. [But] Bheem Singh jee listens to this lady's appeals.[6]

Another means of evasion and manipulation is sheer quarrelsomeness and nuisance value. Amar Singh's aunts, junior to Amar Singh's mother, whose standing is governed by the fact that she is the heir-apparent's wife, feel that there is injustice in the allocation of resources in the house—room, food, and so forth. Their discontents are a constant source of tension and result in deviations from the principle of seniority:

> At Kanota there were my mother, wife and two aunts. These latter two were great pals and there were several quarrels while I was there. These quarrels are a source of great trouble to me. Sometimes I used to get very much put out and it was with the greatest difficulty that I restrained myself from interfering. I am absolutely tired of living with my aunts. My grandfather ought really to separate them now. . . . Fancy the ladies quarreling over the wretched kairs [a fruit used for pickling] . . . the kamdar [estate steward] while distributing them said that [he would] make four shares, two of which would go to the *bara kanwarani jee* [senior wife, Amar Singh's mother] and two to the juniors. On this the latter said that . . . they will have equal shares. . . . This little matter originated a great displeasure.[7]

There are also alternative systems of behavior, well entrenched countercultures that compete with the values enforced by the joint family. Family norms were inimical to expressive behavior, especially by juniors, yet Rajput culture embodies a large element of expressive behavior, including such activities as being entertained by dancing girls, drinking together, and taking opium. Servants strengthen their positions with the *kanwar* (the heir apparent) by making these activities available. Young maharajas need a company of young noblemen around them to make a good party and create a companionable environment for roistering, and young maharajas must be kept pleased even by families who do not approve of expressive behavior in their sons. The political and social power of maharajas and big nobles, of the men's society at the palace, cut across the authority structure of the joint family and created more choiceful environments.

In addition to the constraints on authority exercised by the countervailing interests of related lineages, the capacity of lower participants to evade and manipulate authority, and the competing authority of the court, is a constraint, although a variable and uncertain one. Elders are neither arbitrary despots nor blind conveyors of custom and received wisdom. For example, they must consider the future success of the lineage as a corporate unit by allowing juniors to innovate in ways that will benefit the family. Because forced compliance creates tensions in the joint family household, where even senior males will eventually hear the chatter and resistances of displeased women in the *zenana*, there are incentives for consensual settlements.

These reflections on authority in the patriarchal joint family lead away from its surprisingly persistent image as a microoriental despotism, with an all-powerful ruler and dependent, degraded subjects. Conflict in the joint family is ubiquitous and accepted. Nor is it a tradition bound collectively. The family's scale and complexity, the ambiguity of its many rules, the coexistence of contradictory rules, and the problem of adapting old rules to new facts conspire against propensities toward a closed, highly prescriptive, complaint system. Despite body language, ceremonial conduct, and formal resource allocation that celebrate generational priority, lower participants find ways and means to constrain and manipulate those with authority and to engage in strategic behavior that enables them to pursue and often to realize their purposes.

Adaptation in the Transmission of Values

What patterns characterize the transmission of values among generations in the authority system we have just outlined? The complexity of the system, the coexistence of authority and power, the crosscutting influence of alternate reference groups and senior males, suggest the possibility of variety and innovation in the transmission of values. There are additional sources of adaptation: those arising out of the specific historical opportunities and threats that the Kanota family encountered; those arising out of the structure of the joint family—the differences between eldest and younger sons, between the talented and less talented, between men and women; those arising from the range and flexibility the family achieves through its capacity to add fictive family members; and those that arise from deliberate joint family decisions to allow one or more sons to pursue risk-taking possibilities that require new outlooks and skills.

A guiding principle of value transmission in this lineage, as in the other lineages in princely India that we have studied, is lineage survival and success. Values are not perpetuated without regard to consequences. The costs of conserving old values and the benefits of adapting to new ones are closely calculated. Adherence to status group norms and well-being of the lineage are often coincident, but when they are in contradiction, success and survival count heavily.

These remarks are especially true of "service" families, what we have described elsewhere as bureaucratic lineages in princely India. The Kanota family was one such lineage. Service in the context of princely rule and patrimonial administration required more skill and achievement for survival and success than did landholding, the other principal source of wealth, status, and power in princely India, and probably more than characterizes administrative classes in bureaucratic settings where tenure and promotion are guaranteed by law and seniority. Recruitment, tenure, and promotion were uncertain, the outcome of not only favor and good fortune but also skill and effectiveness.

The historical setting of the Kanota family set parameters for the transmission of values. The three Champawat sublineages of which Kanota is one are not merely large landholders, but together constitute one of the most important service families in the substantial princely state of Jaipur. The Champawats had provided the prime minister and the two senior ministers in the nineteenth century reign of Maharaja Ram Singh, who died in 1880. Grandfather Zorawar Singh was minister of the Bakshi Khana, the office that controlled the *Jagirs* (estates) of the nobles of Jaipur. Father Narain Singh was *Nazim*, administrative and police chief of Shekhawati, a "lord of the marches" in that Shekhawati was both peripheral and the most turbulent Jaipur province. Son Amar Singh is being groomed to revive the family's distinguished role in the court of Jaipur. Family fortunes suffered after the death of their ruler and patron, Ram Singh. The new maharaja, Madho Singh, has a different outlook, tastes, and friends, and the three lineages are replaced in favor and office by others. They hope nevertheless to return to favor and power as a result of the cycles to which careers of service families at Majasthan courts were subject. The present is highly uncertain: Maharaja Madho Singh, adopted son of Maharaja Ram Singh, seeks to deprive the three allied families of their fortunes and estates, alleging that they were fraudulently acquired. The ensuing twenty-year court battle ends when the (British) government of India finds Madho Singh's case (improbably) an invention. Madho Singh is prevented from confiscating the

Champawat lineage's estates but is in a position to exile father Narain Singh—who takes service in another state—and to refuse to appoint the diarist Amar Singh to service in Jaipur state despite his outstanding qualifications and pressure from the Viceroy, Lord Curzon.

The Jaipur court, its servants and nobility, have learned to adapt to the requirements of a dual cultural and political context: British culture and political power penetrate and influence the princely states, less forcefully than they do British India, but with marked effects nevertheless. The setting is a recapitulation of a pattern of cultural and political dualism that characterized Rajasthan generally and Jaipur particularly from the fifteenth century, when the Moghuls established an empire that created a similar dual political and cultural environment for the princely states of Rajasthan. On the one hand, there is considerable continuity between the fifteenth and twentieth centuries in Rajput culture and life-style; on the other, the Rajput rulers and noblemen adapt to the aesthetics, administrative arrangements, and language of the imperial power, Moghul between the fifteenth and seventeenth centuries, British between the eighteenth and twentieth. In this dual political and cultural context, the range of possible choices before the Kanota family, particularly as it seeks to repair its fortunes after the death of Ram Singh, is considerable.

In most Rajput families, which have been governed since at least the early nineteenth century by primogeniture, value transmission varies between eldest and younger sons. The former will remain on the estate, ultimately to inherit the title and revenue-paying lands. The latter will go out to seek their fortunes in princely or jagir service or stay at home, where their fate will depend on the good will of a father or eldest brother. The *bara bhai* (eldest brother), becomes the *thakur*, the dynastic heir, who occupies the father's property and niche in the social order of the Rajputs. He becomes master of a landed estate, the leader of a territorial community, a member of the royal court and its society and, perhaps, the occupant of a lucrative office. In these statuses and roles the emphasis is on continuity of values and skills. There can be strains in the socialization of the eldest son. Resentful or jealous fathers, anxious to avoid somehow the son's day of authority, enforce obedience with a fierceness that does not prepare the heir for the responsibilities to come. The future *thakur* is apt to be inducted into an Indian version of the Squire Western model, a "country" rather than a "court" point of view, that is, one that favors the nobles' rights as against the court's prerogatives (although in Rajasthan as in eighteenth century England there were plenty of "Tory" *thakurs*), the cultivation of localism, agriculture, hunting, police and judicial work, and indifference toward education and the cosmopolitan outlook associated with it.

Chotai bhaiyon, younger sons, by contrast, were often subject to more varied expectations. They might choose or be forced to live in dependency first on father, then on eldest brother, hoping at best to exercise personal influence on the *thakur*. Thus Amar Singh's second brother (the third eldest son) becomes the *kamdar*, estate agent, of Kanota, not as a nominal appointment or sinecure, but as its active manager. Others may opt to leave the estate and live by their wits or training, often enhancing their value to the family and their influence over it by developing an independent economic or political base. Such a course calls for innovation, for new skills, and, often, new values. The *thakur* might choose to educate his younger sons more extensively than his eldest to fit them for new opportunities. With the founding of Mayo College in the 1870s, the British pressed hard for the education of the eldest sons of rulers and *thakurs* as well, so that they might better be or become the natural rulers and loyal allies they valued.

In Amar Singh's family, the uncertainty of family fortunes and the possibility that the estate might be confiscated leads to the education of all sons fit for it in some form of English higher secondary institution. All fit sons are educated as though they were younger sons who need to be readied for service or new opportunities. The eldest, Amar Singh, and the second, are sent to the Imperial Cadet Corps. Two others are educated at Mayo, the "Eton of the East," and one is sent on to an agricultural college.

Language shaped world view and values and was an important social marker. Hindi was generally thought sufficient for the eldest son, who would inherit the estate, although the emergence in the 1880s of an English-style club society at Jaipur, with its implications of cultural and political advantage, gave an impetus to English even among eldest sons. Younger sons going into the world needed English. Urdu was thought essential by grandfather Zorawar Singh, particularly when he entertained thoughts about Amar Singh becoming the *diwan* (prime minister) at Jaipur or another princely state. Urdu, the language of Moghul rule and society and, for a long time, the language of British local administration and courts, had been in his day a necessity for a princely state service career. But Amar Singh, although sporadically fascinated with Urdu, thought English and Hindi better suited for the new era. He pursued his studies of Urdu with much less diligence than his study of English, a diligence that had the happy result of his keeping a diary. After an initial six years of English-medium primary education and another six years of tutorial with the remarkable Bharat Ram Nath ji, himself perhaps the first person to be educated outside Rajasthan in an English-medium university, Amar Singh supplemented his grandfather's and father's teachings with an alternative source of manners, morals, and values: he read English novels, histories, and moral treatises avidly, at the rate of sixty or seventy books a year.

Ordinarily, there were important differences within Rajput families with respect to the transmission of values, conservation for eldest sons and adaptation for (some) younger sons being among the most important. This expectation was altered in the Kanota family because, in the face of a threat to its survival, it emphasized adaptation across the board; all sons who could respond were pressed toward educations that would equip them to serve outside of Jaipur state.

Another obvious difference in the transmission of values was that between men and women. Whatever innovative features may have been introduced in the raising of some sons, conservation was the dominant theme in the raising of daughters. Daughters were an element in the success of the lineage; their favorable marriages were markers in the pursuit of consolidation of social mobility. But to be successfully married, they required world views and forms of socialization that were far more continuous between generations than those of the men. They lived in *purdah* (behind the curtain), remained with their husbands' families when and if their husbands took up careers in other states, and were not under pressure to adapt to new contexts. (The need to adapt to a husband's household and the authority of a mother-in-law was, of course, often traumatic psychologically but did not in itself involve value change).

The scope and variety of value transmission was enhanced by the paraprimary group character of the joint family; with the lineage as a core, fictive family members could be added to meet new needs. Fictive members equipped the joint family with capacities one might have supposed only secondary organizations could supply. Biographical material on prominent Rajput families of Rajasthan in the twentieth century, both princes and nobles, suggests that about half the successions were by adoption. This form of expansion of the primary biological unit followed blood lines, in general providing for the adoption of the relative closest to the main stem, but suggests nevertheless the flexibility and instrumental nature of the notion of a son. Fictive family membership might also include persons not related by affinal or consanguinous ties. Amar Singh, for example, was apprenticed (somewhat in the manner of a medieval page) at the age of ten to a father surrogate who had a profound influence on his character and values. Sir Pratap Singh was for over forty years the regent of Jodhpur state, a leading figure in Victorian Anglo-Indian society, and a man of great influence and standing in princely and British India. He had become a close friend of Amar Singh's father when both lived at the court of Maharaja Ram Singh at Jaipur, Sir Pratap in temporary self-exile from Jodhpur, Amar Singh's father in service to the Maharaja. By the time Sir Pratap became the leading figure in the government of Jodhpur, it had become apparent that he would have no legitimate sons. On a visit to Jaipur, he took a fancy to young Amar Singh at a time when the Kanota family's fortunes had fallen on evil days. When Narain Singh "gave" Amar Singh to Sir Pratap, he did so because he had confidence in his friend and because a powerful sponsor might save Amar Singh even if the rest of the lineage went down.

Sir Pratap raised Amar Singh in ways a Rajput father of that time might have done, in the martial arts and in a code of conduct that featured valor and honor. Amar Singh became, like Sir Pratap, an accomplished huntsman, polo-player, rider, and swordsman. Amar Singh acquired some values from Sir Pratap that he would not have gained at Kanota. Sir Pratap was an early and influential follower of the Hindu reform sect, the Arya Samaj. Combining its teachings with some inspirations of his own, he became contemptuous of Hindu idols and coldly anti-Brahman. He had little regard for the niceties of purity and pollution among castes, which mattered a good deal to grandfather Zorawar Singh of Kanota and to Zorawar Singh's master, Maharaja Madho Singh of Jaipur. His life-style was ascetic, that is, he practiced as well as favored simple living and opposed the conspicuous display and debauchery common at many Rajput courts.

The women at Jaipur regarded as irreligious and improper the reformist simplicity that Sir Pratap introduced into Amar Singh's life. On Amar Singh's trips to Jaipur, they tried to make up for the rituals and ceremonies he had missed or avoided by being at Jodhpur. Amar Singh's wedding, which Sir Pratap sponsored, was a particularly glaring example of Vedic simplicity and martial austerity. Amar Singh, who favored Sir Pratap's world view, handled contextually the conflicts between his surrogate father and his joint family over matters of religion and life-style: in Jodhpur and while traveling with Sir Pratap, he followed one code, and in Jaipur another, allowing himself to be drawn into rituals at Jaipur and strictly observing caste avoidance rules. Only his aversion to debauchery was uncontextual. He was happily monogamous and only gradually overcame a dislike of dance and music, which he associated with dancing girls and court prostitutes.

The family at Jaipur put up with the somewhat anomalous consequences of Sir Pratap's education—father Narain Singh because he shared some of Pratap's outlook, grandfather Zorawar Singh because he had consented, in the interest of the lineage, to his grandson and heir's apprenticeship to so distinguished and influential a person as Sir Pratap.

The family extends to include the dependents and servants who often play a significant affective role and share in the transmission of values and knowledge to the young. Servants are a part of the household; they transmit their household offices to their sons even as their masters transmit their estates to their sons. Their interest and that of the family are strongly identified. Among service families, for example, it was not uncommon for a fourteen-year-old son to be assigned an important administrative office away from home. A senior retainer who knew the work well was expected to administer it even while training his young master.

In Amar Singh's case, his second father surrogate was the very uncommon traditional bard, Bharat Ram Nath ji. He was a retainer on Sir Pratap's staff at Jodhpur. In another society, Amar Singh might have encountered him as a tutor at an Oxbridge college. In Jodhpur he was part of Sir Pratap's household, sharing its interest and affective life. He taught Amar Singh to appreciate English and Hindi literature and history and shaped his moral being in an industrious, purposeful, and conscientious direction. Both Ram Nath ji, the bard, and Sir Pratap, the prince regent, were absorbed into an expansive conception of the Rajput joint family that suggests its flexibility and range.

We have emphasized the openness and flexibility of the Rajput joint family in princely Rajasthan, even while depicting it as both conservative and adaptive in the transmission of values. The chapter began by examining authority in the joint family, emphasizing the priority accorded to the eldest male and, more generally, the importance of compliance by youngers to elders. We then noted that those with authority sometimes lacked power and examined how strategic behavior, particularly the use of alliances and coalitions, enabled younger and/or female members of the family to evade, manipulate, constrain, or resist authority. We next attended to the reasons why and the ways in which Rajput extended families prepared for and adapted to change. We noted that the joint family's capacity to expand itself by adding fictional family members added to its adaptive capacity. While recognizing the centrality of conservation in the transmission of values, we have featured the degree to which and the ways in which the joint family can be adaptive in the transmission of values. We have done so not only because that is how it was portrayed by Amar Singh in his diary but also because so much of the literature wrongly depicts the oriental joint family as despotic or tradition-bound.

Notes

1. Suzanne Rudolph and Lloyd Rudolph, "Rajput Adulthood: Reflections on the Amar Singh Diary," *Daedalus*, Spring 1976.

2. Suzanne Rudolph and Lloyd Rudolph, "Bureaucratic Lineage," *Journal of Asian Studies*, 1975.

3. Jaipur, "Notes about My Last Visit to Mount Abu," 26 "Life with My Father." July 7 and 11, 1905.

4. Meerut, "Notes about My Christmas Vacation," V, "My Grandfather," 7, "My Wife" January 4, 1905.

5. Ibid., 7, "Mookend Singh jee" and 8, "Bhoj Raj Singh jee."

6. Kanota, "Notes about My Ten Days Leave," 16, "The Thakoor of Nawalgarh" 10 April, 1905.

7. Mount Abu, "Notes about My Last Stay at Kanota," 16, "The Ladies" 16 June 1905.

12 Sexual Politics and Social Reform: Jane Addams from Childhood to Hull House

Dominick Cavallo

Introduction

In 1880 one of the ablest members of the Rockford College debating team, twenty-year-old Jane Addams, addressed her schoolmates on a subject that in one way or another would engage the curiosity, passion, and anxiety of Americans for the next hundred years—the "new woman." Addams told her audience at this small, northern Illinois woman's college that educated women must perceive themselves as more than future homemakers and mothers. Although more "intuitive" and emotional in their thinking than men, educated women had the same responsibility as their male counterparts to direct their intellectual energies into the mainstream of modern empirical and scientific thinking. Addams told her listeners that new social roles and careers for women would embellish rather than diminish the new woman's femininity. Indeed, far from denying her femininity the new woman "wishes not to be a man, nor like a man, but she claims the same right to independent thought and action. . . . [O]n the one hand, as young women of the nineteenth century, we gladly claim these privileges, and proudly assert our independence, on the other hand we still retain the old ideal of womanhood—the Saxon lady whose mission it was to give bread unto the household."[1]

As these last lines indicate, young Addams, along with many Americans of her day, assumed that one's sexual characteristics by and large determined one's social role and moral style.[2] Woman—particularly those of the "Saxon lady" persuasion—were vessels of piety, solicitous of the weak and dispossessed, emotional, empathic, loving, maternal, and, above all, incurably domestic.[3] On the other hand, men were empirically oriented, rational, curious about the world, aggressive, ambitious, profane, political, polemical—in a word, worldly.[4]

The problem with Addams's "independent" new woman was that she did not mesh with either masculine or feminine sexual stereotypes. Clearly, Addams was exhorting her young female listeners to summon the courage to venture into what for too long had been a man's world. The educational achievements and social sophistication of educated, middle-class women entitled them to a place in that world. At the same time, however, Addams demanded that they retain and refine their commitment to their "households." But how could educated women achieve and maintain this delicate balance between worldliness and domesticity? At what point would immersion in worldly ambition and realities lead to a diminution of "true womanhood" and a loss of feminine identity? This was a thorny problem, one that generated pain, anxiety, and disillusionment among late-nineteenth-century educated middle-class women like Addams.[5]

Some historians have suggested that the flood of reform movements that swept across the country after 1890 to some extent resolved this dilemma. According to these historians, the social settlement movement in particular allowed middle-class women such as Addams to mobilize their considerable intellectual skills in a war against the staggering social, economic, and political problems confronting American cities. But while the social settlement was a forum for heated ideological debates about, and coldly objective sociological analyses of, urban society, it was also a kind of neighborhood household. Through settlement work female residents whose ambitions transcended homemaking found an opportunity to nurture an entire neighborhood and thus expand their "innate" maternal propensities beyond the confines of the nuclear family. In other words, the social settlement was a kind of middle ground in that it allowed talented women like Ellen Gates Starr (cofounder with Addams of Hull House), Julia Lathrop, Florence Kelley, Vida Scudder, and others to think scientifically and politically (that is, like men) but confined their thinking within a distinctly feminine (that is, household) setting.[6]

On the surface there is much to be said for this interpretation (particularly John Rousmaniere's, which is extraordinarily subtle and perceptive). However, it lacks explanatory depth for a number of reasons, not the least of which is that it cannot account for the large number of males who participated in the social settlement movement. We will not understand the roles played by middle-class men and women in the social settlement movement if we place too great a reliance on the explanatory qualities of the cluster of stereotypes embodied in nineteenth-century images of "true womanhood" and aggressive masculinity. For example, between 1889 and 1914, 40 percent of settlement residents were male.[7] Unlike their female colleagues, male settlement workers like Robert Woods of Boston's South End House and Graham Taylor of Chicago Commons were not subjected to sex-role identity confusion simply because they went to college. Nor, of course, did they have to face the crudities of sex discrimination or the subtler slings and arrows of the domestic piety syndrome. Yet these men saw their social settlement work in much the same light as Addams and other female reformers.

Thus, if Addams exhorted Hull House residents to exhibit a kind of maternal empathy with people of the slum, to be "swallowed" and "digested" by the people, so too Robert Woods used nurturant-empathic symbols to describe the moral role of South End House residents.[8] The resident (male or female) must not only be concerned with the welfare of those in his or her neighborhood, he or she must achieve "absorption" into "the momentum of the personality which is to be influenced." The settlement house should strive to revive the flow of "moral menstruum" into the city's morally desicated streets and tenements.[9] Politically, however, Woods perceived the settlement as a "scientific laboratory" whose purpose was to devise social policy based on a hard-headed, empirical sociological analysis of pertinent social "facts."[10] As we shall see, Addams was equally committed to the ideal of the settlement as a kind of scientific halfway house between the laboratory and society. Thus, like Addams, Woods blended supposedly antithetical feminine and masculine qualities in the ideal settlement resident.

This confluence of culturally prescribed gender characteristics becomes less confusing if we approach the concept of culture from the perspective provided by the sociologist Kai T. Erikson. Erikson defines culture as a "moral space," which both shapes and delimits the behavior of people. Culture is a cluster of inhibitions, rules, languages, and values "that promote uniformity of thought and action."[11]

Thus far Erikson's definition of culture is hardly unique. But he goes on to argue that forces besides those generating uniformity are at work in all cultures. Culture affects not only how people think and feel, but also how and what they imagine, and "it is one of the persisting curiosities of human life that people are apt to imagine the complete contrary of the ideas and attitudes that figure most significantly in their view of the world."[12] That is, the counterpart of a value is implicit in the minds of its adherents, so that wherever "people devote a good deal of emotional energy to celebrating a certain virtue . . . they are sure to give thought to its counterpart." Value and countervalue, then, become cultural partners, leading to what Erikson calls an "axis of variation that cuts through the center of a culture's space" attracting "attention to the diversities arranged along it."[13]

The stereotyping of feminine and masculine moral and social styles common in nineteenth-century America can be seen as an example of Erikson's axis of variation hypothesis. The demand that men be assertive and ambitious implied the fear that they might fall short of these ideals and succumb to a "feminine" passivity. The notion that women were emotionally and intellectually suited to be masters of the household contained, however implicitly, the fear that under certain circumstances they might aspire to be masters of the world outside the household. In short, these stereotypes contained ambiguities, and Erikson's analysis of how individuals and societies deal with ambivalence is worth noting:

These contrary tendencies are reflected at many different levels within the
social order. At the individual level . . . they are experienced as a form of
ambivalence. When a person is caught between two competing strains in his
cultural surround and can find no way to resolve the dilemma, he can be
said to suffer from inner conflict. When he is able to attune himself com-
fortably to one or another of these strains, *or manages somehow to com-
bine them into a new and more coherent whole,* he can be said to have
achieved ego-integration (emphasis added).[14]

In this essay I will argue that from early childhood Jane Addams was
exposed to this type of cultural ambiguity with regard to masculine-
feminine moral styles, that the ambiguity was implicit in her broader
cultural milieu as well as in her idiosyncratic familial setting, and that her
decision to found Hull House was, for her and her society, a creative resolution of this ambiguity. During childhood and adolescence Addams walked
the tightrope of a feminine-masculine "axis of variation," and experienced
intense moral and social conflict because of an inability to adaptively integrate within her personality competing feminine-masculine moral
prescriptions, that is, she was not consistently sure when or how she should
act like a "true" woman. But as her personal crisis deepened during the
1880s, so too did the social and moral crisis of urban America. Her response
to the urban crisis not only led to the founding of Hull House in 1889 but
helped her achieve what Kai Erikson calls "ego integration." In Addams'
case, ego integration consisted of a viable synthesis of feminine-masculine
ethical strains into a new and dynamic moral vision of urban America, one
that combined a commitment to what she called a "social" (feminine)
morality, with an equally intense faith in the social and moral utility of the
scientific methods and bureaucratic techniques (with their emphasis on
hard-headed masculinity).

Of course, Addams's conflicts and crises were idiosyncratic, and we
cannot assume that all social settlement workers experienced the same conflicts in the same fashion. Settlement workers were a disparate group
characterized by a variety of political and economic persuasions, and further research is needed to ascertain the relevance of Addams' conflicts to
the experience of other settlement workers.[15]

Finally, a word about the methodology employed in this study.
Although aspects of psychoanalytic theory are used to interpret Addams'
opinions and behavior as a youth and adult, it must be made clear at the
outset that no simple, linear correlation exists between the problems of her
youth and her adult behavior and political opinions. Addams behavior as
an adult was not a product of youthful problems, conflicts, or traumas.
Adult patterns of behavior are not necessarily echoes of infantile psychosexual or psychosocial oral, anal, or phallic experiences, notwithstanding
the genetic approach to life histories employed by many psychoanalysts and
psychohistorians.[16]

This is not to say, of course, that a person's past is irrelevant to her future. The issue is not the relevance of past to present but the meaning of that relevance. The responses of a child to parental treatment, developmental changes, or social pressures may develop into more or less stable structural patterns of coping with inner stresses and external stimuli. These patterns, however, are neither one-dimensional nor inflexible. Their meaning and value within the "psychic economy" change as the person's internal and social environments change. In short, the meaning and utility of early adaptational patterns may be very different for the adult than they were for the infant or youth.[17]

This means that the psychobiographer not only must isolate the subject's significant psychological patterns, but also must be sensitive to their transformations over time. In Addams's case, her life history to 1889 provided her with a repertoire of potential values and behaviors. At various moments in her development these potentials intersected with specific social events or inner developments that were independent of, and not contingent on, the events or problems of her earlier years. Taken together these two independent factors provided the groundwork for her development of a social philosophy as well as for her participation in the social settlement movement. The social events and psychological patterns of her early years did not—could not—determine how she would respond to unanticipated future events.[18]

The Early Years

Addams was born in 1860 in Cedarville, Illinois, a small town in the northwestern corner of the state. Her mother, Sarah Weber Addams, who died two years later giving birth to her ninth child, came from a middle-class background in Pennsylvania. Although Sarah Addams entertained "no thought of a 'career' excepting that of mother and homemaker," she had attended boarding school and obtained what for those days was considered a good education for a woman.[19]

Because her mother died when Jane Addams was two years old, and her father remained unmarried until 1868, she centered on him "all that careful imitation which a little girl ordinarily gives to her mother's ways and habits."[20] According to his daughter, John Addams became the "dominant influence" in her life. It was her idealized image of his character, behavior, and status that "first drew me into the moral concerns of life."[21]

Addams's childhood attachment to her father was so intense that her nephew said it amounted to a "possession."[22] As a child she was continually abashed by what she perceived as her unappealing physical appearance and by the physical contrast between herself and her handsome father. She was horrified at the thought that strangers might guess "the ugly, pigeontoed little girl, whose crooked back obliged her to walk with her head held very much to one side,'' was the daughter of such a dignified, respected, and handsome man.[23] These inferiority feelings toward her father were a constant theme of Addams's childhood ruminations. One Sunday during her eighth year (it may be significant that it was the same year John Addams planned to remarry) she appeared before him in a new cloak "gorgeous beyond anything I had ever worn before." For some reason she wanted to appear particularly attractive when they went to church. However, her father admonished her that the cloak was too ostentatious and might make the other girls at Sunday school feel inferior. Sorely disappointed, Addams agreed to leave her new garment at home.[24]

The man whose character his daughter idolized was in many respects the embodiment of his era's ideal of success. John Addams was a miller's apprentice prior to settling in Cedarville in the 1840s, but he quickly took advantage of the many opportunities offered by a burgeoning economy. By the late-1850s Addams was president of the Second National Bank of Freeport, Illinois. He was president of a life insurance company and owner of lumber and flour mills as well. Politically he was conservative and very influential in Illinois politics. He was a friend and political ally of Lincoln and served as a Republican member of the state legislature from 1854 to 1870. Addams was a practical man who spurned political and religious extremism. His political philosophy revolved around the ideals of equal opportunity, individual initiative, and local control of the economy. As a father he has been described as "austere" in his relations with his family: he expected, and usually received, the obedience and loyalty of his children.[25]

In fact, John Addams exemplified the virtues of the nineteenth-century "rugged individualist." As a young pioneer he exorted himself in his diary to ignore opinions and enticements that threatened his principles. He was a man who took advice "only from his own conscience."[26] Since he seldom troubled himself over questions of religious dogma, his description of himself as a Quaker assumes meaning when viewed from the perspective of his moral individualism. Nor, except in business affairs, did he offer advice to others. Accustomed to living by his private "inner light," and convinced that the great duty of man was to secure and preserve his moral integrity, " 'Honest John Addams' refused to interfere with the spiritual affairs of others."[27]

As she neared adolescence Addams's moral precepts were dominated by an idealized image of her father's character. She identified with, admired, and tried to emulate those facets of his character that made him socially and economically successful: "I doubtless contributed my share to that stream of admiration which our generation so generously poured forth for the self-made man. I was consumed by a wistful desire to apprehend the hardships of my father's earlier life in that faraway time when he had been a miller's apprentice."[28] Accordingly, she sought out the books, ideas and ideals that influenced him as a young man. Whenever possible she emulated him. Sometimes her passion for emulation assumed extreme form, such as waking up at three o'clock in the morning because he did so. Addams wanted to expose herself to her father's experiences to "understand life as he did."[29]

Her father's ideals may have dominated Addams's childhood values and behavior, but they did not monopolize them. Although Sarah Addams died when Jane was two years old, Sarah, or at least her death, had considerable impact on her daughter. Death at any age was a common occurrence in the world Addams grew up in. Of nine children born to Sarah and John only four lived beyond sixteen years of age.[30] But death's pervasiveness did not dull its impact on Addams when her mother died. Indeed, her nephew James Weber Linn said that Addams remembered her mother's final hours and, in her desire to be at her mother's side, she pounded on the bedroom door.[31]

Half a century later Addams provided indirect evidence of the impact her mother's death had on a vulnerable two year old. In 1916, at the age of 56, she published a book called *The Long Road of Woman's Memory*, a sensitive, moving description of the physical and psychological degradation experienced by Western women. In the final chapter Addams discussed an eerie experience she had while visiting Egypt some years after founding Hull House. The ancient Egyptians' religious and artistic responses to death aroused within her "an unexpected tendency to interpret racial and historic experiences through personal reminiscences."[32] Perhaps this feeling was a natural response to the artistic splendor of Egyptian tombs.

> Nevertheless, what I, at least, was totally unprepared to encounter, was the constant revival of primitive and overpowering emotions which I had experienced so long ago that they had become absolutely detached from myself and seemed to belong to someone else—to a small person with whom I was no longer intimate, and who was certainly not in the least responsible for my present convictions and reflections. It gradually became obvious that the ancient Egyptians had known this small person quite intimately and had most seriously and naively set down upon the walls of their temples and tombs her earliest reactions in the presence of death.[33]

In their tombs the Egyptians "painstakingly portrayed everything that a child has felt in regard to death." In their ardor to overcome the finality of death, the ancient Egyptians and the modern child "often become confused" and "curiously interrelated."[34] Children and "primitive" peoples shut out death, the child through magical thinking, the "primitives" by erecting "massive defences" like the pyramids.[35]

These thoughts sparked another memory in Addams. When she was six or seven the mother of a classmate died, and the students were brought to the cemetery for the final rites. Young Addams had believed the dead went straight to heaven and was "totally unprepared to see what appeared to be the person herself put deep down into the ground." She became "suddenly and brutally" aware of the finality of death, and for weeks her "days were heavy with a nameless oppression and the nights filled with horror." During these painful weeks the question of what her motherless classmates could do to help themselves haunted her. But not for long. That dread was soon "translated into a demand for definite action on the part of the children against this horrible thing which had befallen their mother."[36]

What are we to make of these memories? It may seem odd that Addams's memory of her first confrontation with death's finality occurred at the funeral of someone else's mother. Nevertheless, it is understandable. It was unlikely that Addams's Egyptian experience would lead to a direct confrontation with her mother's death. This is so for two reasons.

First, a two year old is not mature enough to deal with loss of a loved one. The impact of object loss depends on the person's level of development. While a two year old's psychic development can be retarded by loss of her mother, the child is too immature to effectively deal with the loss. Also, what a child of that age loses by her mother's "absence" is not a fully internalized object (part of her superego motive system, which at age two is in a primitive state of development) but a comforting nurturer. If the child is fortunate enough to have competent "mother surrogates" at hand, as Addams did in her older sisters and father, the impact of the loss is mitigated. The child might experience something akin to grief (rather than mourning), but permanent psychological damage can be avoided.[37]

Second, the memory awakened in Egypt was that of her classmate's mother because the visual impact of the internment "suddenly and brutally" brought six-year-old Addams face to face with something she hitherto denied: the finality of the loss of her own mother. It also resuscitated the memory of her response to that loss. Her feelings were translated, as she put it, into definite "action." She was now a child of six or seven and infinitely more capable than four years earlier of feeling adrift in the absence of a mother, of feeling different from children whose mother had not "deserted" them, and of feeling vaguely culpable that she was somehow unworthy of having a mother.

Such feelings are not unusual in a motherless or fatherless six year old.[38] What is significant was Addams's capacity to cope with her crisis, to respond realistically (within the parameters allowed by her culture) to the fact that she and her siblings were motherless and her father a widower. She coped with this situation by identifying with the virtues, attitudes, and duties her society associated with femininity and motherhood. As we have seen, during these years she doted on her father, adored him, and wanted to appear attractive to him. In her autobiography she recalled feeling "a curious sense of responsibility" during her sixth or seventh year. Her almost missionary solicitousness was pervaded by feelings of "feminine" sensitivity and maternity and was made even more intense because it coincided with unresolved oedipal tensions and with her recent discovery at the "other" mother's funeral that Sarah Addams was gone forever:

> I dreamed night after night that everyone in the world was dead excepting myself, and that upon me rested the responsibility of making a wagon wheel. The village street remained as usual, the village blacksmith shop was 'all there.' even a glowing fire upon the forge and the anvil in its customary place near the door, but no human being was within sight. They had all gone around the edge of the hill to the village cemetery, and I alone remained alive in the world. I always stood in the same spot in the blacksmith shop, darkly pondering as to how to begin, and never once did I know how, although I fully realized that the affairs of the world could not be resumed until at least one wheel should be made. The next morning would often find me, a delicate little girl of six, with the further disability of a curved spine, standing in the doorway of the village blacksmith shop, anxiously watching the burly, red-shirted figure at work. I would store by mind with such details of the process of making wheels as I could observe, and sometimes I plucked up courage to ask for more. "Do you always have to sizzle the iron in water?" I would ask, thinking how horrid it would be to do so.[39]

This recurring dream, along with recollections of her confrontation with death, indicate that however powerful her identification with her father's aggressive, "inner light" moral style may have been, "feminine" counteridentifications were active in Addams quite early. And although one need not be a Freudian to discern the sexual symbolism in her dream, along with the not very subtle hints that she had taken her mother's place in the household, of much greater significance is that Addams's dream conveys, however impressionistically, one way socially prescribed feminine roles became intertwined with the idiosyncratic experiences of a female child left "alone" with her widowed father.

This material does not indicate that Addams was neurotically inclined. Her attempts to cope with death appear to have been adaptive—given the society she lived in. They also appear to have initiated a process of learning to cope with the inevitability of death. By the time she was fifteen, Addams saw death as a "relentless and elemental" force. "[O]nce to be young, to grow old, and to die, everything came to that!"[40] But as we shall see, this was not her last brush with the anguish of death and was only the beginning of her confusion over feminine and masculine moral styles.

The Adolescent Years

When she was seventeen Addams entered nearby Rockford Seminary, a non-degree-granting woman's college that specialized in missionary training.

She wanted to go to Smith College because it was one of the few institutions offering the B.A. to women, but her father insisted she attend nearby Rockford. As usual she obeyed him.[41]

On the surface at least, Addams appeared as attached as ever to the moral, social, and political ideals of John Addams through most of her four years at Rockford. She resisted her teachers' attempts to "convert" her, because she believed that like her father she could live a morally upright life without adhering to externally imposed denominational discipline. Also, her social and political views, as expressed in her school work, for the most part faithfully reflected the critical elements of the elder Addams' world-view: hard work, personal initiative, and asceticism. As late as the mid-1880s she still thought of herself as a high-tariff Republican.[42]

But alongside these "masculine" identifications "feminine" counteriden-tifications were reawakened during the Rockford years. Perhaps it would be more precise to say her feminine identifications attained a new level of development and began to assume a form quite alien to the pliant, would-be mother of the blacksmith dream. Addams could no more accept Rockford's conventional ideals about woman's social roles as either homemaker or missionary than she could accept its conventional religious wisdom. Her exposure to the major intellectual currents of the day, particularly Darwinism, convinced her that the study of science might open social and political doors hitherto closed to women. By studying science woman's "intuitive" mind could be trained to function empirically and concretely. The educated woman should not limit her aspirations to traditional social roles, but "convert" her "wasted force to the highest use."[43]

If Addams's vision of woman's expanded role in American society went far beyond the prevailing domestic piety image of women, it did so, as J.O.C. Phillips has pointed out, in terms of women's social rather than sexual role. While higher education provided some women with skills that allowed them to seek rewards outside the home, it also expanded the scope of their alleged innate nurturant propensity. An enlarged social role for women gave them the opportunity to bring their nurturant skills to bear on perplexing social and political issues.[44]

Once Addams began to think of feminine nurturance as a political force instead of a means of exerting a benign influence on children and husbands within the home, she ran the risk of open conflict with her father's moral style. In almost every way the nurturant propensities of what Addams called the "truest womanhood" that "can yet transform the world," clashed with the moral consciousness of John Addams.[45] The notion of feminine nurturance was far removed from the morally privatized world of her father. Indeed, the ideals of the socially oriented, "Saxon lady" moral style she increasingly identified with during her college years were explicitly opposed to the "masculine" traits of social individualism, unrestrained ambition, and the subjective "inner light" moral style. Thus, even before she graduated from Rockford in 1881, the year her father died, Addams was already reassessing her commitment to John Addams's moral style and, consequently, found herself in the midst of a struggle between antipodal masculine and feminine moral styles.

It is difficult to pinpoint the reasons why this conflict surfaced at Rockford. Undoubtedly, the college's missionary atmosphere was permeated with visions of woman's destiny as savior of a forlorn, materialistic world. And although Addams was relatively immune to the religious-messianic ambiance within which Rockford's image of woman's destiny was immured, it would be a short step for this rather secular young person to apply feminine nurturant themes to social and political issues.

But a more compelling reason for the surfacing of moral conflict in these years was that she was in college. Addams was a member of the first generation of middle-class women to attend college in significant numbers.[46] Because she was a college student the possibility existed that she might develop skills and ambitions that would make her dissatisfied with traditional feminine social roles. In fact, her college experience might make those roles singularly unattractive and spark a desire to explore vocational possibilities previously monopolized by men.

Had Addams resigned herself to becoming a mother and homemaker conflicting masculine-feminine moral styles might be handled with relative ease. Her nurturant propensities would be exercised within the home and there would be little conflict in her believing, for example, in a high tariff, since this was a worldly, nondomestic issue that fell within the masculine (nonnurturant) sphere. On the other hand, if for some reason Addams as homemaker opposed a high tariff, she could exert her feminine influence in the home and try to change the opinions of "her men." In either case she would remain within the bounds of her assigned feminine sphere. But once Addams confronted the possibility that as a college-trained woman she might have to find a place for herself in the masculine world, the struggle between feminine and masculine moral styles could become acute. If college broadened her vocational horizons, if it created the potential for careers previously unavailable to a woman, it inevitably forced Addams to deal head-on with the conundrum of masculine and feminine roles and values. Could she be a "true" woman and work in the "outside" world? Could she adhere to John Addams's moral style and maintain her femininity? If she went into the masculine world armed with the nurturant values she said could "yet transform the world," would she thereby have to turn away from her beloved father's moral style—a style she had cherished and tried to emulate all her life?

The dilemma would be intensified by the crisis of adolescence. Indeed, the adolescent experience must have been far more painful for young women in Addams's situation that it had been for women in other classes or in earlier years. An educated middle-class woman and adolescent living in the last quarter of the nineteenth-century was confronted with the difficult task of becoming something other than her mother had envisioned—and perhaps something other than she herself had envisioned a few short years before. In Addams's case, the combination of moral ambivalence and adolescent uncertainty provided the foundation for her prolonged existential crisis, which began in 1881 and persisted until 1889.

As profound as her confusion over these issues had been during the Rockford years, the death of her father in 1881 exacerbated the problem. In that year she entered a phase in which she felt herself "absolutely at sea as far as any moral purpose was concerned." Following a one-year residence at Woman's Medical College of Philadelphia, Addams became mired in a prolonged period of lassitude and "melancholy." To an extent her suffering derived from a chronic spinal deformity, but the depth of her depression and her profound confusion about vocational goals and moral styles convinced her that the malaise was not caused by physical problems.[47] "However, it could not have been due to my health for as my wise little notebook sententiously remarked, 'In *his* own way each *man* must struggle, lest the moral law become a far-off abstraction utterly separated from *his* active life.' " (Italics added.)[48]

Year by year during the 1880s her inability to transcend depression, or make her moral life less "abstract," increased. In a letter of 1884 to her former Rockford classmate Ellen Gates Starr, Addams confided that her ill health and vocational uncertainty were symbols of a failure of will: she lacked the confidence to make a vocational choice.[49] Two years later she complained to Starr that her "faculties, memory, receptive faculties and all" had become "perfectly inaccessible locked up away from me."[50] That year she reached "the nadir of my nervous depression and sense of maladjustment."[51]

Passivity and inertia were accompanied by a revulsion against the cultural attainments of young men and women of her class. The literary and artistic world she was exposed to at school and during trips to Europe enhanced her alienation from the "real" world. Literary and artistic endeavors seemed to "cloud the really vital situation spread before our eyes," especially when intellect was perceived as distinct from moral concerns and consequences.[52]

Addams's late-adolescent crisis lasted eight years. During this period she was unable to make vocational plans, which is to say she could not confront her future. Why? Is there a connection between her inability to face the future on the one hand, and her adolescent crisis and the masculine-feminine moral conundrum that left her morally "at sea" on the other?

There is a connection between time—psychic time—and the moral dilemmas confronting adolescents. The superego, particularly the ethical values of the ego ideal, stands for the person's future. Conscience "speaks to us from the viewpoint of an inner future," pointing in the direction of what the person should become and generating anxiety and loss of self-esteem should she fall short of the idealized future. In this sense, superego represents the young person's future.[53]

Addams's prolonged time of troubles represented a need to suspend her future. It was, therefore, a profoundly moral crisis. She was unable to make a final choice between the moral styles reflected in feminine nurturance and her father's ethical individualism. Consequently, she lacked the will to be anything but passive. Not only were her cognitive and moral faculties "inaccessible," but she was pendant in time, unable to respond autonomously or actively to the "external" world. The psychoanalyst Paul Seton has aptly described the relationship between this passivity and the crumbling of parental ideals during adolescence:

> Without past or future or both, there can be no experience of duration and no sense of one's own history. The timelessness has not been an eruption of the unconscious or a decomposition of ego functioning, but is frequently a suspension of superego operations because one needs to suspend a sense of closure . . . .[54]

In Addams's case, these normal difficulties were compounded by her father's death, which occurred in the midst of her moral reassessment. Feelings of loss and mourning inherent in the adolescent task of turning away from at least some paternal ideals was heightened for her by John Addams's death. The inevitable guilt experienced by a youth who, like Addams, was reevaluating significant aspects of her father's values, was exacerbated by loss of the one who personified those values. The anxiety and fear of abandonment that often accompanies the adolescent moral reevaluation was intensified by the guilt Addams may have felt because her doubts about the paternal system of values appeared to be answered by his death.[55] For her to turn away from those values now was tantamount to having wished his death. In short, Addams could neither let go of the paternal moral style nor subscribe to it. The result was her long bout with depression.

Although her crisis was not fully resolved until the opening of Hull House, the outline of her resolution assumed shape by the mid-1880s. As we have seen, nineteenth-century Americans associated John Addams's privatized moral consciousness with the "masculine" traits of rationality, inner control, and a cool, objective analysis of social reality. By contrast, the "feminine" moral style was "social," because it was rooted in an intuitive, emotional, and empathic insight into the needs and feelings of others, particularly one's children and husband. Thus, there was a spatial as well as a gender dimension associated with specific forms of moral evaluation: an "inner," personal (masculine) form, and an "outer," empathic, social (feminine) orientation. Addams, in effect, commented on this spatial bipolarity in 1883 when she wrote Starr that from "babyhood" the altruistic impulses of female children were cultivated, and they were "taught to be self-forgetting and self-sacrificing, to consider the good of the [social] whole before the good of the ego."[56] As Addams took the first tentative steps in the mid-1880s to resolve her moral dilemma, her ideas about moral evaluation tended to be broached in terms of this inner-outer moral bipolarity.

For example, the spatial parameters of her crisis were poignantly revealed in her correspondence with Starr during these years, especially when they discussed religion. "I am always blundering," wrote Addams, "when I deal with religious nomenclature . . . simply because my religious life has been so small; for many years it was my ambition to reach my father's moral requirements, and now when I am needing something more, I find myself approaching a crisis."[57]

The significance of Addams's religious speculations lies in its spatial imagery. Her letters to Starr are replete with images depicting tensions between inner (masculine) and outer (feminine) moral styles. For instance, on one occasion she confessed to Starr that the difference in their approaches to religion was that Starr desired to experience an inner, "beautiful faith," whereas Addams felt only the need for "religion in a practical sense," as a guide to social action.[58] According to Addams, Starr needed religion to attain inner peace and harmony, and she instead sought a practical faith useful for arbitrating everyday moral problems. The inner-outer bipolarity in Addams's ethical perspective was reflected in her discussion of the Incarnation:

> I don't think God embodied himself in Christ to reveal himself, but that he did it considering the weakness of man; that while man might occasionally comprehend an abstract deity he couldn't live by it, it came to him only in his more exalted moments, and it was impossible for his mind to retain his own conception of God. . . . If a man can once see God through Christ then he is saved for he can never again lose him as Christ is always with him.[59]

In other words, a God that is wholly other and can be "seen" only through an abstract, subjective blind act of faith is inadequate as an ethical guide. Only a divinity embodied in Jesus—in the life of a real person engaged in a network of social and moral relationships—could be relevant to ethics, because the individual can "see" Jesus and use the facts of his life as a behavioral model. "I believe more and more," she wrote Starr in 1885, "in keeping the . . . facts of Christ's life before us and letting the philosophy go."[60] Facts, in short, were inexorably objective, outer and social, and thus far removed from the inner-directed subjectivity of faith.

Addams's confusion, at least on the religious front, was eased somewhat in 1885 when she became a Presbyterian. Although her conversion was bereft of intense emotional upheaval, joining the church alleviated to some degree her morbid sense of a discrepancy between "What I am and what I ought to be," as she put it. Significantly, Addams also felt that by becoming a Presbyterian she entered a community of "fellowship" that was "almost early Christian in its simplicity." This bond of fellowship allowed her to "give up one's conceit," something John Addams would never have surrendered. By opting for a modern counterpart to primitive Christianity, instead of becoming a Quaker like her father, Addams in effect was calling into question his privatized, "inner light" perception of moral rectitude. Instead, she chose a church that satisfied her craving for "an *outward* symbol of fellowship, some bond of peace, some blessed spot where unity of spirit might claim right of way over all differences." (Italics added.)[61]

Perhaps the most striking and significant insight into Addams's adolescent crisis is provided by a letter she wrote Starr in August 1879. Characteristically, Addams was discussing her moral dilemma: how could personal religious values be related to everyday social encounters? She then described a short-lived psychic experience of "peace" during which the dualisms and conflicts of her moral crisis were temporarily eased. Her description of this transient experience provides us with precious insights into the phenomena at the root of her crisis, adolescence, and confusion over masculine and feminine moral styles: "Lately, it seems to me that I am getting back of it—superior to it, I almost feel—Back to a great Primal Cause, not Nature exactly, but a fostering mother, a necessity, brooding and watching over all things, above every passion and yet not passive, the mystery of creation . . . the idea embodied in the Sphinx—peace."[62]

It is essential to understand what an adolescent torn between conflicting moral configurations meant by saying she was going "back to Primal Cause . . . a fostering mother." As mentioned earlier, the ego ideal represents the ethical dimension of the individual's future, and it is important to keep in mind that its origins can be traced to the second half of the child's first year. We have also noted that through childhood and adolescence Addams's ego ideal was the scene of a battle between masculine and feminine moral styles, although until her final two years at Rockford the masculine style appears to have dominated. What, then, is the connection between her experience of being pulled back to a primal cause and her moral dilemma?

Adolescent regression to preego ideal states is both normal and common.[63] Because superego becomes less efficient in fulfilling its roles as regulator of self-esteem and appraiser of behavior during adolescence, the ego, whose task is to guide the person through the maze of often conflicting demands made by her "inner voice" and external reality, is "left weak, isolated and inadequate.''[64] Set adrift, with little guidance from superego, the ego may seek refuge at one or another preadolescent levels of development, probably a level where her doubts and conflicts were less intense. This form of regression is necessary for the youth's stability and future development, because it allows her to revisit (in a sense relive) those infantile interactions with parental figures that generated superego in the first place.[65] In effect, regression allows the youth to reevaluate past moral commitments in light of her present needs.

Addams's regression took the form of going back to a ''fostering mother'' because it is on the ''earliest wishful fantasies of merging and being one with the mother'' that ''the foundations on which all object relations as well as all future types of identifications are built.''[66] Once the primal union of mother-infant begins to crumble around the second half of the infant's first year, and the child begins to realize, however vaguely, that she is a separate entity from what Addams called her primal cause, the ego ideal emerges as a substitute for the lost ideal state of unity. From now on the child's self-esteem is based on the congruence between her behavior and the internalized ''omnipotent'' parental images with which she identifies.[67]

In getting back of it all through reunion with her primal cause (and in her conversion to Presbyterianism as well) Addams recreated the experiences of union, separation, and reunion that preceded formation of her ego ideal. Regression and recreation allowed her to discard questionable aspects of the paternal superego, reexternalize them as it were, and create the possibility of reevaluating her commitment to his moral style.[68]

As the 1880s wore on she discarded those aspects of John Addams's moral style that encouraged moral autonomy. Paternal moral patterns were gradually replaced by ''feminine'' social-organic concepts of morality. Her conversion to a denomination that in her eyes evoked images of early Christian communitarianism, symbolized her desire to live by ''the simple social relationships in the way in which he connects with his fellows.''[69]

By creating what she called a ''code of social ethics,'' or a ''social'' (nonindividualistic) morality, the dualisms at the heart of her crisis, masculine-feminine, inner-outer, and subjective-objective, could be resolved. Addams was convinced that such dualisms caused many of her middle-class contemporaries to experience the same difficulties in relating private ideals to social behavior. Years after her crisis was over, she summarized the nature of the problem:

> They fail to be content with the fulfillment of their family and personal obligations, and find themselves striving to respond to a new demand involving a social obligation; they have become conscious of another requirement, and the contribution they would make is toward a code of social ethics. The conception of life which they hold has not yet expressed itself in social changes or legal enactments, but rather in a mental attitude of mal-

adjustment, and in a sense of divergence between their consciences and their conduct. They desire both a clearer definition of the code of morality adapted to present day demands and a part in its fulfillment; both a creed and a practice of social morality.[70]

We must, of course, keep in mind that Addams's moral crisis was rooted in her idiosyncratic childhood and family experiences. Yet we should also remember that the moral vocabulary (if I might put it that way) of her crisis was social as well as personal: changes in her moral vocabulary had echoes in the changing structure of American society. The increasingly corporate tendencies of American business, the monumental problems spawned by overcrowded and unsanitary conditions in cities, and the social, economic, and educational problems generated by the presence of "unassimilated" immigrants from Asia and Southern and Eastern Europe had to affect the sensibilities of this intelligent young woman. Specifically, these conditions indicated that the country was becoming too complex and, as she would put it, too "interdependent" to accommodate the moral individualism and subjectivity of her father. The old frontier virtues of "thrift, industry, and sobriety," she later wrote, pertained only to the individual and to a decentralized economy in which "each man had his own shop." But as society and industry become more organized "life becomes incredibly complex and interdependent," and, therefore, moral values must shift away from personal needs or beliefs and toward society "as a whole."[71] It was her desire to extend her own "social," empathic, organic (feminine) morality to the rest of society, as a means of making "social intercourse express the growing sense of economic unity" in society, that prompted her to open Hull House.[72] And it is to this relationship between her personal crisis and her perception of urban-industrial problems that I will direct my final remarks.

Conclusion: The Meaning of Hull House

Addams found an ideal form to express what she called "both a creed and a practice of social morality" in 1889 when she and Starr opened Hull House in Chicago. Unquestionably, the social settlement symbolized for Addams the domestication of her worldly skills. She and Starr were "ready to perform the humblest" services, "wash the new-born babies, and prepare the dead for burial, nurse the sick and mind the children."[73] When discussing the role of the settlement in urban society she often employed images consistent with her adolescent recreation of union with her fostering mother. She informed Hull House residents that they must be "swallowed," and "digested," and "disappear into the bulk of the people."[74] The residents should view the city as "organic" and sedulously strive to prevent it from becoming "over-differentiated." They must persuade urbanites that "individual morality" and pride in personal achievements were irrelevant "in an age demanding social morality and social adjustment."[75] She was certain that these aspects of the reform impulse were rooted in feminine, maternal sentiments.

> Maternal affection and solicitude, in woman's remembering heart, may at length coalesce into a chivalric protection for all that is young and unguarded. This chivalry of women expressing protection for those at the bottom of society, as far as it has already developed, suggests a return to that idealized version of chivalry which was the consecration of strength to the defense of weakness.[76]

Hull House represented Addams's rejection of her father's moral insularity in favor of a social morality. On the other hand, her equally compelling belief that social settlement workers should undertake "objective" analyses of social data constituted a rejection of the stereotypically passive, emotional female role in favor of an allegedly masculine rationality needed to make scientific, objective evaluations of people and things. Settlement workers should make scientific studies of the causes and consequences of urban poverty, political corruption, and the like, because only unprejudiced, rational, objective analyses of the "facts" could uncover the underlying causes of urban problems.[77] More significantly, residents must focus their attention on the concreteness, factuality, and immediacy of the social experiences of their clients, for "we do not believe that genuine experience can lead us astray any more than scientific data can."[78]

Thus Addams's social philosophy blended a spatially outward, or communal (feminine), moral style with a (masculine) empirical orientation. Both tendencies pointed in the same direction: each emphasized the centrality of facts, objectivity, and experience while, implicitly denigrating the personal and the subjective, especially in the areas of morality and social analysis. "Action" she wrote, "is indeed the sole medium of expression for ethics."[79] What people did, in contrast to what they felt or thought, was what mattered ultimately, because "the deed often reveals when the idea does not."[80] What the deed reveals is the actor; and what the abstraction of personal morality and intellectual ideas often conceal is the private, insular moral precipitates of behavior. Addams's "pragmatic" interest in results, her quest to have the social settlement "test the value of human knowledge by action and realization," was a reflection of the shift from "inner" control to "external" conformity that occurred in her moral and social perspectives during the 1880s.[81] Nor were these sentiments peculiar to Addams. As Allan Davis has pointed out, social settlement workers, male and female, exhibited an unmitigated faith in the truth-revealing power of unadorned facts and statistics, as well as in the reform potential of administrative techniques.[82]

The shift from inner control to social morality was implicit in Addams's moral crisis. But the empathic "feminine" morality that influenced Addams' perceptions of ethics and women's social roles during adolescence may not have had so powerful or lasting an impact on her adult behavior had not changes in the structure of American society and in attitudes about economic intercourse occurred in the 1870s and 1880s. In other words, things did not have to turn out the way they did. Any number of viable combinations of masculine and feminine moral and social attributes could have prevailed in Addams. Thus, in a society less in need of organization, or less congested, or less ethnically heterogeneous Addams might have tilted toward the insular morally and socially insular facets of her father's masculine code. Modern forms of economic and social organizations were as antithetical to moral individualism as the notion of feminine empathy. But feminine empathy was not incongruous with a (masculine) empirical orientation, for both stressed the moral and social relevance of animate and inanimate environments. Indeed, the emphasis on people as actors and morality as a network of facts must have seemed a highly adaptive response to the rather chaotic social and economic circumstances of modern America.

At any rate, once these two streams of thought and feeling converged, as they did in Addams's moral style and social philosophy, it was a short step to the notion that "scientific" control of the person's environment could determine his personality development, thus creating an atmosphere conducive to social reform. "We don't expect to change human nature," Addams said of social workers shortly before her death in 1935, "but we do expect to change human behavior."[83]

Notes

1. Adams quoted in J.O.C. Phillips, "The Education of Jane Addams," *History of Education Quarterly* 14 (Spring 1974):63.

2. On the issues of masculine and feminine social roles and sentiments see Peter Gabriel Filene, *Him, Her, Self: Sex Roles in Modern America* (New York: Harper and Row, 1974); Ann Douglas, *The Feminization of American Culture* (New York: Alfred Knopf, 1977); Barbara Welter, "The Feminization of American Religion: 1800-1860," in *Clio's Consciousness Raised* ed. Mary Hartman and Lois W. Banner (New York: Harper and Row, 1974); "The Cult of True Womanhood: 1820-1860," *American Quarterly* 18 (1966):151-174; Christopher Lasch, *The New Radicalism in America* (New York: Alfred Knopf, 1965), pp. 3-68; Anne Kuhn, *The Mother's Role in Childhood Education: New England Concepts, 1830-1860* (New Haven, Conn.: Yale University Press, 1947).

3. Ibid.

4. Douglas, *Feminization*, p. 176.

5. Jane Addams, *Twenty Years at Hull House* (New York: MacMillan, 1910), pp. 94-95.

6. Lasch, *New Radicalism*, pp. 3-37; John Rousmaniere, "Cultural Hybrid in the Slums: The College Woman and the Settlement House," in *Education in American History*, ed. Michael Katz (New York: St. Martins Press, 1973), pp. 122-138; Phillips, *"Education of Jane Addams,"* pp. 50-60; Jill Conway, "Jane Addams: An American Heroine," *Daedalus* 93 (Spring 1964).

7. Rousmaniere, "Hybrid," p. 123.

8. Addams quoted in Morton White and Lucia White, *The Intellectual versus the City* (Cambridge, Mass.: Harvard University Press, 1962), p. 154.

9. Robert Woods, *The Neighborhood in Nation-Building* (Boston: Houghton Mifflin, 1923), pp. 106-109.

10. Ibid., pp. 9, 43.

11. Kai T. Erikson, *Everything In Its Path* (New York: Simon and Shuster, 1976), p. 81.

12. Ibid.

13. Ibid., pp. 81-82.

14. Ibid., p. 82.

15. Allen F. Davis, *Spearheads for Reform: The Social Settlements and the Progressive Movement* (New York: Oxford University Press, 1967), pp. 111-112.

16. For an incisive discussion of these issues see Lois B. Murphy and Alice E. Moriarty, *Vulnerability, Coping and Growth* (New Haven, Conn.: Yale University Press, 1976), pp. 171-198.

17. Ibid., pp. 173-175.

18. In effect, this means that the resolution of Addams's moral crisis was contained within the boundaries of her childhood and adolescent repertoire of potential values and behaviors, but not determined by any one of them. Which values prevailed would depend less on genetic considerations than on the interplay between her potential values and her perceptions of the current imperatives and promises of American life and her role in helping fulfill those imperatives and promises in the future.

19. Marcet Halderman-Julius, "The Two Mothers Of Jane Addams," *Addams Papers*, Swarthmore College Peace Collection, pp. 3-5.

20. Addams, *Twenty Years*, p. 25.

21. Ibid., pp. 1-2.

22. James Linn, *Jane Addams, A Biography* (New York: MacMillan, 1938), p. 26.

23. Addams, *Twenty Years*, p. 7.

24. Ibid., pp. 26-27.

25. Ibid., p. 16; Allen Davis, *American Heroine: The Life and Legend of Jane Addams* (New York: Oxford University Press, 1973), pp. 4-6.

26. Linn, *Addams*, p. 16.

27. Ibid., pp. 17-18.

28. Addams, *Twenty Years*, pp. 12-13.

29. Ibid.

30. Halderman-Julius, "Two Mothers," pp. 4, 11.

31. Linn, *Addams*, p. 22.

32. Jane Addams, *The Long Road Of Woman's Memory* (New York: MacMillan, 1916), p. 141.

33. Ibid., p. 142.

34. Ibid., pp. 145-146.

35. Ibid., pp. 147-149.

36. Ibid., pp. 154-157.

37. Adele Scharl, "Regression And Restitution in Object Loss," *Psychoanalytic Study of the Child* 16 (1961):479; Margaret Mahler, "On Sadness and Grief in Infancy and Childhood," *Psychoanalytic Study of the Child* 16 (1961):337-343.

38. Gregory Rochlin, "The Dread of Abandonment," *Psychoanalytic Study of the Child* 16 (1961):452-453.

39. Addams, *Twenty Years*, p. 22.

40. Addams quoted in Linn, *Addams*, p. 39.

41. Lionel C. Lane, "Jane Addams as Social Worker" (Ph.D. dissertation, University of Pennsylvania, 1963), pp. 6-7.

42. Addams, *Twenty Years*, pp. 49-50; Davis, *Heroine*, pp. 20, 35-36.

43. J.O.C. Phillips, "The Education of Jane Addams," *History of Education Quarterly* 14 (Spring 1974):50-60.

44. Addams quoted in ibid., p. 63.

45. Linn, *Addams*, p. 63.

46. John Rousmaniere, "Cultural Hybrid," pp. 124-127.

47. Addams to Ellen Gates Starr, 7 January 1883, *Starr Papers*, Sophia Smith Women's Collection, Smith College.

48. Addams, *Twenty Years*, p. 16.

49. Addams to Starr, 8 June 1884, *Starr Papers*.

50. Addams to Starr, 7 February 1886, *Starr Papers*.

51. Addams, *Twenty Years*, p. 77.

52. Ibid., pp. 70-71, 76-77.

53. Paul Seton, "The Psychotemporal Adaptation of Late Adolescence," *Journal of the American Psychoanalytic Association* 22 (1974):797-804.

54. Ibid., p. 816.

55. Rochlin, "Dread of Abandonment," p. 461; Martha Wolfenstein, "How Is Mourning Possible," *Psychoanalytic Study of the Child* 21 (1966):113-115.

56. Addams to Starr, 2 December 1883, *Starr Papers*.

57. Addams to Starr, 6 December 1885, *Starr Papers*.

58. Addams to Starr, 29 January 1880, *Starr Papers*.

59. Ibid.

60. Addams to Starr, 30 March 1885, *Starr Papers*.

61. Addams, *Twenty Years*, pp. 78-79.

62. Addams to Starr, 2 December 1883, *Starr Papers*.

63. Peter Blos, "Character Formation in Adolescence," *Psychoanalytic Study of the Child* 23 (1968):253; Edith Jacobsen, "Adolescent Moods and the Remodeling of the Psychic Structure in Adolescence," *Psychoanalytic Study of the Child* 16 (1961):180.

64. Peter Blos, *On Adolescence* (New York: The Free Press, 1962), pp. 73, 193.

65. Blos, "Character Formation," p. 253.

66. Edith Jacobson, *The Self and the Object World* (New York: International University Press, 1968), p. 39. One need not take this genetic sentiment literally to justify the act of regression.

67. Calvin Settlage, "Cultural Values and the Superego in late Adolescence," *Psychoanlytic Study of the Child* 27 (1973):80-81.

68. Jacobson, *Self*, p. 121.

69. Addams, *Twenty Years*, p. 96.

70. Jane Addams, *Democracy and Social Ethics* (New York: MacMillan, 1902), p. 4.

71. Ibid., pp. 212-213.

72. Jane Addams, *Philanthropy and Social Progress* (New York: MacMillan, 1893), p. 1.

73. Addams quoted in Lane, "Addams," p. 59.

74. Addams quoted in White and White, *Intellectual*, p. 154.

75. Addams, *Twenty Years*, p. 100; *Democracy*, pp. 2-3.

76. Addams, *Long Road*, pp. 82-83.

77. Addams, *Democracy*, pp. 64-68.

78. Ibid., pp. 6-7, 273-275.

79. Ibid., p. 273.

80. Jane Addams, "A Function of the Social Settlement," *Annals of the American Academy of Social and Political Sciences* 13 (May 1899):326.

81. Ibid.

82. Davis, *Spearheads*, p. 173.

83. Addams quoted in Linn, *Addams*, p. 416.

13 Women's Diseases before 1900

Edward Shorter

If women in past times have been unequal to men, it is partly because they have been so vulnerable to their own bodies. Their inferior status in the eighteenth and nineteenth centuries resulted, in some measure, from their victimization by their reproductive organs in a way that men have never been victimized. This vulnerability has several dimensions:

1. Women's exposure to an unending series of pregnancies, as a result of both their husbands' "conjugal rights" over their bodies and rape, which makes them immediately vulnerable to male violence.

2. Women's exposure to death, terrible pain, and mutiliation in childbirth, a vulnerability to the forces of nature that men, of course, escape, and that is inflicted on women as a consequence of their sexual contact with men.

3. Women's vulnerability to a whole range of diseases of the reproductive system for which there is no male counterpart in urology. If the first two aspects of misadventure have received some treatment in the scholarly literature, women's diseases have, among historians of women, excited no attention at all. They are the subject of this chapter.

Even today women are more exposed to illness than men as a result of the reproductive system. In 1976, for example, a survey recorded forty-eight days of "restricted activity" owing to acute genitourinary disorders for every hundred women interviewed, only twelve for every hundred men.

Another survey of "chronic" conditions of "prostate" and "female trouble except breasts," as the survey put it, uncovered a similar difference.[1] I shall argue in the following pages that in North America and Western Europe before 1900 the difference in "morbidity" status between men and women was even more glaring and that if women were obliged to take secondary roles in traditional society, it was partly because they were constant prey to nutritional disorders and pelvic diseases that left them more enervated than men in their daily lives; that made them highly apprehensive about their sexual relations with men; and that helped convince them that femininity was a curse imposed on womankind by God.

Of course other reasons exist for the subordination of women in times past, such as the teachings of the Catholic Church or the formidable networks of male bonding arrayed against women. My purpose is not to make physical vulnerability the chief explanation of women's ritual subservience, their legal status as minors, or the constant victimization of their daily lives. It is rather to show that at the level of disease they were not only worse situated than men but often the direct victims of male sexuality. This is a more modest undertaking than documenting the roots of sexual subservience and often benumbingly technical. But I remind the reader of two larger perspectives in "mentalities," which I hope the medical evidence in this chapter will help open up: (1) that women themselves felt deeply debased and humiliated by these gynecological afflictions that were their lot all along, a further spur for them to comply voluntarily with patriarchy; and (2) that a precondition for the explosion of modern feminism has been the abolition of these various vulnerabilities, through birth control, through what has become virtually risk-free childbearing, and through the medical alleviation of most of the pelvic pathology we shall encounter here. Alas, not all. I shall not discuss gynecological cancer, that "angel of death of the woman's world," because the historical evidence on prevalence rates is just too skimpy.[2] And I shall omit all those new "diseases of civilization," such as anorexia nervosa, to which women have been newly subject.[3] Two other disease conditions will also be omitted from consideration:

1. Hysteria—simply because the diagnosis was too unreliable. When nineteenth-century doctors use the term, they lump together a number of different psychiatric symptoms and then hopelessly discredit their own usefulness as observers by attributing the whole thing to the uterus. What is one to make, for instance, of the following utterance, from a "medical topography" of Wurzburg in 1805:

> Among the female gender the so-called nervous diseases are to be encountered among all classes, yet with some differentiation. Marriage, with all its consequences, is often the best remedy for hysteria. Often, however, the disease makes such strides, especially among single women, that all efforts of the doctors are unable to prevent its transition into an incurable malady. . . . Hysterical women suffer especially in the period of the monthly cleansing, which often is combined with great pain.[4]

We have no way, moreover, of knowing how common hysterical symptoms were among men. I am inclined to dismiss as hopeless any effort to reconstruct the epidemiology of women's mental health from sources like these. (My confidence in this whole range of psychiatric labels has been further shaken by the recent discovery that a specific "menopausal" syndrome, on which doctors have until recently relied heavily, simply does not exist.[5])

2. Uterine malpositions—especially retroversion, which is the backward-tilting of the uterus. Nineteenth-century medicine was obsessed with malpositions, but we now know that how the uterus rests in the body is responsible for very few symptoms perceived by the women themselves. (Gravest is that a retroverted uterus might drag down the ovaries into the

"pouch of Douglas," resulting in painful coitus.) I have decided simply to ignore the whole question.

Let me avert a possible misunderstanding or two. My aim is not to write a puff piece for the "marvels of medical science," which (it could be argued) has inflicted a sort of cultural disaster on attitudes to our bodies and to death in the twentieth century. Nor is it to present evidence of women's attitudes to their bodies in traditional times, because we have no way of knowing what most of these women actually thought as their uteruses started to prolapse or as the dull pains of cervical cancer started to announce themselves. At present we are reduced to inferring what they might have felt about their relations with men, about the "joy of sex," and about the very nature of femininity itself as they brushed against the various disease conditions that are the subject of this chapter. Ultimately, whoever wants to write about the impact of disease on women's lives will be obliged to find information on the attitudes of the women themselves. By declaring as "provisional" and "interim" my findings, and by clearly posting as "speculative" the bridges to mentalities constructed here, I have hoped for the moment to elude this responsibility.

A brief word about the sources. Historians have paid little attention to several varieties of medical treatises that convey considerable information about the lives of women in times past. We have, for one thing, the hundreds of medical topographies written in the years after 1778, when the French Royal Academy of Medicine asked provincial doctors to send in reports on the diseases, hygienic conditions, and folkways of the local populations.[6] A similar kind of literature seems to have started out quite independently in Germany and in other countries as well.[7] Then too, around 1840 numerous doctors began to publish statistical reports on the patients in their clinics. Remember that only in the first half of the nineteenth century does the "clinic," as opposed to the general hospital for the poor, really get going. So thereafter a quite rich literature on, let us say, the epidemiology of the contracted pelvis or the ovarian tumor becomes available. Previous students of women's health have dwelt almost entirely on gynecology and obstetrics textbooks, to the exclusion of this rich data on the incidence of disease in the female population as a whole.[8]

Well, the reader might object, were the lives of women in past times really so different from our own days? Have "narrowly defined sex roles" and "male chauvinism" not been the main affliction of women since time out of mind? The following description of women's health in the small town of Sigmaringen early in the nineteenth century suggests that women's problems may have been more complicated than their inability to get into law school:

The main causes of poor (female) health here are:

The laborious field and house work, which generally fall upon the women and from which otherwise women even in primitive societies are exempt.

> You can see pregnant women here reaping the grain harvest, bundling up and hauling away the sheaves, mowing, carrying fodder, wood and water, and during the winter they're constantly threshing.
>
> Intercourse right up to the end of pregnancy.
>
> The mean, insufficient diet of the women, in that the men spend every evening at the tavern, and the women and children content themselves at home, year in and year out, with a miserable *Wassersuppe*.
>
> Lack of proper rest, care and treatment when they get sick, whereby they continue to work, without any help at all, as long as possible before . . . the doctor is called.
>
> The delay in summoning the midwife.
>
> Their impregnation again immediately after giving birth, whereby the incompletely recovered uterus receives the ovum not in the proper place, not in the fundus, but on one side, or deeper down in the lower uterine segment.[9]

(This latter is apparently a reference to a complication of pregnancy called "placenta previa," in which the placenta implants itself near or across the mouth of the cervix, making the mother liable to sudden hemorrhaging.)

The point running through this chapter is that if women in places like Sigmaringen were callously treated by their husbands, weary of the burden of children, and attentive to the parish priest's declamations about the special burden God had placed on Eve, it was partly because the illnesses of their own frail bodies had ground much of the joy of life, the young confidence, the easy autonomy, out of their existence.

Sigmaringen, and many accounts like it, help us to construct a larger picture of the health of women before the twentieth century. My discussion will center on four areas: (1) diseases arising from the nutritional deficiencies to which women were more subject than men; (2) "Leukorrhea," a whitish, glutinour vaginal discharge; (3) such sequellae of pregnancy as fistulas and perineal tears; (4) a whole range of uterine and ovarian pathology, such as giant tumors, painful menstruation, and uterine prolapse.

Deficiency Disorders

A prefatory point—the most serious deficiencies of nutrition fell on women during pregnancy and in the puerperium, which I have omitted from this chapter on the grounds that they erupted only momentarily—although often with fatal results—rather than dragging on the life long. Of the many diseases arising from vitamin and mineral shortages that we could consider here, such as women's higher susceptibility to tuberculosis, I focus on two: iron-deficiency anemia and pelvic contractions arising from childhood rickets.

So rare has iron-deficiency anemia become in our own time that we are inclined to ascribe its physical symptoms in the past to Victorianism or to the oppression of women. In fact, many of the real world counterparts of these literary heroines, with their pale faces, their easy fatiguability, and their inconstant appetites, were suffering from anemia, the chronic depletion of the body's iron stores (although the cause was unknown). This deficiency, as seen in young women, was called "chlorosis."[10] The same pattern of description appears again and again: pallid color, irregular menstruation, weariness, and some kind of puslike vaginal discharge indicating the presence of an infection (which would further exacerbate the anemia).[11] Hysteria is often mentioned too, although whether the doctor understands by that wide swings of personality, the tremor arising from some kind of functional disease, or the muscular rigidity associated with classical descriptions of hysteria is impossible to say. A typical quote is that of Dr. W.W. Johnson of Washington, D.C. written in 1888: "Confirmed ill health . . . is common after the establishment of the marriage relations and after childbirth among American women. . . . The principal manifestations of this persistent ill health are chronic anemia, with malnutrition, and impaired or altered function in all the organs, especially in those of the nervous system."[12] And just to show that these descriptions are not merely the sexist fantasies of a gaggle of society gynecologists, anemia was endemic toward the turn of the century also among working-class women. For example in Leipzig female subscribers to the local Health Insurance Fund missed work much more frequently than male subscribers because of "weak blood" and "anemia" (*Blutarmut und Bleichsucht*): ages fifteen through nineteen fifty times as often, ages forty-nine and older seven times as often. These were mainly women working in the textile and garment industries.[13]

I think it possible that many of these early accounts confuse anemia with early tuberculosis, and the real incidence may therefore be somewhat lower. But the fatigued, undernourished women we encounter recovering from childbirth in Lyon's Croix Rousse suburb, where they worked in the silk industry, show too clearly the hallmarks of anemia.[14] A vast pool of iron-deficient women clearly existed among the working classes.

But just women? To the extent that worms of chronic infection were the source of the anemia, we have no reason for thinking that men as well were not anemic. One factor in anemia, however, was exclusively female: iron loss through pregnancy and childbirth. Today an average, well-nourished North American woman will be unlikely to store in her own bone marrow the 800 milligrams or so of iron she needs for a typical pregnancy, and to offset the huge iron demands that both the fetus and her own hemoglobin mass make, women currently ingest large amounts of supplementary iron.[15] Now, let us recall the following:

1. Even though iron as a cure for anemia has been used since time out of

mind, in traditional dosages it seems to have done little good. And the biochemistry of anemia was not understood until the 1890s.[16]

2. The intestinal worms that plagued much of the population prevented the gut from absorbing a good deal of the natural iron that people got in their diets. Although in England (at least) normal iron intake was sufficient by modern standards, worms would have prevented the body from utilizing it.[17] The natural history of worms has yet to be written, but so many medical topographies comment casually upon "Wurmer" or "vers" in infants and adults that we must conclude the incidence was substantial.[18]

The average woman was likely to have between six and twelve pregnancies in her lifetime, her iron deficit deepening with each (and further exacerbated to the extent that she breastfed).[19]

The conclusion is inescapable that iron-deficiency anemia was another of those burdens that nature had allocated especially to women, making them more irritable, more anorexic, more tired, more flatulent, more subject to vasomotor disturbances such as "hot flashes," more prey in general than men to nameless aches and pains and unspecific tinglings—all of which are the classic symptoms of iron-deficiency anemia.

Only around 1918 was it established that vitamin D and sunlight are essential to the intestine's absorption of calcium, which, in turn, is vital for proper bone growth.[20] The "beading" of the ribs and the bowlegs symptomatic of rickets occur, of course, among both boys and girls. But only among women does the twisted growth of the pelvis have such grisly consequences—in childbirth. Victims of rickets exhibit a "flat" pelvis, in which the sacrum at the rear grows too close to the pubic bone at the front, narrowing the space through which the infant's head may pass in its descent along the birth canal. These deformed pelves give rise to the nightmare of "dystocia," protracted, agonized labors, as in endless hours of bearing down the mother is simply unable to force the infant's head through the birth canal. Or the fetal head might not even engage in the pelvic inlet, so narrow are the bones. When this happens, her birth attendant has to either tug the fetus out with high forceps, or reach in and pull out manually the infant's feet. Or in extreme cases simply let the mother die undelivered.

Here is Guillaume Mauguest de la Motte, a small town doctor in late-seventeenth-century Normandy, encountering a typical contracted pelvis: "On 23 March, 1694, I was called to deliver a woman in the parish of Teil, two leagues from here (Vallognes), who had started in labor the previous day and whose waters had burst, the hand of the fetus protruding." We have here, in other words, an "arm presentation," in which the mother is unlikely to deliver the child spontaneously because its neck and shoulder are lodged against her pelvic inlet. "I introduced my hand in her vagina easily and pushed it up to the top part of her sacrum . . . which I found curved inward, leaving so little space between it and the pubic bone that I was obliged to try more than four times to get hold of the infant's feet." De la Motte was trying to perform an obstetrical operation known as "version," turning the infant feet first, to prepare it for delivery, the mother's pelvis being highly contracted. Finally however he succeeded in getting one foot between his two fingers and the other foot, lying close by, followed. He then pulled the child slowly from the womb. The mother survived, but the baby died a quarter of an hour later.[21]

It is thus clear that contracted pelves represented a serious problem for women: they increased the incidence of malpresentations in childbirth, which in turn increased the maternal mortality; a flat pelvis, or a pelvis with severe inlet or outlet contractions, would almost certainly cause labor to be protracted, stretching possibly over several days, further increasing the risk of death or infection; and a contracted pelvis might oblige the midwife or accoucheur to use instruments in the delivery, indeed to cut the fetus into pieces in order to extract it, thereby enhancing again the mother's risk. (Only about half of mothers with contracted pelves delivered spontaneously.)[22] Although the problem is, strictly speaking, obstetrical, the woman whose pelvis had grown badly in childhood would remain deformed all her life. A permanent organic lesion, these pelves distinguished women clearly from men in terms of risking medical misadventure.

What percentage of women before World War I had contracted pelves? Here we must renounce any pretense at precision because, even though a "pelvimeter" had been devised late in the eighteenth century, only in the 1850s did studies on how to classify pelvic abnormality begin to appear.[23] Before then, contractions were spotted only if they were grossly apparent to the naked eye, the mother's hips twisted and misshapen, or if they became evident as a result of obstructed labor. Even later on, measurements are difficult to compare because different obstetricians report different kinds of pelvic diameters.

I am going to advance the view that a sizeable minority of all women in those pre-1900 centuries suffered serious contractions, but it should first be observed that the distribution of pelvic deformities was highly uneven, both by class and by region. In some areas local doctors reported no pelvic bone problems at all, such as Berlin's H. Wollheim, writing in 1844. Only 1.6 percent of his clinic patients had contracted pelves, "and also in private practice, according to the experience of the busiest accoucheurs, obstetrical operations arising from pelvic deformities belong to the rarest of cases." Women in the Swiss valley of Lotschental had traditionally been free of pelvic problems, and in eighteenth-century Chambery local mothers were reported as having "large and well shaped pelves." The obstetricians at Avignon's lying-in hospital reported in 1905 that "pelvic contractions are unusual in the Midi, and seldom observed at the *Maternite* of the Vaucluse." And less than 2 percent of the women birthing at Munich's lying-in hospital, 1859 to 1879, were found to have deformed pelves.[24]

Such cases, however, are a minority. A far greater percentage of doctors report "pelvic bones squeezed together" and "difficult labors" as, if not the norm, at least the lot of many women. Table 13-1 compiles the pre-1920 reports in which systematic clinical data are available, indicating for a wide variety of cities and small towns pelvic contractions in 8 to 40 percent of all mothers. Rather than affecting an isolated group of women, pelvic deformity in the past struck perhaps one woman in four, a staggering incidence.

Although the biochemistry of rickets is still not entirely clarified, we do know that to grow properly, bones require calcium salts, and calcium is metabolized in the body through the aid of vitamin D. Of the possible sources of vitamin D, such as fish-liver oil, not least important is exposure of the skin to the sun's ultraviolet rays. Hence social historians have, for a long time, associated rickets mainly with the smoky industrial cities of Victorian England, where dirt particles in the air presumably filtered out much

Table 13-1
Percent of Parturient Mothers with Contracted Pelves, Pre-1920 Data

Author	Date	Number	Population	Place	Percent of mothers with contracted pelves
Wegelin[a]	1789	100	private practice	St. Gallen district	19
Michaelis[b]	1877	300	OB clinic	Munich	19
P. Muller[c]	1870s?	1177	OB clinic	Berne	40
Ahfeld[d]	1881-1882	275	OB-GYN clinic	Giessen	20
Flint[e]	1897	10,233	maternity hospital	New York	8.5
Crouzet[f]	1898	?	private practice	Lodeve	"on constate . . . hanches resserrees . . . uncorps rachitique"
Davis[g]	1900	1224	hospital	Philadelphia	32
Kipping[h]	1905-1908	2941	OB clinic	Freiburg	1st class (highest) 1
					4th class (lowest) 21
Thoms[i]	1909-1913	4000	university hospital	Baltimore	24 (white = 13) (black = 40)

Table 13-1 *(Continued)*

Author	Date	Number	Population	Place	Percent of mothers with contracted pelves
Williamson[j]	1918	1579	maternity hospital	New York	2.8

[a]Adrian Wegelin, "Bemerkungen uber den Geburtszustand in St. Gallischen Landen nebst aufrichtiger Darstellung des verschiednen Erfolgs bey hundert Geburten," *Johann Christian Starks Archiv fur die Geburtshulfe* 2 (1789):85.

[b]Cited in Rudolf Dohrn, *Geschichte der Geburtshulfe der Neuzeit*, vol. 2 (Tubingen: 1904) pp. 226.

[c]Cited in ibid., p. 227.

[d]F. Ahlfeld, *Berichte und Arbeiten aus der geburtshulflichgynaekologischen Klinik zu Giessen, 1881-1882* (Leipzig:1883), p. 10. Of the 54 contracted pelves, the two most common types were the "generally contracted" (27) and the rachitic (13).

[e]Cited in John T. Williams, "Normal Variations in Type of the Female Pelvis and Their Obstetrical Significance," *American Journal of Obstetrics and Gynecology* 3 (1922):345. The original study, which I have not seen, was published in the *Report of the Society of the Lying-In Hospital* (New York: 1897), p. 258.

[f]Jean-Auguste Crouzet, *Topographie medicale et statistique comparee de Lodeve (Herault)* (Montpellier: 1912), p. 117. The context suggests that contracted pelves are highly frequent, and further down the same page the author speaks of "accouchements laborieux . . . etroitesse du bassin." On p. 217: "Les jeunes filles ont les hanches un peu resserrees." Writtin in 1898.

[g]Edward P. Davis, "The Frequency and Mortality of Abnormal Pelves," *American Journal of Obstetrics* 41 (1900):12.

[h]Cited in Max Hirsch, "Frauenarbeit und Frauenkrankheiten," in Josef Halban and Ludwig Seitz (eds.), *Biologie und Pathologie des Weibes: Ein Handbuch der Frauenheilkunde und Geburtshilfe*, vol. 1 (Berlin: 1924), p. 937. "Arbeiterinncn" had a contracted-pelvis frequency of 22.9 percent, "Landwirtefrauen" of 34.3 percent.

[i]Herbert K. Thoms, "A Statistical Study of the Frequency of Funnel Pelves and the Description of a New Outlet Pelvimeter," *American Journal of Obstetrics* 72 (1915):123. J. Whitridge Williams, in a subsequent review of the same data, found the incidence of pelvic contractions among white women for 1896-1910 to be 14.9 percent, for black women, 39.5 percent. "A Statistical Study of the Incidence and Treatment of Labor Complicated by Contracted Pelvis in the Obstetrics Service of the Johns Hopkins Hospital, from 1896 to 1924," *American Journal of Obstetrics and Gynecology* 11 (1926):736.

[j]Cited in Williams, "Normal Variations in Female Pelvis," p. 346. The author included only cases in which the sideways (transverse) diameter of the pelvic outlet was 8 centimeters or less, a relatively rigorous criterion.

ultraviolet radiation, and where children got out relatively little to play in parks and such (hitched, as they were, to pullcarts in the mines).

But that view is incomplete. Rickets abounded in parts of Europe hundreds of miles from the nearest smoking chimney. Here, for example, is Doctor Olivet, reporting in 1819 on the town of Montereau (Seine-et-Marne): "Children become liable at the age of 8, 10, 14, 16 or 20 years to rachitic deviations of the spine, to the turning inward of the sternum, two circumstances which give rise to a number of hunchbacks quite considerable for a town as small as Montereau. This bone disease, when it arrives late, strikes almost exclusively young women . . . who experience difficult menstruation, deforming their shape. Nature will suffice to cure them, provided they endure their fate with corsets . . . " But it was most unlikely that nature "cured" the pelves of many, which doubtless had been misshapen from birth. (Some people do, however, recover from childhood rickets.) How else are we to interpret the information that among infants in Montereau rickets were "almost universal," that at the age of twelve months many children had as yet made no effort to walk, and that others still experienced difficulty at twenty-four months. Their dentition was "irregular." Their "pelvic bones appear greatly emaciated, and the skin of their thighs forms folds that are disagreeable to the eye."[25]

These accounts could be multiplied by the dozens for other parts of Europe, for staid administrative cities like Konigsberg where "very many" young girls were considered "deformed," for schoolchildren in Victoria (Australia), of whom in 1910 to 1915, 20 to 30 percent were estimated to suffer from rickets. The proportion of rachitic infants toward the end of the nineteenth century in Europe's big cities ranged form 8 percent in Basel to 28 percent in London, to 31 percent in Prague.[26]

Unlike leukorrhea or uterine prolapse, rickets leaves telltale skeletal remains, which permit us to plot a rough history of the disease. The late Calvin Wells, a paleopathologist, commented on the "very low incidence" of rickets in prehistoric and early historic times, seeing then a slow increase through the Middle Ages and a dramatic explosion in England during the period of the industrial revolution. "A major factor in this was that owing to the gravitation of women to the factories, few infants were breast-fed."[27] In view of the substantial implantation of rickets during the nineteenth century in decidedly unindustrial rural and artisanal areas, I am disinclined to share Wells' emphasis on the "industrial era." Yet to go by a Swedish time series, the disease does seem to peak in the mid-nineteenth century, in Hamburg evidently several decades earlier.[28]

I should like to be able to argue that the difference in rickets between males and females supports the proposition that women have been historically less well nourished than men, a proposition for which there exists, I think, independent evidence.[29] Unfortunately, the data on bone diseases do not unambiguously support this hypothesis. Paleopathological studies of several early populations have shown the kinds of bone defects normally associated with malnutrition to be higher in female skeletons than male.[30] In late nineteenth-century Europe, however, boys suffered from rickets more often than girls, which suggests that at least female children, (whatever the nutritional lot of adult women might have been), were not systematically underfed.[31] Unlike men, however, women paid the price of their rickets in childbirth.

Leukorrhea

Leukorrhea means simply some kind of whitish or puslike vaginal discharge, and is not, in contrast to what eighteenth- and nineteenth-century doctors thought, a disease in itself. The wide range of illnesses that give rise to these discharges may be divided into two categories, vaginal infections and infections elsewhere in the pelvis, which drain through the vagina. Consider, for example, the multitude of microorganisms in the vagina itself which can cause leukorrhea:

1. Trichomonads, tiny flagellate protozoa that cause a yellow-greenish or purulent discharge, constant itching, painful urination, general pelvic pain, and a fetid odor.

2. Candida albicans, a yeastlike organism that produces a thick, caseous, yellow-white discharge that resembles cream cheese. The disease is called "moniliasis," and is experienced as a sharp burning sensation, together with itching and pain in intercourse. Infants born to women with candida infections often developed a similar fungal growth in their mouths called "thrush," and, in the eighteenth century, died of it in massive numbers.[32]

3. Hemophilus vaginalis, and a host of other bacteria called staphylocci and stretococci, that infect the vagina, causing itching and burning, pain on pressure, and unpleasant exudates: white in the case of hemophilus vaginalis, sticky and purulent for "staph" infections.

Those are just the chief pathogens that can produce "vaginitis," the market-basket term for all the pelvic itching we have been discussing. Infections elsewhere in the pelvis can produce another long series of leukorrheas, but since the doctors of the time were incapable of diagnosing any of them on the basis of the agent involved, little point is served in detailing all the things that can go wrong with the cervix and the uterus, or in describing the pockets of pus that accumulate alongside the ligaments in the pelvis. For the time being we just note that many different infections, not the least of which is gonorrhea, produce the cervicitis and endometritis that eighteenth-century doctors, with their unsterilized probes and primitive speculusm, lumped together as the single disease "leukorrhea." (They did, however, distinguish gonorrheal infections from other varities).

I wish to make two larger points about vaginal infection. The first is that the existence of leukorrhea may point to some more fundamental organic disease of interest to us. And even though their doctors often dismissed their complaints as "hysterical," and thus automatically the lot of women, the women themselves who had leukorrhea seemed to have known that something graver was wrong. In the folklore of Finland around 1914, for example, it was said that leukorrhea was "a serious sickness, a defect which weakens the woman generally, finally rendering her infertile."[33]

The second point is that leukorrhea was enormously widespread. Today perhaps one of every four gynecology patients has some kind of leukorrhea, which is quickly treated and cured.[34] Estimates for pre-1900 Europe appear considerably higher. Consider, for example, Berlin at the end of the eighteenth century: "The female sex here suffers commonly from a disease which more than any other has recently increased among the general population. There are, among all classes, only a few women entirely exempt from this condition. . . . The consequences of leukorrhea are by no means insignificant . . . in that the patients look pale and sickly, are plagued by attacks of hysteria, and are usually infertile."[35] Before we dismiss this as the exaggeration of a society gynecologist describing a clientele of languishing bankers' wives, let's listen to Dr. Zengerle, investigating fifty years later the cottage-industrial workers around Wangen in Wurttemberg: "One of the most frequent diseases among our female population is the so-called 'white-flowers' [leukorrhea], and there are perhaps few regions in our fatherland where one encounters so many female individuals suffering from this malady, young girls as well as married women. . . . The cause of the high incidence of this disease [is] the lifestyle of constant sitting, and the accompanying enormous consumption of food. For the female part of our population is, from October until April, almost continually occupied with spinning, sewing or knitting from early morning until late evening, in overheated living quarters. . . ."[36]

I am unable to put my finger on a single doctor who, in commenting on women's diseases, does not mention how common leukorrhea is: Schubler and Cless in Stuttgart called it "very widespread"; Schneider in Ettlingen remarks on its "stubbornness" and how it often makes women infertile; Rouger in Vigan, Gard department, considers it "highly frequent at all ages and among all classes"; Metzger in Konigsberg, Klinge in the mining districts of the Oberharz, Herz in Prenzlau, Crouzet in Lodeve, all comment on its typicality.[37] Dr. Ely van de Warker, who in 1877 did a gynecological survey of about a quarter of the women in the Oneida Community (before he was stopped by John Humphrey Noyes), reported that 42 percent of the women had more than "small" amounts of leukorrhea.[38]

Some of these cases are clearly consequences of infected abortions, others of gonorrhea, others of "trich" infections, which husbands had picked up from prostitutes and transmitted to their wives. We learn, in short, little about the history of disease from studying leukorrhea, for these discharges represented so many different diseases. But for the women afflicted with them, the pruritis and vaginitis, the malodor, and the embarrassment they may have felt from their husbands, doubtless made these infections a major moment in their intimate lives, a moment for which there is no real male equivalent.

Perineal Tears and Fistulas

In poorly managed deliveries the mother's birth canal and perineum are often torn, and although this type of injury would normally belong in a discussion of obstetrics, the scars and lesions of these tears may remain with the woman all her life, an enduring reminder of the potential consequences of sexuality. I have therefore decided to include them among the maladies that may affect women's attitudes to men and to their own bodies.

Our sources speak of two kinds of childbirth lesions in particular: tears of the birth canal, including ruptured uteruses, torn cervixes, and lesions in the septum between vagina and bladder (vesico-vaginal fistulas) or between vagina and rectum (recto-vaginal fistulas), to scarred-over vulvas; and ruptures of the perineum, which is the skin extending from the base of the vagina to the anus. Tiny perineal tears are quite common in childbirth even today, and to make their repair easier, accoucheurs often perform routinely "episiotomies," which means cutting a small incision into the perineum with a pair of scissors, to facilitate the passage of the fetal head, then stitching it up again afterwards. Major perineal tears are another problem, however.

Because most births, in the years before 1900, were managed by midwives, who intervened rarely with foreceps to accelerate an obstructed labor (or who, when they intervened, would wreak considerable damage), the incidence of lesions in childbirth seems to have been fairly high. This is a sensitive subject, the competence of midwives and "grannies."[39] And while the midwives of traditional Europe do indeed seem to have been competent to handle normal deliveries (having a stillbirth rate of 5 percent, perhaps, and a maternal mortality of 1 percent), they were usually at a loss to manage birth complications, especially dystocias, when the fetus ceases to advance along the birth canal, its head lodged in the vagina perhaps, or pounding repeatedly against the pelvic floor, or stuck in some malposition in the pelvic outlet.[40] An obstructed labor of this nature can result in ruptures and tears in several ways:

1. The accoucheur (or midwife) reaches into the uterus to perform version, grabbing the infant's feet and pulling it out. A clumsy version can easily rupture the mother's uterus or her incompletely dilated cervix.[41]

2. The midwife attempts manually to dilate the vagina (doctors, whatever their flaws, had enough training at least to realize the vagina was undilatable) and bruises and tears the whole vulvar area. De la Motte, for example, tells of a woman he went to deliver in 1698 who had been "all torn up" (*toute dechiree*) at the hands of an incompetent midwife. Three months later he was again summoned because the woman's vagina had sealed together completely as a result of the scars. "I found a woman in terrible

convulsions, complaining in the intervals that these convulsions caused her intolerable pain in her private parts and in her whole abdomen.'' De la Motte opened her up again with a lance, a huge quantity of ''thick, black blood'' flowed out, and she became well again, going on to bear another child.[42]

3. As the fetal head lodges in the vagina, the cells on the membranous wall dividing the vagina from the bladder start to die and slough off, finally opening up a hole, called a ''fistula.'' Although holes between vagina and rectum may be opened too, leaving women with vaginas ''full of feces,'' the most common variety by far is the bladder-vagina lesion.[43] Here is a German doctor's description of fistulous women, around 1836: ''A sadder situation can hardly exist than that of a woman afflicted with a vesicovaginal fistula. A source of disgust, even to herself, the woman beloved by her husband becomes, in this condition, the object of bodily revulsion to him; and filled with repugnance, everyone else likewise turns his back, repulsed by the intolerable, foul, uriniferous odor.'' The basic problem with this sort of fistula, it must be explained, is that the urine trickles uncontrollably from the vagina, rather than from the urethra.

> The labia, perineum, lower part of the buttocks, and inner aspect of the thighs and calves are continually wet, to the very feet. The skin assumes a fiery red color and is covered in places with a pustular eruption. Intolerable burning and itching torment the patients, who are driven to frequent scratching to the point of bleeding, as a result of which their suffering increases still more. . . . The refreshment of a change of clothing provides no relief, because the clean undergarment, after being quickly saturated, slaps against the patients, flopping against their wet thighs as they walk, sloshing in their wet shoes as though they were wading through a swamp. The bed . . . is quickly impregnated with urine and gives off the most unbearable stench. Even the richest are usually condemned for life to a straw sack, whose straw must be renewed daily. One's breath is taken away by the bedroom air of these women, and wherever they go they pollute the atmosphere.[44]

How common were such fistulas? A cure had already been developed for them, and obstetrics in general enormously improved, by the time we get systematic statistics. Only two vesico-vaginal fistulas were reported to the Medical Society of the Middlesex East District of Massachusetts, for example, among 2,666 childbirth cases between 1855 and 1882. But those were all physician-assisted deliveries.[45] Another study during the 1890s at the Vanderbilt Clinic in New York found only one vesico-vaginal fistula among 398 gynecology patients (and one recto-vaginal fistula too). The author speculated that ''the early use of the forceps probably accounts for the rarity of this accident at the present time.''[46] Other North American doctors argued late in the nineteenth century that vaginal fistulas were becoming uncommon.[47] And a 1920's survey of women in New York City seeking birth control advice found vaginal fistulas in only 1.5 percent of the 8,300 clients examined.[48]

But in traditional Europe, at least, fistulas seem to have been quite common. Although a statistical estimate is impossible, in 1860, the Finistere's Dr. Caradec included fistulas in a list of accidents of delivery that he considered "frequent." The British obstetrician Fleetwood Churchill, writing earlier on, declared them "not very rare." And the seventeenth-century Parisian accoucheur Paul Portal included fistulas among the horrors that happened easily if too much force were used in the delivery.[49]

What these fistulas represented for the lives of common women can scarcely be imagined today. Women were reduced to desperate extremities to avoid them, subjecting themselves to incredibly painful operations (likely to be unsuccessful at best, fatal at worst) for their repair. One Austrian woman, for example, whose fistula had been operatively closed underwent caesarean section rather than risking another, at a time when the mortality from caesarean sections was around 25 percent.[50]

4. The cleaving open of the perineum from vagina to anus was a possible consequence of bearing an infant with a large head. In contrast to fistulas, these perineal ruptures were highly frequent. Philadelphia's Barton Hirst, writing in 1917, speculated that "of the 2,500,000 women delivered in the United States annually, a million or more or less are added every year to the ranks of the comparatively unfit from this preventable cause."[51] He includes the genital canal as well as the pelvic floor in this estimate.

These injuries often happened because the fetal head was permitted to pop out too quickly; and their consequences endured because the birth attendant failed to stitch the mother back up. Both are signs of incompetent obstetrics, and both happened often among the women of the popular classes. As Thomas Madden wrote in the 1870s of Dublin:

> The after-effects of lacerations of the perinaeum are even more distressing with patients of the working class than is the case with women of a higher social condition. . . . Increased experience of the intimate domestic habits of the wretched denizens of the crowded tenements of the lanes and back streets of the capital of the poorest country in Europe has confirmed the observation—the wives of our artisans and labouring men undergo far more hardship and privation, and at the same time perform as much labor as their husbands. The whole of the domestic duties of women of this class, such as washing, cooking, carrying children, etc., all act as powerful predisposing causes of prolapse of the womb; and, therefore, when the support that should be afforded by the perinaeum is taken away by the accident we are now considering . . . the tendency to prolapse [is] increased. . . .[52]

We shall consider uterine prolapse in more detail in a moment. The points I wish to make here are that (1) perineal tears were quite common, and (2) their long-term effects on the lives of women could be devastating.

In 1671, for example, a woman who had given birth nine years earlier, came to see the Parisian accoucheur Francois Mauriceau. Evidently as a result of the large size of her infant's head, she seems to have suffered a third-degree perineal tear, which would mean that her anal sphincter muscle had torn in two, leaving her unable to control defecation. Mauriceau describes this as a "simple deformity" which gave her "une extreme chagrin." But by the time she saw him the rupture had formed a rigid scar, and could not be reopened and repaired properly without "une incision tres-douloureuse." So she went away resigned. But, just imagine, for nine years she had endured this torment in silence.[53]

Uterine-Ovarian Disorders

Given the medical ignorance of the doctors, the embarrassment of the women afflicted, and the primitive means of diagnosis available, we can say little about the epidemiology of uterine and ovarian disorders. A minimal solution is simply to review the most common complaints that women would mention to the doctors.

First, there were anomalies of menstruation. If we may take Marie Kopp's survey of New York women seeking birth control advice in the 1920s as a "modern" baseline, around one fifth of all older married women complain of "irregular menstruation."[54] Whether that is intracycle bleeding, which would be extremely useful in diagnosing tumors or cancer, heavy periods, or just lack of regularity in their arrival is unclear.

We may infer from earlier doctors' qualitative accounts that considerably more than a fifth of their patients complained of menstrual irregularity. Berlin's Dr. Wollheim wrote in 1844 that "disorders of menstruation are extremely common; the suppression or delay (of the menses) happens more often than does an excessive flow." Doctor Lavergne of Lamballe indicated in 1787 that "nothing was more common than irregular menses and amenorrhea (a missed period). This latter accident afflicts above all the women of the lower classes, who are exposed to it by their work." Similar remarks could be quoted from late-eighteenth- and nineteenth-century medical topographies for the mining communities of Klausthal and the Oberharz, Stuttgart, Wurzburg, Hamburg, and Hanau.[55] Whether in all these cases more than a fifth of all married women had such complaints is impossible to say. We know only that these problems appear often in the patients' minds, and in the doctors'.

Painful menstruation, another harbinger of some graver problem, appears often in these accounts. Only 6 percent of all older married women suffered it in the 1920s birth control survey.[56] For the cottage workers of early-nineteenth-century Wangen it was "quite frequent"; de la Motte reports "some" young unmarried women suffering the kind of pain and vomiting in menstruation that a mother endures in labor.[57] And so on. Nothing systematic can be made of such testimony, but we are alerted that dysmenorrhea is, at least, not a "disease of civilization."

And what of the whole complex pathology of tumors and growths in the ovaries and uterus? The world of pain that contemporary gynecology texts take hundreds of pages just to classify? Here we descend into the truly unknown. The Kopp survey put noncancerous uterine tumors at 4.2 percent of the 8,300 women examined; the birth-control doctors didn't classify ovarian tumors separately, probably because they're so difficult to palpate in a routine bimanual examination.[58] Other gynecologists, writing around the turn of the century, found 12 to 14 percent of their patients to have fibroid tumors (the most common variety of uterine growths).[59]

Fehling comments that before 1800 the medical literature contains almost no reference to ovarian cysts as a pregnancy complication and speculates that during the nineteenth century they may have become more common. And Lubben's study of morbidity early in the nineteenth century in Germany's impoverished Rhon district found uterine disorders, most of which were (presumably) tumors, "exceptionally frequent."[60] Aside from these wisps of smoke, the medical literature I have seen reports only isolated case studies of ghastly ovarian cysts that swelled up to 40 pounds and the like. We are left puzzling to what extent this pelvic pathology represented a debilitating irritant in the lives of normal women.

Given the large number of births to older married women, the gruelling regimen of work to which they were subjected, and the custom of not sparing oneself at all during pregnancy, we would expect a high incidence of uterine prolapse, which in fact happened. Prolapse occurs through the weakening of the cardinal ligaments, which hold the uterus in place within the abdomen, or through the weakening of the muscles on the pelvic floor, which gives support from below. The result is that the uterus begins to slide down the vagina, in extreme cases (called "procidentia") making the woman look as though she had an elephant's trunk hanging down between her legs. The condition represents both a serious medical problem, involving leakage of urine or infection of the ulcerated cervix and collapsed vaginal walls, and a striking dilemma in the psychodrama of sexual relations. What must a woman with a badly prolapsed uterus feel about sexual relations with her husband or imagine that he feels about her?

The 1920s Kopp survey of New York women found 8.6 percent of them to have prolapsed uteruses.[61] Although the repair of prolapse had become, by that time, a simple procedure in gynecological surgery, we might assume that most of the poorish, immigrant women on whom these birth control clinics drew put this kind of surgery low on their list of priorities. So the one-in-ten figure for prolapse approximates roughly the "traditional" level.

So common was prolapse among the working-class women in Manchester that the first major procedure for its repair, developed in the 1890s by two local gynecologists named Archibald Donald and William Fothergill, was called the "Manchester Operation."[62] Indeed, prolapse might result in part from the demands of factory life where women could pass their pregnancies standing interminably in front of their machinery. Elsewhere uterine prolapse was associated with roughly managed deliveries, incompetent midwives, and the ensuing weakening of the pelvic floor (as, for example, through major perineal tears).[63] Prolapse has, par excellence, been one of those constants in women's lives that reminded them how much more vulnerable they were than men to the blank face of fate.

Antibiotics have made us forget today about that vast armada of pathogens that invaded uterus and adnexa to produce infections, the mildest of which merely created a sensation of "heaviness," the most severe of which—as in "puerperal fever"—might often end in the woman's death. They were a daily affliction for lower-class women, as Max Hirsch testified in his survey of the occupational diseases of factory women early in the twentieth century: "The uterus becomes swollen, painful on pressure; the patients claim about congestion in the lower abdomen and about pains up and down the back . . . All these conditions, from simple endometritis (an infection of the lining of the uterus), to chronic metritis, retroflexio and parametritis (pockets of pus accumulating in the uterine ligaments) are to be found among female workers who spend long hours sitting with their upper bodies bent over or who just stand for long periods. . . ."[64]

Rather than assailing the reader with further quotations about uterine and adnexal infections, I shall make just one brief point: many of the infections from which these women suffered were undiagnosable by the medicine of the time and instead dismissed as "neurotic symptoms." Chronic pelvic infection produces no external signs, such as leukorrhea; nor are its victims likely to have a high temperature or high sedimentation rates (tests of infection available to late-nineteenth-century medicine). Yet movement, intercourse, and defecation are all likely to be painful for them. They will feel enervated and inclined (if possible) to take to their beds for rest. They will in short, exhibit all the symptoms that nineteenth-century women's doctors were inclined to write off as "neurosis" or "hysteria," which some twentieth-century historians have accepted as evidence of doctors convincing women they were invalids to better dominate them.[65] If in fact these middle-class valetudinarians really were suffering from "endometriosis" (the spread of endometrial tissue outside the lining of the uterus to attack other pelvic organs, first diagnosed in 1922) or from pelvic inflammatory disease, it would behoove us as historians to be more sympathetic to the doctors, who were guilty mainly of a sort of condescending incompetence, and to their patients, who knew that they themselves were experiencing genuine pain, and that they were not "overanxious," although no one would believe them.

Conclusion

Much speculation has recently been devoted to the evident sexual uninterest of married women in their husband during times past. The scholarly journals have bulged with tales of nineteenth-century women "who aren't supposed to feel sexual desire," or who were counseled "surtout ne bougez pas" during intercourse. Three explanations have been offered for this:

1. That a chauvinistic male society systematically repressed women's sexuality, persuading them that the world of eros was soiled and disgusting, and that female purity could only be maintained through failure to lubricate.[66]

2. That men were normally so brutal and clumsy in intercourse that women's best interest would be preserved in avoiding the entire business entirely and retreating instead to the company of one's sisters.[67]

3. That women felt uneasy about sex because of the grim physical consequences that pregnancy, birth, and abortion could have for their bodies and their lives in general.[68]

The purpose of this chapter is to reinforce the third interpretation, by stressing that not only were women vulnerable to men through the sex act and the impregnation likely to ensue, but they were also vulnerable to men at many somatic levels: in being subjected to nutritional disorders that men did not experience; in having a whole range of genital equipment liable to fall into disrepair in a way that did not happen to men; and in being liable to various pelvic exudates and prolapses that would make them feel uneasy about their naked bodies in intimate contact with men. I argue that among the historical consequences of this vulnerability were a female preference for abstinence as a means of birth control, for the company of other women as opposed to "family togetherness," and for an intense religiosity, which maintained that if God had imposed such burdens on womankind, it could only be because He was testing them.

Notes

1. See U.S. Department of Health, Education, and Welfare, *Acute Conditions: Incidence and Associated Disability, United States, July 1975-June 1976* (Vital and Health Statistics: series 10; Data from the National Health Survey, no. 120; US-DHEW publication no. /PHS/ 78-1548,

National Center for Health Statistics, Hyattsville, Md., January 1978), p. 10. See also U.S. Department of Health, Education and Welfare, *Prevalence of Chronic Conditions of the Genitourinary, Nervous, Endocrine . . . Systems and Other Selected Chronic Conditions, United States, 1973* (Vital and Health Statistics: series 10: Data from the National Health Survey, no. 109; US-DHEW publication HRA 77-1536), pp. 44-45.

2. Hermann Fehling, *Entwicklung der Geburtshilfe und Gynakologie im 19 Jahrhundert* (Berlin: 1925), p. 233. "Wurgengel der Frauenwelt."

3. See, for example, A.H. Crisp et al., "How Common Is Anorexia Nervosa? A Prevalence Study," *British Journal of Psychiatry* 128 (1976):549-554. Calvin Wells argued, however, in a letter to me, "I think there is substantial evidence of anorexia nervosa in earlier case histories, though it may not have been common."

4. Phil. Jos. Horsch, *Versuch einer Topographie der Stadt Wurzburg in Bexiehung auf den allgemeinen Gesundheitszustand* (Arnstadt: 1805), p. 185.

5. See the review of research by J.R.W. Christie Brown and M.E. Christie Brown, "Psychiatric Disorders Associated with the Menopause," in *The Menopause: A Guide to Current Research and Practice*, ed. R.J. Beard (Baltimore: University Park Press, 1976), pp. 57-80.

6. See *Travaux proposes aux Medicins et physicians regnicoles et etrangers, par la Societe Royale de Medicine . . . 1778;* chap. 1 is entitled "Sur la Description Topographique et Medicale de la France," p. 1.

7. Alfons Fischer, *Geschichte des deutschen Gesundheitswesens*, vol. 2 (Berlin: 1933), pp. 37-38, 113-120. Fischer claims that the idea originated in Germany and seems unaware of the entire French contribution. Arthur Imhof has recently begun an extensive analysis of the German topographies. See pp. 50-62 of the introduction to the volume he edited, *Biologie des Menschen in der Geschichte: Beitrage zur Sozialgeschichte der Neuzeit aus Frankeriech und Skandinavien* (Stuttgart-Bad Cannstatt: Friedrich Fromann Verlag, 1978).

8. See G.J. Barker-Benfield, *The Horrors of the Half-Known Life: Male Attitudes toward Women and Sexuality in Nineteenth-Century America* (Champaign-Urbana, Ill.: University of Illinois Press, 1974); Stephen Kern, *Anatomy and Destiny: A Cultural History of the Human Body* (Indianapolis, Ind.: Bobbs-Merrill, 1975).

9. Franz Xaver Mexler, *Versuch einer medizinischen Topographie der Stadt Sigmaringen* (Freiburg: 1822), pp. 155-156.

10. For a historical overview see W.M. Fowler, "Chlorosis: An Obituary," *Annals of Medical History* 8 (1936):168-177. For more recent literature, see Karl Figlio's excellent article, "Chlorosis and Chronic Disease in Nineteenth-Century Britain: The Social Constitution of Somatic Illness in Capitalist Society," *Social History* 3 (1978):167-197, and Robert P. Hudson, "The Biography of Disease: Lessons from Chlorosis," *Bulletin*

of the History of Medicine 51 (1977):448-463, who argues that "iron played only a small role in the disappearance of the disease" (p. 459).

11. Among many accounts, here is D. Pfieninger, writing in 1834: "For the female gender anemia and interruptions in menstruation which stand in a reciprocal relationship with hysteria are very common in Stuttgart. The widespread belief that hysteria is to be found more among the upper than the lower classes appears to be without foundation." *Beschriebung von Stuttgart hauptsachlich nach seinen naturwissenschaftlichen und medicineischen Verhaltnissen* (Stuttgart: 1834), p. 116.

12. "Chronic Anemia and Wasting in Newly Married Women: Some of the Causes of their Persistence and Incurability," *American Journal of Obstetrics* 21 (1888):113.

13. Max Hirsch, "Frauenarbiet und Frauenkrankheiten," in Josef Halban and Ludwig Seitz (eds.), *Biologie und Pathologie des Weibes: Ein Handbuch der Frauenheilkunde und Geburtshilfe*, vol. 1 (Berlin: 1924), p. 940.

14. "Nous noterons ici le nombre tres-restreint de femmes qui ont nourri leurs enfants, soit par faiblesse, soit per necessite de travailler; il est inutile de parler de la faible constitution de ces malheureuses meres de famille, la population de la Croix-Rousse est assez connue par sa mauvaise conformation et le grand nombre de ses phthisiques." F. Guyenot and Ch. Pujo, *Etude clinique sur les suites de couches: Compte-rendu de la maternite de l'hopital de la Croix-Rousse durant l'hiver 1867-68* (Lyon: 1869), p. 76.

15. 800 megagrams figure from Louis Hellman and Jack A. Pritchard, *Williams Obstetrics*, 14th ed. (New York: Appleton-Century-Crofts, 1971), pp. 763-764.

16. Fowler, "Chlorosis," p. 172.

17. Jack C. Drummond and Anne Wilbraham have estimated that the diet of better-off people in seventeenth-century England would have provided perhaps 6 to 12 megagrams in available iron a day, depending on the proportion of bread in the diet. Men in twentieth-century English middle-class families have access to virtually the identical amount of available iron (11 mg.), women 8 mg. *The Englishman's Food: A History of Five Centuries of English Diet* (London: Cape, 1939), p. 156.

18. J.W. Consbruch, for example, wrote of the county of Ravensberg, "Worms and their traces are very frequently found among the rustics, a consequence of the numerous flour-based dishes they consume. In some regions . . . a strikingly large number of tapeworms are to be noted." *Medicinische Ephemeriden, nebst einer medicineischen Topographie der Grafschaft Ravensberg* (Chemnitz: 1793), pp. 57-58.

19. The average number of live births in family reconstitution studies of French and German villages ranges from about five to eight. If we add on an additional 30 percent to represent pregnancy wastage and stillbirths, we get six to twelve as the average number of pregnancies of a typical married woman who survives to the menopause.

20. For the story see recently (Dame) Harriette Chick, "Study of Rickets in Vienna, 1919-1922," *Medical History* 20 (1976):41-51.

21. *Traite complet des acouchemens*, rev. ed. (Leiden: 1729), p. 344.

22. For various clinical reports see Carl von Hecker, *Beobachtungen und Untersuchungen aus der Gebaranstalt zu Munchen, 1859-1879* (Munich: 1881), pp. 84-129; Franz Torggler, *Bericht uber die Thatigkeit der geburtshilfichgynakologischen Klinik zu Innsbruck, 1881-1887* (Prague: 1888), pp. 84-96; Ernst Kummer, "Die Prognose der Geburt bei engem Becken," *Zeitschrift fur Geburtshulfe und Gynakologie* 12 (1886):418-429.

23. The classic treatise is Gustav Adolf Michaelis's, *Das enge Becken nach eigenen Beobachtungen und Untersuchungen* (Leipzig: 1851).

24. H. Wollheim, *Versuch einer medicinischen Topographie und Statistik von Berlin* (Berlin: 1844), p. 69; Carl Muller, *Volksmedizinisch-geburtshilfliche Aufzeichnungen aus dem Lotschental* (Stuttgart: Hans Huber, 1969), p. 136; Joseph Daquin, *Topographie medicale de la ville de Chambery* (Chambery: 1787), p. 79; Emile Estachy, *La Maternite de Vaucluse: Historique, statistiques* (Montpellier: 1905), p. 37; Hecker, *Gebaranstalt zu Munchen*, p. 10.

25. Ms. in Paris Academie de medecine, Societe de l'ecole de medecine de Paris, memoires OP, received 25 February 1819.

26. Joh. Dan. Metzger, "Medicinische Topographie von Konigsberg," *Archiv der parktischen Arzneykinst* 2 (1786):299; Milton James Lewis, ' "Populate or Perish': Aspects of Infant and Maternal Health in Sydney, 1870-1939" (Australia National University, diss., 1976), p. 37; August Hirsch, *Handbuch der historisch-geographischen Pathologie, vol. 3: Die Organkrankheiten*, 2d ed. (Stuttgart: 1886), p. 516.

27. "Prehistoric and Historical Changes in Nutritional Diseases and Associated Conditions," *Progress in Food and Nutrition Sciences* 1 (1975):753-754.

28. Jonas Frykman, *Horan i bondesamhallet* (Lund: Hum. diss., 1977), p. 77, graph of "Horeskaver. Meddelare med angivna fodelsear, 1824-1890"; Johann Jakob Rambach, *Versuch einer physisch-medizinischen Beschreibung von Hamburg* (Hamburg: 1801), pp. 175-176.

29. For detailed evidence that women in, for example, Norway and Iceland were not only thought to need less but actually got less food at table before World War I, see Lily Weiser-Aall, "Die Speise des Neugeborenen," in Edith Ennen and Gunter Wiegelmann (eds.), *Festschrift Matthias Zender: Studien zu Volkskultur, Sprache und Landesgeschichte*, vol. 1 (Bonn: Rohrscheid, 1972), pp. 543-544.

30. See Calvin Wells, "Ancient Obstetric Hazards and Female Mortality," *Bulletin of the New York Academy of Medicine* 51 (1975):1235-1249. Wells concludes that "the pattern of illness in these children reflects the difference between relatively well-fed boys—the up-and-coming warriors and

patriarchs—and the marginally fed or frankly undernourished girls—the future drudges and mothers" (p. 1248).

31. See the statistics in Friedrich Prinzing, *Handbuch der medizinischen Statistik*, 2d ed. (Jena: 1931), pp. 212-215.

32. In the manuscripts of the "Vicq d'Azyr" collection in the Paris Academie de Medecine there are, for example, numerous reports from local doctors writing late in the eighteenth century that "le muguet," the French word for "thrush" (Monilia, candida albicans) was exacting a heavy mortality toll among the neonates of their locality. See especially the cartons SRM 175-185.

33. E. Pelkonen, *Uber volkstumliche Geburtshilfe in Finnland* (Helsinki: 1931), p. 30.

34. "One in four," see Robert W. Kistner, *Gynecology: Principles and Practice*, 2d ed. (Chicago: Year Book Medical Publishers, 1971), p. 79.

35. Ludwig Formey, *Versuch einer medicinischen Topographie von Berlin* (Berlin: 1796), p. 196.

36. (Dr.) Zengerle, "Auszug aus einer . . . statistisch-medicinischen Topographie des Oberamtsbezirks Wangen (Schluss)," *Medicinisches Correspondenz-Blatt des wurtembergischen arztlichen Vereins* 18 (1848):255.

37. G. Cless and G. Schuber, *Versuch einer medizinischen Topographie . . . Stuttgart* (Stuttgart: 1815), p. 76; P.J. Schneider, *Versuch einer medizinisch statistischen Topographie von Ettlingen* (Karlsruhe: 1818), p. 339; Francois-Alexandre Rouger, *Topographie statistique et medicale de la ville et canton du Vigan* (Montpellier: 1819), pp. 99-100; Metzger, "Konigsberg," p. 305; Johann Heinrich Wilhelm Klinge, *Fragmente aus dem Tagebuch eines Arztes auf dem Oberharz* (Stendal: 1812), p. 34; Simon Herz, *Versuch einer medicinischen Ortbeschreibung . . . Prenzlau* (Berlin: 1790), p. 83; Jean-August Crouzet, *Topographie medicale et statistique comparee de Lodeve* (Montepellier: 1912), pp. 128, 217, written 1898.

38. "A Gynecological Study of the Oneida Community," *American Journal of Obstetrics* 17 (1884):785-810, leukorrhea data on p. 804.

39. There is a fiercely partisan feminist literature designed to redeem the midwives from the reproaches of male doctors. See recently, for example, Jean Donnison, *Midwives and Medical Men: A History of Inter-Professional Rivalries and Women's Rights* (New York: Schocken, 1977); Ann Oakley, "Wise-woman and Medicine Man: Changes in the Management of Childbirth," in *The Rights and Wrongs of Women*, ed. Juliet Mitchell and Ann Oakley (Harmondsworth: Penguin, 1976), pp. 17-58; and for a flagrant example, Suzanne Arms, *Immaculate Deception: A New Look at Women and Childbirth in America* (Boston: Houghton-Mifflin, 1975), chap. 1.

40. While stillbirth statistics are readily available, maternal mortality in home deliveries is much harder to determine for pre-1900 Europe. My own

investigations, however, show the normal range to have fluctuated between perhaps 0.5 and 3.0 percent of all births. In a group of Baden counties around 1800, to take one example, maternal mortality was perhaps 1 percent of all births. Karlsruhe, Generallandesarchiv, 74/9071.

41. Among many horror stories, see for example that in De la Motte, *Traite complet des acouchemens*, p. 275.

42. Ibid., pp. 508-510.

43. See, for example, J. DeLee, "Six Cases of Caesarean Section," *American Journal of Obstetrics* 51 (1905):738.

44. J.F. Dieffenbach, quoted by Harold Speert, *Essays in Eponymy: Obstetric and Gynecologic Milestones* (New York: Macmillan, 1958), pp. 442-443.

45. "A Summary of Obstetric Cases Reported by Members of the Middlesex East District Medical Society, and Compiled by Dr. Samuel W. Abbott," *Boston Medical and Surgical Journal* 57 (1882-1883):5.

46. William S. Stone, "A Review of Five Years' Experience with Pelvic Diseases at the Vanderbilt Clinic (cont'd)," *American Journal of Obstetrics* 41 (1900):803, 805.

47. See Thomas Addis Emmet, "The Necessity for Early Delivery, as Demonstrated by the Analysis of 161 Cases of Vesico-Vaginal Fistula," *American Gynecological Society, Transactions* 3 (1878):124, 126. This kind of evidence, unhappily, provided an overly vigorous push for the kind of "meddlesome midwifery" that was endemic among American obstetricians in the first half of the twentieth century.

48. Marie E. Kopp, *Birth Control in Practice: Analysis of Ten Thousand Case Histories of the Birth Control Clinical Research Bureau* (first ed. 1934; reprint New York: Arno Press, 1972), p. 156.

49. Louis Caradec, *Topographie medico-hygienique du departement du finistere* (Brest: 1860), p. 80; Churchill, *On the Theory and Practice of Midwifery*, 3d American ed. (Philadelphia: 1848), p. 467," . . . one of the most distressing and intolerable accidents to which females are subject; and the more so, as a cure is but seldom affected" (p. 467); Paul Portal, *La Pratique des accouchemens* (Paris: 1685), p. 10.

50. Torggler, *Bericht Klinik Innsbruck*, p. 141.

51. "Fifteen Years' Experience with the Intermediate Repair of the Injuries of Childbirth," *American Journal of Obstetrics* 75 (1917):755.

52. "On Lacerations of the Perinaeum, Sphincter Ani, and Recto-Vaginal Septum: Their Prevention and Surgical Treatment," *American Journal of Obstetrics* 5 (1872-73):53.

53. *Observations sur la grossesse et l'accouchement des femmes* (Paris: 1694), pp. 39-40.

54. *Birth Control in Practice*, p. 84.

55. Wollheim, *Topographie Berlin*, p. 310; Louis Marie Lavergne, *Topographie medicale de Lamballe et de ses environs en 1787* (Lehon: les presses d'Entre-Nous: journal de l'hopital psychiatrique Saint Jean de Dieu, 1959), p. 33; Friedrich Benjamin Lentin, *Merkwurdigkeiten von der Witterung, der Einwohner zu Klausthal, in den Jahren 1774 bis 1777*; I have quoted from passages excerpted in *Archiv der praktischen Arzneykunst* 1 (1785):312; Klinge, *Oberharz*, p. 34; Cless and Schubler, *Stuttgart*, p. 75; Horsch, *Topographie Wurzburg*, p. 185; Rambach, *Beschreibung Hamburg*, p. 335; Johann Heinrich Kopp, *Topographie der Stadt Hanau, in Beziehung auf den Gesundheits—und Krankheitszustand der Einwohner* (Frankfurt/Main: 1807), p. 160.

56. Kopp, *Birth Control in Practice*, p. 88.

57. Zengerle, "Topographie Wangen," 255; *Traite complet des acouchemens*, p. 71.

58. *Birth Control in Practice*, p. 156.

59. James N. West, "What Shall We Perform Myomectomy and When Hysterectomy in Uterine Fibromyomata?," *American Journal of Obstetrics* 56 (1907):701, 702 for the two estimates of 12 and 14 percent.

60. *Entwicklung der Geburtshilfe*, pp. 116-117; K.H. Lubben, *Beitrage zur Kenntniss der Rhon in medizinischer Hinsicht* (Weimar: 1881).

61. *Birth Control in Practice*, p. 156.

62. Speert, *Essays in Eponymy*, pp. 108-115; see also De la Motte, *Traite complet des acouchemens*, p. 651, who saw a good deal of prolapse among unmarried women.

63. See, for example, Metzger, "Topographie von Konigsberg," p. 305. For a world overview see Heinrich Ploss and Max and Paul Bartels, *Das Weib in der Natur- und Volkerkunde*, rev. ed. by Ferd. v. Reitzenstein, vol. 3 (Berlin: 1972), pp. 105-106.

64. "Frauenarbeit," p. 961.

65. Ann Douglas Wood, for instance, writes of ". . . a nightmare vision of sick women dependent on male doctors who use their professional superiority as a method to prolong their patients' sickness and, consequently, the supremacy of their own sex." The cure for many of these diseases turns out, unsurprisingly, to be "female strength." "'The Fashionable Diseases': Women's Complaints and Their Treatment in Nineteenth-Century America," *Journal of Interdisciplinary History* 4 (1973): quotes from pp. 43, 47.

Barbara Ehrenreich and Deirdre English go even further in their discussion of "male" medicine in nineteenth-century America. "[It] made very little sense as *medicine* [italics in original], but it was undoubtedly effective at keeping certain women—those who could afford to be patients—in their place." They go on to say that "prescribed bed rest was obviously little more than a kind of benign imprisonment." Finally they declare, "The more the doctors 'treated', the more they lured women into seeing themselves as sick. The entire mystique of female sickness—the house calls, the tonics and medicines, the health spas—served, above all, to keep a great many women busy at the task of doing nothing." *Complaints and Disorders: The Sexual Politics of Sickness* (Old Westbury, N.Y.: The Feminist Press, Glass Mountain Pamphlet no. 2, 1973), pp. 35-37.

66. Most recent in a long line of authors to take this approach is Lawrence Stone, *The Family, Sex and Marriage in England, 1500-1800* (New York: Harper and Row, 1977), pp. 673-677.

67. Again, in a venerable historiographical tradition, see most recently Linda Gordon, *Woman's Body, Woman's Right: A Social History of Birth Control in America* (New York: Viking/Grossman, 1976), pp. 104-115.

68. This, generally, is the approach I have taken in *The Making of the Modern Family* (New York: Basic Books, 1975), and in "Maternal Sentiment and Death in Childbirth: A New Agenda for Psycho-Medical History," in Patricia Branca (ed.), *The Medicine Show: Patients, Physicians and the Perplexities of the Health Revolution in Modern Society* (New York: Science History Publications, 1977), pp. 67-88.

Index

*Contribution to the Critique of
Political Economy* (Marx), 22
Cooper, James Fenimore, 104
Cosway, Maria, 99
Cottle, Tom, 88
Coward, Rosalind, and John Ellis, 79
Crouzet, 194

Davis, Allan, 178
Deficiencies, nutritional, diseases from,
    186-192
de la Motte, Guillaume Mauguest, 188-
    189, 195-196, 199
Depression, neurotransmitters and,
    55-56
Depth psychology, 61
Development, historical, 24
Dialogue, nature of, 132-133
Diary (C.F. Adams), 126
Diaspora Jews, 85
Dicks, Henry V., 72-73
Donald, Archibald, 200
Dreams, 65, 98, 107-108; archetypes in,
    122
Drives, instinctual, 16, 25, 122
Durkheim, Emile, 28

Economic action, 28, 32
Edel, Leon, 107-108
Edinger, Lewis, and Donald Searing,
    61
Education (Henry Adams), 127
Ego: functioning, 28, 31, 32, 34; id
    and, 15-16
"Eight stages of man," xii, 62-63
"Elites," 58
Empathy, 37-38, 56
Engels, Friedrich, 12-13, 84, 85-86
English Civil War, 73-75, 76, 77
Environmental experiences, 120, 122
Erikson, Erik, xii, xiii, xiv, 45, 54, 97,
    99, 100-101, 103, 104, 112, 131,
    143, 147; dreams and, 98; and
    eight-stage theory, xii, 62-63; and
    Freud's work, 5-9; identity forma-
    tion, 11; psychohistory, 3-19
Erikson, Kai T., 163-164

Family, value transmission in, 131-142;
    joint, 143-160
Family myth, 124-126
Fathers and Children (Rogin), 99
Feinstein, Howard, xv, 131-142
Fenichel, Otto, 55
Feuerbach, theses on (Marx), 23-24
Fistulas, 195-198
Forster, E.M., 112
For Whom the Bell Tolls (Hemingway),
    105
Fothergill, William, 200
French Royal Academy of Medicine,
    185
Freud, Anna, 85, 122
Freud, Sigmund, xi, xii, xiii, 3, 16-17,
    55, 62, 75, 97, 98, 102-103, 104,
    120, 121, 122, 144; ego functioning,
    28-29, 34; id, 15-16, 29, 30, 33, 34;
    and Lamarckism, 7, 14; linear
    materialism and, 24-25; and Marx,
    21-26; Oedipus complex, 15, 30;
    personality structure and, 27-30;
    psychosexual deviation and, 54; sex-
    uality, childhood, 11, 13; social
    theory, 6-7; superego and, 29-30,
    34; totem murder, 6-7; weakness in
    work of, 5-9; and Weber, 27-35
Frost, Robert, 100

Gadamer, Hans-Georg, 79
Galle, J.G., 121
Gandhi, Mahatma, xii, 45, 63
Gandhi's Truth (Erikson), xii
Generativity, 54
George, Alexander, 60
Goering, Hermann, 73
Gould, Roger, 64
Grant, Ulysses S., 110
Grant study, 54
Greenstein, Fred, 58, 59, 60
Group-self, 44-45
Guntrip, Harry, 50

Habermas, 79
Hamilton, Alexander, 99
Hampstead Nursery Group, 54

About the Contributors

Dominick Cavallo, Ph.D., teaches American history at Howard University. Dr. Cavallo has written numerous articles on childhood and American education in such journals as *The History of Education Quarterly* and *The History of Childhood Quarterly*. He is author of *The Progressive and the Playground: Urban Reform and Children's Play 1880-1920*. Dr. Cavallo is currently doing research on the history of American prostitution.

Erik H. Erikson, a pioneer in the field of child psychology and psychohistorical studies, is perhaps the most influential psychoanalyst in the world today. Among his numerous works are *Childhood and Society, Young Man, Gandhi's Truth, Insight and Responsibility, Identity, Youth and Crisis, Life History*, and *The Historical Moment*. Professor Erikson recently edited *Adulthood*.

Howard Feinstein, M.D., Ph.D., teaches psychology and American studies at Cornell University. Dr. Feinstein is a leading scholar on the family of William James.

Joel Kovel, Ph.D., teaches psychology at the Albert Einstein College of Medicine, Yeshiva University. Dr. Kovel is the author of *White Racism: A Psychohistory* as well as numerous articles and book reviews.

David Musto, M.D., is on the faculty of the Child Study Center at Yale University. Dr. Musto is a leading scholar on the family of John Adams.

Talcott Parsons, Ph.D., was the founder of Harvard University's School for Social Relations. Dr. Parsons was perhaps the best-known social theorist of the past quarter century. He was the author of hundreds of articles and books, including *The Structure of Social Action, The Social System*, and *Personality and Social Structure*. He was the coauthor of numerous works, on every aspect of social life, including *Economy and Society* (with Neil Smelser); *Family, Socialization and Interaction Process* (with R.F. Bales); and *The American University* (with G.M. Platt).

Gerald M. Platt, Ph.D., teaches social theory at the University of Massachusetts. Dr. Platt is the coauthor with Professor Fred Weinstein of *The Wish to Be Free, Psychoanalytic Sociology*, and the "Coming Crisis in Psychohistory," and numerous other works. He is coauthor with Professor Talcott Parsons of *The American University*. Dr. Platt has written articles and reviews for *The American Quarterly, Contemporary Sociology* and other scholarly journals and is on the editorial board of *Psychohistory Review*.

Stanley A. Renshon, Ph.D., is an associate professor of the graduate faculty and the Department of Political Science of City University of New York. Among Dr. Renshon's numerous publications are *The Handbook of Political Socialization* and *Psychological Needs and Political Behavior*. Dr. Renshon is currently the editor of a policy-studies series for Pergamon Books. He is on the editorial board of *History of Childhood Quarterly* (*Journal of Psychohistory*) and the International Association for the Use of Psychology in Politics.

Lloyd I. Rudolph, Ph.D., and **Suzanne Hoeber Rudolph**, Ph.D., teach political science at the University of Chicago. They are renowned scholars on the politics of India and are coauthors of *Modernity of Tradition: Political Development in India* and numerous articles on the Rajput family of India.

Miles Shore, M.D., is a member of the faculty of Harvard University Medical School in the Department of Psychiatry.

Edward Shorter teaches European social and family history at the University of Toronto. Professor Shorter is author of *The Historian and the Computor, The Making of the Modern Family*, and many articles and reviews.

Cushing Strout, Ph.D., is E.I. White Professor of Literature at Cornell University. Dr. Strout has written *The New Heavens and the New Earth: Political Religion in America, Pragmatic Revolt in American History; Carl Becker and Charles Beard*. He is also the editor of *Intellectual History in America, Volume 2, From Darwin to Niebuhr*, and *Hawthorne in England*. Dr. Strout has written articles for *American Quarterly* and numerous other journals.

Fred Weinstein, Ph.D., teaches psychosocial theory and European history at State University of New York at Stony Brook. He is coauthor, with Gerald M. Platt, of *The Wish to Be Free, Psychoanalytic Sociology* and numerous articles. His most recent book is *Germany's Discontents, Hitler's Visions: The Claims of Leadership and Ideology in the Nazi Movement*. Dr. Weinstein is the chairman of the Group for the Use of Psychology in History.

Ernest S. Wolf, M.D., teaches psychology at the Chicago Institute of Psychoanalysis.

About the Editors

Mel Albin teaches political and social theory, and public policy and the history of the family in the Department of political studies at Adelphi University. Professor Albin has published essays and reviews in family studies and on the history of American education. Recently he has coauthored an article on political turmoil (with Gerald Heeger) to be followed by a book on the subject. Professor Albin is completing a manuscript on the political socialization of public school children at the turn of the century. He was director of "Psyche, Society, and Value Change: A Conference on Psychohistory in Honor of Erik H. Erikson."

Robert Devlin teaches in the Department of History at Adelphi University. Professor Devlin's area of specialization is the Russian revolution. He has delivered numerous papers and is completing, with George D. Jackson, *Dictionary of the Russian Revolution* (forthcoming, 1981) and *The Trotsky-Stalin Conflict* (forthcoming, 1981). Professor Devlin has completed a monograph on the working class in the Russian revolution and has coauthored, with Mel Albin, "Petrograd Workers: Affect, Ideology, and Consciousness in the Russian Revolution." He was coordinator of "Psyche, Society, and Value Change: A Conference on Psychohistory in Honor of Erik H. Erikson."

Gerald A. Heeger, Ph.D., is a specialist on South Asian politics, political development, and the study of political violence. Dr. Heeger is the author of *The Politics of Underdevelopment* and several articles and reviews. He has taught at the University of Virginia and at Adelphi University. Currently he is dean of University College, Adelphi University.